3 FEET TO THE LEFT

A NEW CAPTAIN'S JOURNEY FROM PURSUIT TO PERSPECTIVE

CAPTAIN KORRY FRANKE

Library of Congress Control Number: 2018910945

ISBN 978-1-7326954-0-5 (paperback)
ISBN 978-1-7326954-1-2 (ebook)
Published in Bath, PA 18014

www.korryfranke.com
korry@korryfranke.com
Editor: Stephanie M. Scott

Title page photography courtesy of Captain Karl Novak © 2015

Note: Charts featured on cover are not intended for navigation.

To Jen,
for her unrelenting willingness
to be my partner in life and discovery.

And to the scenic route,
whose wisdom is profound.

AUTHOR'S NOTE

To write this book, I relied upon my personal journals and photographs, researched facts when I could, consulted with many of the people who appear in the book, and called upon my own memory of these events and this time of my life. Quotations should be interpreted only as being representative of the spirit of the conversations. I have changed the names of many, but not all, of the individuals in this book, and in some cases I also modified identifying details in order to preserve anonymity. On a few occasions, I used composite events to aid in simplicity and readability. I occasionally omitted people and events. But none of the changes I made impacted either the veracity or the substance of the story.

While United Airlines is featured heavily in the pages that follow, United has not endorsed any of the events described in this book as being representative of current corporate policies or procedures. Importantly, my perspective is mine alone, completely independent of any United Airlines affiliation.

Without United Airlines, however, I never would have had the amazing opportunity to live this story. That's why for the first ten years of publication I will donate 10% of the net author proceeds from this book to the *United We Care Employee Relief Fund* and an additional 10% of the net author proceeds to the *Captain Jason Dahl Scholarship Fund*. Information about how you can help donate to these charities is found in the *Acknowledgments* section at the end of the book.

"The greatest journey an airline pilot
ever takes is the one to the captain's chair
three feet to the left."
- *Unknown*

Flights Operated by Captain Korry Franke

July 28, 2013 - August 2, 2014

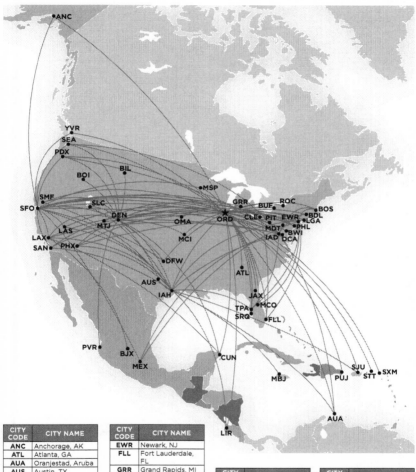

CITY CODE	CITY NAME
ANC	Anchorage, AK
ATL	Atlanta, GA
AUA	Oranjestad, Aruba
AUS	Austin, TX
BDL	Windsor Locks (Hartford), CT
BIL	Billings, MT
BJX	Guanajuato (Leon), Mexico
BOI	Boise, ID
BOS	Boston, MA
BUF	Buffalo, NY
BWI	Baltimore, MD
CLE	Cleveland, OH
CUN	Cancun, Mexico
DCA	Washington, D.C.
DEN	Denver, CO
DFW	Dallas-Fort Worth, TX

CITY CODE	CITY NAME
EWR	Newark, NJ
FLL	Fort Lauderdale, FL
GRR	Grand Rapids, MI
IAD	Dulles (Washington, D.C.), VA
IAH	Houston, TX
JAX	Jacksonville, FL
LAS	Las Vegas, NV
LAX	Los Angeles, CA
LGA	New York, NY
LIR	Liberia, Costa Rica
MBJ	Montego Bay, Jamaica
MCI	Kansas City, MO
MCO	Orlando, FL
MDT	Harrisburg, PA
MEX	Mexico City, Mexico

CITY CODE	CITY NAME
MSP	Minneapolis-St. Paul, MN
MTJ	Montrose, CO
OMA	Omaha, NE
ORD	Chicago, IL
PDX	Portland, OR
PHL	Philadelphia, PA
PHX	Phoenix, AZ
PIT	Pittsburgh, PA
PUJ	Punta Cana, Dominican Republic
PVR	Puerto Vallarta, Mexico
ROC	Rochester, NY

CITY CODE	CITY NAME
SAN	San Diego, CA
SEA	Seattle, WA
SFO	San Francisco, CA
SJU	San Juan, Puerto Rico
SLC	Salt Lake City, UT
SMF	Sacramento, CA
SRQ	Sarasota, FL
STT	St. Thomas, U.S.V.I.
SXM	St. Maarten, Netherland Antillie
TPA	Tampa, FL
YVR	Vancouver, Canada

FOREWORD

Brett Snyder
Author of the *Cranky Flier* Blog

The 737 whizzed by the window, hovered over the runway in Los Angeles, and then gently reunited with *terra firma*. Once the aircraft was out of view, I swiveled my head back around to re-engage with Korry Franke about his career and this very book, *3 Feet to the Left*, which tells the story of Korry's first year as the youngest captain flying for United Airlines. It was the first time we had ever met.

Two months prior to that day was when I first heard Korry's name. He had reached out to me personally, asking if I would be interested in reading his book and then possibly writing a foreword for it. As author of the *Cranky Flier* blog, I'm used to getting requests to read manuscripts, but being asked to write a foreword? I wasn't sure what to say. After all, I didn't even know this guy. In the blog, I've written about the airline industry for 12 years, but that largely focuses on the business of flying, not the *ACTUAL* flying. Having a background on the commercial side of the industry, doing pricing for America West and marketing for United, among others, shaped my views. And those views about the business weren't necessarily aligned with the views in the cockpit. I couldn't help but wonder why Korry wanted someone who had never flown an airplane involved in his project.

Fortunately, with a vacation coming up, I decided that at the very least, I could spend some time reading the manuscript. Korry had taken the time to seek me out, and he seemed to value my opinion.

I figured reading his memoir would at worst be a mildly interesting way to spend an afternoon on the beach.

As I read the book, I began to understand more about why Korry had reached out to me. One thing that has always driven my writing is the pursuit of shedding light on why things happen the way they do in the airline industry. This book tries to do that very thing, and Korry, being a new captain at the time, makes it seem like we're learning right along with him.

For the airline employee, frequent flier, or just casual observer, Korry's anecdotes will prove to be fascinating. Long gone are the days of the "Sky Gods," where captains knew everything and were never to be questioned. Instead, today, we have pilots trying to manage situations and coworkers in a delicate dance. They are not perfect, and this book puts a human face on those people who may seem invincible in their sharp uniforms.

In some cases, the stories are strangely comforting. For example, my heart started to race and my palms began to sweat as I read the tale of Korry and his first officer flying around an intense thunderstorm cell near Mexico City. Yet the matter-of-fact way they went about doing their jobs as if solving a puzzle calmly and efficiently made it seem, well, routine. Most people don't get to see that side of pilots.

But this book is about more than just being an airline pilot. This is a much broader general business book about managers trying to find their way through difficult situations.

Take, for example, Korry's experience on an evening flight out of Washington's Dulles Airport that really stuck with me. A late-arriving passenger on a first class fare had walked on the airplane and started complaining about how the flight attendants said there was no room for his bag in the overhead bin. Frequent fliers have seen this story a million times but not from the perspective of a pilot. It was eye-opening to watch Korry wrestle with what, on the surface, seemed like a simple, insignificant decision. Few of us may find ourselves in the exact same situation, but Korry's thinking in making the time-sensitive, difficult choice as well as dealing with the consequences of that decision can be applied to any industry where new managers are trying to find their footing and learn how best to run a team.

It doesn't stop there. As Korry makes his way through his first few months as a captain, we can see that he's searching for something. In the end, Korry comes to an understanding about how he wants to live his life, particularly about how he wants to define success, and that's something that others who are seeking order might find valuable as well.

There's a lot to like about this book, but the simple act of humanizing a captain and the cockpit experience would make this worth reading on its own. For more than a decade, I've tried to demystify parts of the airline industry for people who want to better understand how it works, but I've never flown an airplane myself. I can interview people, but I can't give the captain's eye view of why things happen the way they do. Korry Franke makes that happen with a book that has appeal far beyond the airline industry.

When Korry flew 6 hours just to have lunch with me that day we first met (before turning around and flying right back), I knew that he was serious about making this book a success, so serious that he was willing to spare a precious day off to come speak with me. I'm no longer confused about why Korry asked me to write this foreword. I'm now just glad he did.

Brett Snyder
Author, Cranky Flier

PROLOGUE

Departure

"And suddenly you know:
It's time to start something new
and trust the magic of beginnings."
- Meister Eckhart

Chicago, Illinois – February 2013

The lid of my laptop closes with a gentle *thap*. The sound cuts through the still air of my Chicago apartment as cleanly as the information I've just read on my laptop's screen has cut through me.

I recline into my black leather high-backed chair, which, along with my desk, is wedged into the corner of my apartment's cramped spare bedroom. My slender fingers slide through my short strawberry-blond hair, lacing together along the nape of my neck. I let a long, drawn-out breath escape through my pursed lips as I stare at the apartment's exposed concrete ceiling.

This changes everything, I think.

I know I've said the same thing to myself in the past, but this time it feels different, like it's not an overreaction. This time, it seems more real. And after repeating the affirmation several times in my head, it starts to sink in that the moment I've dreamed about for fourteen years since I was a high school junior is finally here.

I close my eyes and watch the surreal scene from that November day in 1998 play out again in my mind. I see the flight attendant

1

approaching my family's row in the back of the giant Boeing 747. I notice her smile as my face lights up with elation after she relays the captain's generous invitation. I feel the thumping in my chest as I follow behind her toward the front of the plane before climbing the steps to the upper deck. We walk past the cushy first-class seats to the narrow cockpit door, and as it swings open, a giant burst of light greets me. I'm immediately overwhelmed by the dizzying collection of knobs, switches, and buttons. One of the pilots folds down an extra flight deck jumpseat for me. He straps me in and hands me a headset to wear. To my novice ears, the air traffic control communications I hear sound like an indecipherable foreign language at rapid-fire pace. I'm in awe of it all—the complexity, the novelty, and most of all, the spellbinding panoramic view around me.

It's the English countryside. Oddly shaped fields, each a different shade of green and separated from the others only by narrow tree lines and fencerows, fashion a vibrant patchwork quilt across the rolling hills. Tiny clumps of towns are speckled about, each with twisting roads and densely packed homes capped with reddish-brown roofs. Gradually, the empty fields give way to London's labyrinth of city streets. One of the pilots points out the Thames River, and then the Tower Bridge, Big Ben, and the tennis courts of Wimbledon. But when it comes to spotting Heathrow, its massive parallel runways are impossible to miss.

The jumbo jet lumbers toward the extended pavement ahead of us. The captain calls "gear down," and as the wheels lock into place, the white noise of the rushing wind intensifies. The jet shifts about as the captain moves the control wheel left and right. We jostle in our seats, growing closer and closer to the ground. We drift above the airport's perimeter fence, and then over the runway's threshold. Then I feel the rumbling that indicates the jet's eighteen wheels have settled onto the runway. Our transatlantic journey from Washington, D.C., is complete. And in that single moment, I know my life has changed forever.

Back in the confines of my Chicago apartment, I open my eyes, wondering where I would be now without that fortuitous moment and thinking what a shame it is that the passengers I now carry as a United Airlines pilot can't experience things like that anymore. But in the post-9/11 airline world, it's completely understandable. Before that fateful day, the cockpit door existed primarily to partition the flight deck from the cabin so as to create a distraction-free work environment for the pilots. Now, it's also a bulletproof barrier protecting the flight crew from unscrupulous individuals wishing to do unthinkable harm...and a reinforced reminder of the day the airline industry—and the fabric of our nation—changed forever.

My eyes drift around the bedroom, and I notice the well-worn flight logbooks stacked on the side of my desk below the edge of a framed Boeing 767 cockpit poster. The blue logbook, roughly the size of a folded sheet of printer paper, chronicles my first flight lessons, which I began the summer after my flight to London. It sits atop a larger black one, which details the lion's share of my flights as a flight instructor during college and immediately afterwards. And on top of both of them is a stack of several maroon pocket logbooks that I've meticulously maintained over the past nine years as an airline pilot, all of them as a first officer, or what is often referred to as a co-pilot. Their pages are dingy and their corners are bent from being repeatedly stuffed into the right breast pockets of my crisp white uniform shirts and carried with me on jaunts to small towns and major cities all around the globe.

Oh, if these books could talk, I muse nostalgically, leaning forward to pick one up. I flip through its pages as though it's an animated tale, thinking, *In a way, I guess they do.*

The three-letter airport codes stand out to me, with each line triggering a highlight reel of memories, like the dust trails I saw extending behind the army tanks crawling across the open fields of Fort Hood, Texas, as I peered through the right side window of the Saab 340B prior to my first landing as a regional airline pilot in 2004. Or the excitement I felt from hearing the high-pitched whine of the Embraer 145's engines spooling up on my first takeoff in a jet a year later. Or the way the brilliance of the sunrise over the craggy Irish coastline seemed dreamlike on my first transatlantic crossing in a Boeing 767 in 2006. Countless inflight landscapes, each one more beautiful than any that a master painter could create. Vivid moments that I know will remain with me forever.

The names I see in the books stand out to me, too. They're the pilots with whom I've flown. Some names seem to have melded together over time, but for many, I can still see the pilots' faces in vivid detail. I can hear their voices and remember the stories they told as we droned along at 38,000 feet, our feet propped up on the lower dashboard footrests, passing the time between Dallas and Des Moines or New Jersey and the Netherlands. I can still taste the curry we consumed in Manchester and the souvlaki we sampled on a hot July evening at the crew hotel's rooftop restaurant overlooking the Parthenon in Athens. It's as though those moments were yesterday, and I'm so thankful to have their memories permanently cached in my mind.

I flip a few more pages, smiling as I recount moments of laughter in Lisbon and picnics in Paris. And then it dawns on me that the names I see printed in my little logbooks have a strong connection with the message I just read on my laptop's screen.

This really does *change everything*, I remind myself again.

For a day I have dreamed about for nearly a decade and a half, it seems ironic that I have never given much consideration to how this moment would feel when it actually arrived. I'm confident, however, that I never expected it to feel so matter-of-fact.

But matter-of-fact it had been. There was no fanfare. No grand ceremony. Just a simple message on the United Airlines crew communication website, announcing that the final results for Bid 14-02 were out.

Alone in my apartment, I searched for my name within the 199-page PDF document, just as I had done on so many other previous bid awards. And on page 79, I had found it listed along with those of other pilots flying Boeing 737s out of United's Chicago O'Hare pilot domicile. But unlike all the previous bids, this time my name was listed on the left side of the page instead of the right. And as it happens, that is not an insignificant detail at all. In fact, it's actually a detail of momentous proportions.

I set the pocket logbook back atop the rest. Rising from the chair, I leave the bedroom and walk down the narrow entry hallway's wooden floors, past the apartment's modern kitchen, to the floor-to-ceiling windows that look out on the cold and blustery streets of Chicago's financial district from thirty-seven floors above. I stare blankly at the massive stone-, steel-, and glass-covered buildings that consume my view, listening to the muted wave-like rumble of a passing L train one block away.

It doesn't seem possible that I am about to achieve my childhood dream. Making that dream a reality had been my sole professional focus to date. In fact, it had been my life's focus, too. I had researched the possible paths that could lead to my goal, dissecting each one's requisite steps. And once I had settled on the path I believed would be the fastest, I had chased each step with vigor, moving wherever I needed to move and taking whatever job I needed to take, so long as doing so put me one step closer to my dream. Focus and discipline, I had told myself, were the keys to achieving success.

And now, the results of Bid 14-02 reveal my success is at hand. I have climbed the mountain. I have reached my destination. And there is one person with whom I cannot wait to share my news: Jen.

I pull my iPhone from my pocket and dial her work number.

"Hi, Husband!" she answers, using the appropriate, if not overly obvious, nickname she affectionately gave to me the day we were married in 2010.

"Hi, Wife," I respond in kind.

"Well?? Is it out??" she asks, cutting right to the point. Like me, Jen has eagerly awaited the results of Bid 14-02, because she understands the significant effect its results could have on our lives.

"Yep," I reply. "It's out."

"Reallllllly??"

"Realllllly," I say, letting a grin creep across my face as I draw out my big reveal.

"Annnnnnddddd…did you get it????"

"Annnnnnddddd…I got it!!!!"

"YES!!!!" she exclaims, her excitement palpable even over the phone. "You're going to be a 737 captain!"

I smile. "That's right! I'm heading to the left seat!" Three feet to the left of the first officer's seat I have occupied for my entire airline career to this point.

"Congratulations!" she exclaims.

"Thanks!" I reply. "I just barely got it, but I got it."

"Who cares how close you were? Your number was up. That's all that matters," she says, knowing as I do that promotions—and demotions—within the pilot ranks are determined solely by a pilot's position on the all-controlling seniority list. "You must be so excited."

"I am," I tell her, before adding that I'm also a bit terrified. After all, it's a lot of responsibility to place on the shoulders of a 31-year-old.

"Well, dude," she cautions, "don't jack it up!"

I chuckle. "I'm gonna do my best!"

"And don't let this go to your head, either," she adds.

I roll my eyes. "Let's be honest. With you around to keep me in check, I'm confident that won't be a problem."

"Truth!"

I shake my head before suggesting a celebration is in order when she gets home.

"Yeah, dude! Count me in! You may even have to pull out your special bottle of scotch," Jen suggests, referring to the first bottle of whisky I ever purchased—a souvenir I've treasured since a passionate shopkeeper taught me all about the spirit during a 2007 layover in Edinburgh, Scotland.

"You know, I think you're right!"

"As usual."

I roll my eyes again, mumbling, "Mmhmm."

A few moments later, we say goodbye and the line goes silent. For several minutes, I continue gazing onto the urban landscape in front of me. In the distance one of United's jets drifts across the shoreline of Lake Michigan on its final approach to O'Hare.

This is about to get real, I think.

But the truth is I have no idea how real the next year is going to get. I cannot comprehend how much I will be challenged or how much I will grow as a leader and as a man. And perhaps most of all, I have no idea how much my perspective on success and adversity is about to change. Because as I'll soon understand, this moment isn't actually the top of the mountain. And it is most definitely not a destination reached. In fact, if it is anything at all, it is merely another waypoint on an even more important journey—one that will take an entire lifetime to achieve.

This is the story of my first year as a United Airlines captain. It's the story of a new leader who is tasked with stepping up and taking command. And it's the story of a man who is molded and shaped in powerful, unexpected ways that eventually transform his perspective on what success really is.

This story takes place inside and outside of airline flight decks. It flies above mountain ranges and across oceans. It maneuvers through blustery blizzards and around awe-inspiring thunderstorms. And along the way, it presses up against the limits of comfort zones.

It's a story about people—airline people—who are struggling to make sense of their pasts while learning to accept their new realities. It's a story about humility and compassion, a story about joy and pain, and most of all, about how every one of those moments is actually interwoven with the others for a simple and beautiful purpose.

It's a story about me, but it could just as easily be a story about any number of my colleagues at United…or about you, for that matter. Because in one way or another, we are all on our own journeys…three feet to the left.

And so with that, it's time to fly. Welcome aboard.

CHAPTER 1

The Role of the Captain

*"An Air Line Pilot will keep uppermost in his [sic]
mind that the safety, comfort, and well-being
of the passengers who entrust their lives to him
are his first and greatest responsibility."*
- Air Line Pilot Association Code of Ethics

Northwestern Colombia – December 20, 1995

*N*ine minutes to go.

"Pretty night, huh?" asks the captain of American Airlines Flight 965 partway through the Boeing 757's descent. The chaos of holiday travel and the cascading weather delays at Miami International Airport are but a distant memory for the crew, replaced by the serenity of shimmering South American starlight. But the crew is wise enough to know that the serenity will be short-lived, because the approach and landing into Cali, Colombia's Alfonso Bonilla Aragon International Airport includes many challenges—even for the experienced pilots of Flight 965.

For starters, the airport rests along the floor of a narrow valley within the Andes Mountains, where some nearby peaks reach above 14,000 feet—roughly half the height of Mount Everest. Given the moonless December night, the steep, tree-covered slopes will be like invisible canyon walls. Only by precise pilotage along three-dimensional highways in the sky, known as airways[1], can a flight safely navigate over the mountains, through the passes, and into the valley for landing.

To make matters worse, radar coverage within Colombian airspace is spotty in places, which means air traffic controllers cannot always independently verify a flight's position. In those instances, controllers build a mental picture of where a flight is and where it is going by asking pilots to report passing specific points along an airway. These named points, which are known as "fixes[2]," are intersections of latitude/longitude and serve, in essence, as mile markers along the airways. Of course, those "position reports" are useful only if the flight actually is where the crew says it is. And if a crew is unsure of its position, or if the crew members report inaccurate information, there is no way for the controller to know otherwise until the flight returns to airspace with radar coverage.

Adding still more complexity for the English-speaking crew, the primary language for most South American air traffic controllers is

---

[1] Airways are usually defined laterally by specific radials emanating to or from ground-based navigation aids. These are known as Very High Frequency Omni-Directional Ranges, or V.O.R.s. The signals sent by these aids are interpreted by onboard equipment to show pilots whether they are left of, right of, or precisely on a selected radial. Airways are then segmented into sections, using precise distances to or from a V.O.R. or specific crossing radials from other V.O.R.s to identify specific intersections, which are given names and referred to as "fixes." One might think of these as mile markers along a particular highway in the sky. Each section is then assigned a minimum safe altitude to account for terrain or other known hazards (e.g. towers, buildings, etc.). By carefully referencing the lateral and vertical limitations of an airway, pilots can safely navigate without the visual reference of the ground. Today, almost all airliners navigate laterally using high-precision Global Positioning System (G.P.S.) equipment that has significantly simplified aerial navigation; however, the charted airways, the fixes defining their respective segments, and the charted safe altitudes for each section remain functionally unchanged.

[2] See footnote number 1. Additionally, government agencies assign fixes particular names. Sometimes these names are assigned in reference to local geographical features, notable individuals, or even sports teams. At other times, the names of fixes are simply randomly generated combinations of pronounceable letters. Some are even rather humorous.

Spanish. And while international regulations require that all controllers speak English, the extent of their abilities can sometimes make communication challenging and confusing due to misunderstandings arising from the language barrier.

To combat the many challenges, the crew of American Flight 965 plans ahead. The pilots evaluate the weather conditions in Cali and determine that a landing to the north on Runway 1 is most prudent. Then they load their flight computers with the appropriate airways to safely guide them into the valley, beyond the airport, and through the course reversal maneuver to position the aircraft for the expected northerly landing.

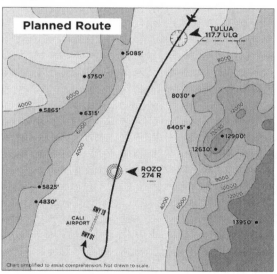

But on this night, things won't go as planned for Flight 965.

Five minutes to go.

"Niner-Six-Five, Cali," the Colombian air traffic controller says over the radio to get the attention of the crew.

"Niner-Six-Five, go ahead, please," the captain replies.

"Sir, the wind is calm. Are you able to approach Runway One-Niner?"

The captain turns to the first officer—the pilot actually steering the jet on the Miami to Cali flight—and asks what he wants to do. On the one hand, landing to the south on Runway 19 is a much more direct route to the airport than the crew's expected northerly landing, saving several minutes of flight time and offsetting some of the departure delay the flight had encountered in Miami. On the other hand, switching to the southerly runway will require many modifications to each pilot's flight computer and navigation instruments. It will also drastically compress the timeline for landing and place the jet well above the desired flight path for that runway. With many factors to consider, including Cali's inherent challenges, the decision of what to do is far from cut-and-dried.

"Uh, yeah," the first officer replies. "We'll have to scramble to get down. We can do it."

The captain accepts the runway change and immediately requests a lower altitude from the controller.

"Roger. Flight Nine-Six-Five is cleared V-O-R D-M-E approach Runway One-Niner. ROZO One arrival. Report TULUA V-O-R."

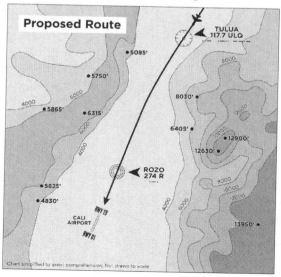

With the new clearance received, the crew members burst into action, rifling through their thick navigation binders to locate the correct approach chart, re-tuning a slew of flight instruments, and typing vigorously on the flight computers' keypads to program the correct airways for the newly assigned routing. Concurrently, the first officer pulls back on a thin handle next to the throttles, extending the speed brakes to hasten the aircraft's descent rate, which causes a rumbling sensation as large metal panels pop up on the top of the wing. As expected, the nose of the airplane drops, taking the jet deeper into the valley and closer to the imperceptible mountains nearby.

Amidst the flurry of activity, the crew members banter back-and-forth amongst themselves and with the controller, seeking clarity about their newly assigned routing, altitude, and present position in relation to where the controller wants them to go. But the last-minute runway change has led to great confusion on the flight deck.

In an attempt to clear things up, the captain asks the controller for permission to fly to a different fix that is closer to the airport. But once again, the controller's response contains non-standard phraseology, which adds to the crew's confusion instead of relieving it. And with each second that passes, the crew's margin for error slips away, while the airplane continues its descent below the jagged mountaintops and toward the undulating valley floor.

Three minutes to go.

"Flight Niner-Six-Five, distance now?" the controller queries, trying to build a mental picture of precisely where American Airlines Flight 965 is at this moment.

"Ummm, what did you want, sir?" the captain asks, still distracted by the myriad tasks on the flight deck.

"Your distance."

"Okay, the distance from CALI is, uh, thirty-eight," signaling the number of miles.

"Roger," the controller replies.

Then the captain looks to the first officer, suggesting a right turn is needed to get back on the flight's assigned course. He presses a few buttons on the flight computer to program what he understands is the new routing, and then he seeks the first officer's confirmation of the change, asking, "Okay, you got it? It's on your map."

The first officer looks to his moving map display. The captain's proposed routing change shows up as a dashed white line. But the direction of the initial turn doesn't jive with what the first officer expects. "It's a left turn," he replies.

"Yeah," the captain says, pausing to reconsider things. "Just doesn't look right on mine. I don't know why."

Two minutes to go.

"So you want a left turn back around to TULUA?" the first officer asks again, referring to one of the named fixes on the flight's assigned airway.

But the captain knows a left turn is incorrect. Something's wrong with the loaded routing, so he says, "Nawww…hell no. Let's press on to…" He pauses again.

"Press on to where, though?" the first officer interjects.

The jet speeds through the dark valley, below the mountaintops, at more than four miles per minute.

"We got screwed up here, didn't we?" the captain asks.

"Yeah."

"How did we get screwed up here?"

One minute to go.

After another request for air traffic control to clarify the flight's routing yields only more uncertainty, the first officer suggests, "Let's just go to the extended centerline."

"Which is ROZO?" the captain asks, referring to the name of the fix just prior to the start of Runway 19.

"ROZO," the first officer confirms.

There are risks to this choice, but the crew members know that if they can navigate to ROZO, they will be back on the airway, protected from the surrounding terrain, and lined up for landing on Runway 19.

Thirty seconds to go.

"I'm going to put that over for you," the captain says, typing into his flight computer the letter "R," which corresponds to ROZO's identifying code on the navigation chart. The problem, however, is that the flight computer's navigation database identifies twelve "R" fixes from which to choose, each one with its own unique seventeen-character latitude/longitude coordinates. Ideally, the captain would compare the coordinates of each fix with the coordinates for ROZO that are published on the approach chart. But there is no time to make such a detailed evaluation. A decision is needed immediately.

Recalling that the computer's logic lists fixes in order of their proximity to the aircraft's present location, the captain assumes the first fix is, therefore, the correct "R" fix for ROZO. Accordingly, he presses the small rectangular button to the left of it two times, first to select the fix and then to insert it at the top of the flight's routing. Then, without asking the first officer to verify the proposed routing change, the captain presses his computer's execute key, confirming the change. Immediately, the autopilot starts turning the plane to the left...toward the wrong "R" fix.

As it happens, the first fix isn't ROZO; it is ROMEO. And while ROMEO is slightly closer to Flight 965 than ROZO, it is well to the east of the plane's location, off the airway selected for purposes of flight safety, and beyond the mountains lining the valley—mountains that are now directly in front of Flight 965 because of the plane's sharp left turn.

Rugged, towering mountains, covered in trees and devoid of any manmade lights that could warn the crew of impending danger. Instead, in the darkness of night, the mountains are like an invisible wall in front of the crew—a wall that may mean the difference between life and death. To prevent catastrophe, the crew must realize its mistake…and fast.

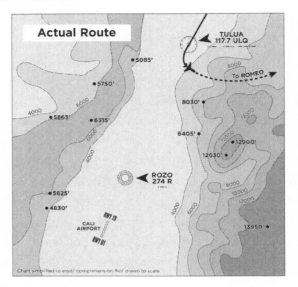

Eighteen seconds to go.

"Niner-Six-Five, distance now?" the controller asks. Without radar, the controller is completely unaware that the 757 has veered off its intended course and is now racing toward the mountains.

But the controller receives no response. Amidst the chaos and confusion on the flight deck, a new voice suddenly begins shouting at the crew. A panicked, computerized male voice, built into the jet to alert the crew of only the direst circumstances, which, of course, these are.

"TERRAIN!! TERRAIN!! WHOOP WHOOP!!" the airplane shouts through the cockpit speakers. American Airlines Flight 965 is fewer than 500 feet above the mountainous terrain—one-third the height of the Empire State Building.

"Oh, shit!" the captain hollers.

Drawing on his prior training, the first officer disconnects the autopilot and shoves the thrust levers full forward, commanding the mighty Rolls-Royce engines to roar at maximum thrust. He pulls back aggressively on the control wheel, pitching the nose of the airplane skyward. But he fails to stow the speed brakes that are extended on top of the wings. And those speed brakes act as yet another obstacle for the plane to overcome as it tries to rise above the jagged peaks that are now perilously close.

"TERRAIN!! TERRAIN!! WHOOP WHOOP!!"

"Pull up, baby!" demands the captain.

Ten seconds to go.

The aircraft is gaining altitude, but not fast enough to outclimb the steep terrain. The harsh computerized voice changes to an even more dire and aggressive "PULL UP!! WHOOP WHOOP!! PULL UP!!" that repeats incessantly.

With the airplane pitched 30-degrees nose high, the automatic stall warning "stick shaker" activates, literally shaking the controls that the first officer clings to and initiating a machinegun-like warning sound that further adds to the chaos. It's as though the plane is begging the crew to lower the nose so the craft doesn't exceed its capability to fly. But the crew needs every degree of pitch it can get. The terrain is closing in on the plane with each passing second.

"PULL UP!! PULL UP!!" the computerized voice demands again and again, unrelenting in its urgency.

Seven seconds to go.

"OK, easy does it, easy does it," the captain cautions. It's as though he's trying to reassure himself that everything will be alright. But his calm demeanor doesn't last long, because the warning continues.

"PULL UP!! PULL UP!! PULL UP!! PULL UP!!"

Five seconds to go.

"UP BABY!" the captain shouts, attempting to will the jet above the terrain as he breathes rapidly, his pupils fully dilated from the adrenaline rushing through his tense body.

"PULL UP!! PULL UP!!"

Suddenly, the crew notices movement out the front windows. It's barely perceptible at first, at the farthest reaches of the white beams projecting from the powerful landing lights. But it's growing steadily. Rapid movement, undulating constantly, almost like the frothy top of a river rapid. But it isn't a river of water; it's a river of trees—the trees upon the mountain's approaching hillside.

Three seconds to go.

"MORE MORE!!!" screams the captain.

Beside him, the stoic first officer grips the controls and grimaces as he fights mightily to keep the plane above the terrain. But the airplane is giving all it can, its performance hindered by the extended speed brakes. And the rushing river of trees grows closer still. It consumes the pilots' view out the front windows, brightly reflecting the full force of the plane's intense landing lights back into the cockpit.

"PULL UP!! WHOOP!! WHOOP!! PULL UP!!"

Two seconds to go.

"UP UP UP!!!" the captain pleads.

But it's too late. The aircraft shakes violently as its tail slices through the treetops. Almost immediately, the tallest branches begin an unrelenting attack against the cockpit windows, quickly shattering them. The engines whine and moan, popping and backfiring as they gag, struggling to chew through the endless river of leaves and limbs. Then the motors rip away from the wings of the jet, shooting spectacular bursts of flame high into the night sky. And finally, the plane itself begins to break apart. The pilots are tossed around like ragdolls, shoving the two men hard against their seatbelt harnesses as they jolt from side to side.

One second to go.

"WHOOP!! WHOOP!! PULL UP!!"

And then silence.

Houston, Texas – June 18, 2013

The training video stops, and the tall, gray-haired United Airlines flight training instructor looks at the fourteen first-time captain "upgrade" candidates sitting in front of him, me included, and suggests, "Let's take a break and then come back to talk about this one."

But no one moves. We sit silently in the dark, windowless classroom, stunned by the harshness and realness of the accident reenactment video.

Just thirty seconds had elapsed between when the captain of American Airlines Flight 965 entered the wrong fix into the flight computer and when the aircraft crashed into the Colombian mountaintop. Thirty seconds. It was the length of a TV commercial. A red light. Less time than it takes for me to brush my teeth, or for Jen and me to ride the elevator down to street level from our 37th floor Chicago apartment. It was nothing, and yet it was everything. And on that day, it was the difference between life and death.

My thoughts turn to the passengers and flight attendants behind the cockpit door. Did they realize what was happening in those thirty seconds? Did it feel normal, or was it terrifying? Did they understand they were crashing into trees? Was their ultimate fate instantaneous? Or were they forced to suffer through some violent and agonizing end? I shudder just thinking about it.

Ultimately, 151 passengers and eight crewmembers died. Miraculously, four people survived.

But what about the families of the unlucky? I picture them waiting with open arms near the terminal in Cali, holding signs and flowers and balloons, eager to share the upcoming holiday together, to open Christmas presents together, to make future plans together. I envision them in Miami or in cities all across American's route network where the passengers originated, waiting for confirmation that their loved ones have arrived safely. How long was it until word trickled out that something had gone terribly wrong with Flight 965? How long was it until the families came to the painful realization that there would be no *together*?

The whole thing makes me sick. And just one all-consuming question occupies my mind and probably those of my colleagues: *could that be me?*

Captain Crawford, the seasoned United captain and instructor of the *Role of the Captain* course, intends to make certain we know that yes, absolutely and without a doubt, that *could* be us. But it doesn't need to be…*if* we manage our flights well. Flights aboard $100-million airplanes, carrying just shy of 200 passengers and crewmembers. Flights operating at all hours of the day and night to locations all over the world, each with its own unique challenges. The responsibility for those people—the passengers, the crewmembers, and their families— will soon rest solely on our shoulders.

After aimlessly milling about in the break area for a few minutes, I return to the classroom, ready to dissect Flight 965. Our discussion will cover the chain of events leading to the accident, but its primary emphasis will be the specific actions or inactions of the captain that had contributed to the descent into danger for a flight that had been well on its way to another routine landing.

In other words, we hope to discover what the role of the captain truly is.

From a legal standpoint, the role of the captain is straightforward. The Federal Aviation Administration (FAA) dictates that every flight must have one and only one Pilot in Command (PIC), defined as "the person who has final authority and responsibility for the operation and safety of the flight." For airlines, that final authority and Pilot in Command is the captain.

United even goes so far as to say that the captain's authority is "absolute" during all flight-related operations, including pre- and post-flight decisions. That means no one can supersede the decisions of a captain—not another crewmember, not the company, not an air traffic controller, not even the FAA itself. No one. From the time the crew boards a flight until the moment the last passenger disembarks, it is the captain's aircraft, and what the captain says goes unquestioned. Clearly, the intent of these provisions isn't to have renegade captains doing whatever they want, whenever they want. Rather, the intent is to provide the captain with the power to manage any situation that might arise in whatever manner the captain deems best. There are no free lunches, of course, and United reminds us, "Use of Captain's authority is inextricably linked to responsibility and accountability." In other words, while captains can do whatever they believe is necessary to meet the needs of a situation, they may have to explain why they did what they did after the fact.

For example, in order to meet the demands of a medical emergency or mechanical malfunction, it may be beneficial to intentionally violate a federal aviation regulation, such as the 250-knot[3] maximum airspeed limit below 10,000 feet. Will paperwork be required? Sure. Is discretion expected when utilizing captain's authority? Absolutely. But the authority is there, and it is final and absolute. I suspect even the President of the United States wishes for this kind of power at work everyday, although Congress would likely have something to say about that!

The captain also serves as the final authority for inflight decision-making. Literally hundreds of people are available to advise and assist a given flight. There are flight dispatchers, load planners, aircraft mechanics, gate agents, air traffic controllers, medical professionals, flight attendants, and, of course, the first officer—the Second in Command—who assists the captain throughout all phases of flight and who, as the title suggests, is next in line should something happen

---

[3] For reference, 1 knot is equivalent to 1.151 miles per hour or 1.852 kilometers per hour.

to the captain. While having those resources available is incredibly helpful and beneficial, it leads to a lot of opinions. Ultimately, someone has to make the final call, particularly when there is insufficient time for discussion. That someone is the captain.

As a first officer, I have been struck by how varied the leadership styles are of the captains with whom I fly. Some are fantastic team builders. Some are authoritarians. Some delegate and encourage debate, while others want to be involved with even the smallest decisions. Some are laid-back. Others are all business. Over the years, some styles have resonated with me more than others, and I have a picture in my mind of which styles I want to emulate when I take command as captain. What strikes me now as I reflect on the reenactment video, however, is how profoundly a captain's style can impact the safety of a flight. And it is through that stylistic lens that our class approaches its discussion of American Airlines Flight 965.

But first, Captain Crawford lays down a few ground rules. "Before we begin, I want to ensure we're all on the same page with something," he says, making eye contact with each of us to convey the seriousness of his words. "We're about to dissect American Nine-Sixty-Five because of its unique lessons regarding the captain's influence on the flight deck. The same goes for Southwest Twelve-Forty-Eight, which we'll discuss next. But we could have picked Eastern Four-Oh-One, United One-Seventy-Three, or one of the other seminal accidents attributed to pilot error. You need to understand that this isn't an American, Southwest, Eastern, or United issue; this is a human issue. It's a cockpit management issue. And I know it's tempting to point the finger and say, 'How could they do this or that?' But when you're out there, strapped into the jet, deep in the heat of battle, no aspersions cast today will keep you and your passengers safe. Only discipline, teamwork, and leadership on the flight deck will. Are we good with that?"

Of course we are good with it. Airline pilots are tribal by nature. We love to root for our own team, pretending some secret sauce available only at our company makes us the best pilots in the world. But we know that isn't the case. We know we share far more similarities than differences with our fellow pilots from other companies. And we recognize that the same things that have caused our counterparts to fail could be the same things that lead us to fail. So with the benefit of hindsight and from the comfort of a classroom, we dig into the tiniest details of a particular accident, reading transcripts from the cockpit voice recorder and scouring clues left behind by the flight data recorder—the two mystical "black boxes" on every airliner. We identify every possible factor and every single decision point. Then we put the pieces together and consider what actions could have been taken to break the fateful chain of events. We do this not so we may cast blame upon our fellow pilots, but so we may learn from their mistakes and hopefully prevent them from ever being repeated. After all, in the airline business, if we wait to learn from our own mistakes, well, we might be too late.

Captain Crawford poses the first question to the group: "What sort of tone did the captain set on the flight deck of American Nine-Sixty-Five?"

The responses are mixed. On one hand, the captain empowered the first officer to make decisions and fly the way he wanted. I knew firsthand how frustrating it was to have a captain constantly telling me how to fly, particularly when the suggestions were technique-related, not procedural. Deferring to the first officer showed the captain trusted his flying partner, which is critical to fostering a high-functioning team. On the other hand, when the captain did assert himself, which was within his right to do as Pilot in Command, he didn't always seek the first officer's opinion or, at a minimum, ask for verification, such as when he made changes to the flight computer unilaterally.

"And what's the danger of not utilizing the verbalize-verify-monitor process?" asks Captain Crawford, referring to United's policy stipulating any changes to the flight computer or autopilot system—or really anything on the flight deck—be verbalized by one pilot, verified by the other pilot, and then monitored by both pilots to ensure that what is expected to happen actually happens.

The danger, classmates respond, is that failing to verbalize-verify-monitor removes layers of safety. It takes one pilot out of the loop, reducing that pilot's situational awareness. And it potentially leads to inputs that may have disastrous, unintended consequences—such as veering sharply off course and heading straight for a mountain.

"So, why do you think the captain let that happen?"

Because he was too focused on completing the mission—landing on Runway 19—we say. He got tunnel vision, which blocked out other perfectly acceptable options and alternatives. And so he rushed, cut corners, and got sloppy.

"Friends, we all know that when we rush, we tend to make mistakes. But as the captain, *you* control the pace at every step, which means you should never, ever feel compelled to rush," Captain Crawford instructs. "Pay attention to the pilot beside you. If either of you are overloaded or reaching capacity, slow down. Set an open tone where your first officer feels free to speak up and admit as much to you. And when that red flag is raised, slow down. Set the parking brake if you're on the ground. Request holding if you're in the air. Do whatever you need to do to avoid rushing at all costs, because the rewards aren't close to being worth the risks."

I can't agree more. I *hate* to rush.

Captain Crawford's questioning continues. "When the crew became confused about their clearance, could they have abandoned the approach, gone around, and set up for it again?"

Absolutely.

"Could they have stuck with Plan A and refused the change to Runway One-Nine in the first place?"

Of course.

"Do you think the passengers and families of Flight Nine-Sixty-Five would have preferred a safe arrival that was five minutes later?"

Unquestionably.

"And if the controller hadn't suggested the runway change, do you think the crew would have voluntarily requested it?"

Probably not.

"And why not?"

Because the crew members were all set up for a landing on Runway 1, and they probably knew the five minutes of time savings wasn't a big deal in the grand scheme of things.

"So you're telling me the crew let someone sitting comfortably on the ground bait them into accepting a clearance they didn't even really want? Why would they let that happen?"

Because they were human. There were benefits to the southerly landing, and the crew probably had past experiences that suggested such last-minute changes would come together just fine.

"Maybe it works 99 times out of 100. Maybe 999 times out of 1000. But why take the chance that your flight is the one that doesn't work out? Friends, you are about to be the captain—the Pilot in Command. An air traffic controller is *never* the P-I-C, regardless of how good his or her intentions may be. A controller doesn't have absolute control over your flight. The controller doesn't dictate the pacing of your flight. YOU control those things," he says, pointing at us with a stern look. "Don't take the bait. Don't let outside forces commandeer your flights. It's your signature on the flight release paperwork accepting responsibility for the plane and its passengers. Be the captain. Maintain the big picture. And put the brakes on when necessary."

Captain Crawford pauses for a moment, stroking his chin as he moves back to the center of the room. Then he offers one last word of caution to wrap up our discussion of American Airlines Flight 965. "This isn't the 1940s anymore. We're not looking for captains with nerves of steel who insist they shouldn't be questioned." The notorious "sky gods" we've all heard about from that era. "Maybe that was needed back then when planes weren't reliable and first officers weren't experienced." His gaze moves slowly and methodically around the room. "But not today." He sits down onto the edge of a table at the front of the classroom. "Now, we want captains who are true leaders in the cockpit, building high-performance teams by leveraging the strengths of their first officers, flight attendants, mechanics, dispatchers, and everyone else on those teams. We want captains who collaborate, not control. We want captains who open the lines of communication among teammates so the right information flows at the right time, making the quality of their decisions better. We want captains who ensure standards are met and limits never exceeded. We want captains who never lose sight of the big picture. And perhaps above all else," he says, placing his hands on his knees and leaning forward intently, "we want captains who do everything in their power to honor and protect the sacred bond that's created the moment a passenger steps aboard the plane and entrusts his or her life to the crew." He stands up again. "Because that, my friends, is the true role of the captain. And that's precisely what we expect of you."

Point made.

The rest of the *Role of the Captain* class zips along thanks to more lively and thought-provoking discussion. Without a doubt, the training is some of the best professional development I've received during my career. It outlines the high expectations United holds for its captains while emphasizing the role's unique challenges and humanizing its responsibilities, risks, and rewards. But perhaps more than anything, it leaves me with the life-and-death reminder of how tremendously important it is for me to do the job well.

As the class draws to a close, Captain Crawford outlines the rest of our month-long captain training. First, we'll review United's operating policies and procedures. Then we'll complete computer-based training covering the systems and components of the 737. After passing written tests on those topics, we'll move on to actual aircraft training in the flight simulators. The pace, he cautions, will be arduous.

"All of you have been assigned training partners who are also upgrading to captain on the 737," Captain Crawford says, holding up the list of pilot pairings. "You'll swap back-and-forth between the left seat as a captain and the right seat as a first officer during each training session. You'll be a team from here on out, so get to know your partner well. Stick together, and help each other grow. This is the time to make mistakes," he reminds us, "because in a few weeks, it won't be training anymore."

Captain Crawford reads off the flight crew pairings and suggests we exchange cell phone numbers and email addresses. My partner is a Houston-based pilot named Chris, who, despite being originally from Maine, wears a Texas-sized smile and drives, fittingly, a Texas-sized pickup truck to match. I'm eager to get to know him, and I'm optimistic we will get along well given his jovial personality.

"There's just one more thing to do before we wrap up," Captain Crawford tells us. "The wing ceremony."

It catches me completely off guard, because I have figured we would get our captain wings at the end of training, not the beginning. But Captain Crawford emphasizes that we need to embrace our new position in order to transform our thinking. We are no longer first officers or merely captain upgrade candidates; we are captains.

"Your passengers don't lower their expectations because you're a new captain," he tells us. "In fact, they expect you'll perform as well as the most seasoned United captains. And United expects the same. I know that's a tall order, but I also know you can do it," he insists, encouraging us to trust the system. "Airlines like United have been training captains for decades and decades, almost like a captain factory. So if you work together with your partner," he says, "I have no doubt all of you will make it through."

In truth, most of us aren't concerned about passing training, but we *are* concerned about the integration. All fourteen captain candidates in the class started with Continental Airlines, which merged with United Airlines in 2010 to create the new United. Three years later, many parts of the new United are fully integrated, but the pilot groups are not. We still wear different uniforms and can't fly the other subsidiary's airplanes. Full integration for pilots will come with a combined seniority list in a few months. Partial integration, however, began when pilots who were on furlough from United on the merger date were recalled onto the Continental side of the new company. Almost all of those returning furloughees were assigned to the 737, which means as 737 captains, we will be on the front lines of integrating our two corporate cultures.

I have no idea what it will be like to fly with the United furloughees. I genuinely worry about how they will take to me, particularly since at 31 years old, I'll likely be significantly younger than most of them. Those, however, are concerns for another day.

Captain Crawford places the box of wings on the table next to him. "This is a big day. You should enjoy the feeling of satisfaction it brings. But remember that while your seniority triggered this promotion for you, it will be your hard work every day from here on out that proves you are actually deserving of the larger paycheck and the fourth stripe you'll wear on your shoulders."

Then he calls us up, one by one, to receive our new captain wings as our classmates applaud. It isn't a fancy ceremony, but it is impactful nonetheless. I feel tremendous pride as I firmly shake Captain Crawford's hand and grasp the folded white card containing my new wings. Emblazoned on the front of the card is the new United's logo, which is a combination of United's name and the blue and gold globe that has been associated with Continental Airlines since the mid-1990s. Inside, the golden captain wings worn by subsidiary Continental pilots are affixed in the center, flanked by a simple message, saying, "Congratulations, Captain Korry Franke."

Captain Korry Franke. It seems funny to see my name written that way. I sit down and stare at my new wings, smiling as I run my thumb across their shiny face, feeling each little indentation of the five-pointed star in the center—the star of a captain—and the woven wreath that is wrapped around it. I think about how different these wings are from the first set I ever received—stick-on plastic wings that a captain gave me when I visited the cockpit of his USAir flight to Orlando in 1986, my first trip aboard an airliner. Those wings represented the start of a lifetime fascination with flight. And my new captain wings represent years of planning and hard work, long hours spent as a flight instructor working for low pay, multiple moves across the country chasing different internships and flying jobs, and, finally, a childhood dream attained.

I catch myself wondering what a particular high school teacher whom I admired would now think of my decision to pursue a career in the airlines. Back then, he had cautioned that the airlines were tough and unpredictable. He had told me that no amount of effort or planning on my part could circumvent the raw and unforgiving power of a seniority list. At the time, it had felt to me like he believed pursuing an airline career was tantamount to throwing my potential away. Now, part of me wonders whether my present success means I have proven him wrong. But if I'm being honest, another part of me—a much quieter part deep within me—wonders whether I have simply proven my teacher's point for him. After all, it was merely my position on the airline's pilot seniority list that has triggered my promotion to captain. And perhaps that means luck was simply on my side.

I shake off the reflection, reminding myself that none of this matters right now, because while I may have captain wings, I won't actually fly as a captain until I get past the Box. And its many daunting challenges await.

CHAPTER 2

The Box

*"Everyone has oceans to fly, if they have
the heart to do it. Is it reckless? Maybe.
But what do dreams know of boundaries?"*
- Amelia Earhart

Houston, Texas – Late June 2013

They look like giant marshmallows on stilts," Jen tells me as we stand on the narrow platform, gazing onto the twenty-foot-tall machines and the wall of windows beyond them. "Or maybe sci-fi aliens."

The two contraptions fill the cavernous space, each one resting atop six stilt-like legs that anchor it to the room's cement foundation.

"These are new ones," I explain. "You can tell because of how rounded their fronts are. That's where the visuals are projected." I describe how the older flight simulators had looked like big boxes, which was how the simulators first earned their unofficial nickname. "The Box has a much nicer ring to it than the Blob, don't you think?"

"Just a bit," Jen replies, shaking her head at my attempt at humor.

Looking closely, we can see both machines jiggling ever so slightly. Then, out of nowhere, one jukes and jives frantically. Its hydraulic legs make high-pitched squeals as fluid compresses through the metal tubes to maneuver the massive box forward and back.

"Probably a landing," I tell her. "And a hard one at that!"

Jen laughs.

"Come on. Let's go find a simulator that's not in use so we can peek inside."

I place my hand on the small of Jen's back and guide her up the short staircase leading to the main artery of the United Airlines Flight Training Center in Houston, Texas. The complex sits directly adjacent to the busy departure runways of the George Bush Intercontinental Airport. Originally, it served the flight training needs of only Continental Airlines pilots; however, after the merger, it became a complement to United's much larger facility in Denver, Colorado. And together, the two training centers provide almost all of the flight training for the new United's 12,000 pilots[4].

Jen has heard me talk about "the schoolhouse" many times in the past, but until today—the start of her three-day trip to Houston during a break in my captain training—she has never visited the facility in person. That's because access to United's simulators requires specific permissions, and only after I jumped through those internal hoops was I able to set up her behind-the-scenes tour.

"It's hard to believe it's already been ten years since I first trained here as a Continental intern," I tell her as we walk down the narrow hallway adorned with framed pictures of the airline's airplanes and various print advertisements from years past. "Of course, it was a lot more fun back then."

The Continental Airlines internship had served as the incredible 4-month capstone experience of my tenure at Embry-Riddle Aeronautical University. From my cubical next to the window on the 43rd floor of Continental's Houston headquarters, I completed an assortment of research and administrative projects for senior leaders of the airline's Flight Operations department. In exchange, Continental granted interns like me a number of perks, including flight deck

---

[4] In January of 2017, United consolidated all of its flight training operations at the Denver facility.

jumpseat access, which allowed us to complete cockpit observation flights all over the country each weekend, and intern education programs, the highlight of which was the MD-80 flight simulator course. Such perks more than made up for the fact the internship was unpaid, but the one that eventually paid the largest dividends for me personally was the preferential consideration given to pilot applicants who were former Flight Operations interns.[5]

I stop suddenly in the hallway, pausing in mid-thought to point out an empty classroom similar to the one my classmates and I had used a few weeks earlier for the *Role of the Captain* course. When I start walking again, Jen asks, "Why do you say it was more fun back then?"

"Because the stakes were so low. Continental's MD-80 simulator was the first jet I ever 'flew,'" I say, holding up two fingers of each hand to make quotation marks in the air. "And flying the simulator was like playing with a shiny new toy—a $20-million toy that could do lots of fun tricks." I point out another room, this one containing training devices for the airline's cockpit flight computers. I continue walking. "So it was exciting and fun to see what the simulator could do, to challenge myself by flying around with a failed engine or trying to land with super gusty winds. But in the back of my mind, I knew I'd never actually have to face those situations in real life, since I wasn't going to fly the real jet. It was like I was playing a sophisticated video game. But now, I know my life and those of my passengers depend on my mastery of the skills I learn in this building. I need to be ready for anything. And so the stakes—and the stress—are much higher."

"I can see that," Jen says.

We walk past the snack area on our way to the staircase leading to more simulator bays. Above the water fountain, an old Continental Airlines sign hangs on the wall, just one of the many clues in the

---

[5] The structure and benefits of United's Flight Operations internship program have changed. Consult United's website for the most up to date information.

building indicating that the complete integration of our two airlines is far from complete.

"Anyway, that MD-80 simulator is long gone now. If memory serves me, I think Continental dismantled it shortly after I flew it during my pilot interview here. That was a few weeks after we first met."

"You mean the day your life changed forever?"

"Yep," I grin. "The day I landed the job I'd been chasing for years."

"Mmhmm," Jen groans as she rolls her eyes and grins at my bad joke.

In truth, however, I know she's correct.

We had met in the hospitality suite of a beachside hotel in Daytona Beach in January of 2006. We were both in town for a statewide conference of Florida resident assistants: Jen as the leader of the delegation of students from the University of West Florida, and me as the speaker scheduled to deliver the keynote address on the conference's final night. I had noticed her as soon as she walked into the suite, but it took some time for me to build up enough courage to go say hello, partially because Jen looked absolutely gorgeous. At 5'4" she was comfortably shorter than me—the perfect height, I'd later discover, for kissing her forehead while wrapping my arms around her in a giant bear hug after coming home from a trip. Her stylishly cut hair—then blond with highlights instead of her natural brunette color, just to keep it fun—perfectly framed the soft features of her face, flowing downward until barely reaching the tops of her shoulders. Her eyes were deep green, and they were as mysterious as they were intoxicating. They pulled me in and convinced me there were many more layers to this woman than were visible on the surface. Like the playfulness that came through when I heard her laugh. It was more of a subdued chuckle, really, which was accompanied by a seemingly endless smile that showcased her brilliantly white teeth. And, of course, there was her figure, complete with curves in all the right places and in just the right proportions. It was all I could do to prevent my eyes from drifting, especially on that first day. But I knew better. Judging from her toned arms, I could tell Jen was one tough woman who would fight for herself, her family, or the causes she believed in at a moment's notice.

The time flew by as we talked that night, late into the evening. When we talked about her studies at UWF, she lit up as she spoke about being the first person in her family to attain a four-year degree or to attend grad school, for that matter. I quickly realized Jen was a woman who never shied away from setting big goals or from working hard to achieve them. So when she mentioned she was training for her first marathon, I wasn't the least bit surprised, since powering through 26.2 miles would be a walk in the park for someone as strong and determined as she clearly was.

As for me, we talked, unsurprisingly, about my work then as a pilot for American Eagle Airlines. I did my best to mask the unglamorous and low-paying truths about the regional airline flying I was doing at the time, but there was only so much I could do to make flying to places like Lawton, Oklahoma, or Shreveport, Louisiana, sound exciting. Worst of all for me, Jen seemed unimpressed by my pilot talk. UWF shared its hometown of Pensacola, Florida, with a major flight training base for the Navy, Marine Corps, and Coast Guard. So Jen had met plenty of pilots, and she had heard plenty of not-so-flattering stories about flyboys and their antics. I could tell she wasn't overly eager to find out if the tall tales she'd heard about pilots were actually true. But I also knew I had never met someone like her, and I desperately wanted to convince her that this flyboy was different and worth a shot. As luck would have it, my speech at the end of the conference gave me the opportunity to do just that.

My speaking slot was less than ideal, right after dinner and just before the end-of-conference dance party. I knew I needed to do something unique to capture the attention of the roughly 400 Florida college students in attendance, so I opened my speech with a popular rap song whose lyrics I had carefully rewritten for the occasion. It was far from what the crowd—or Jen—had expected from me, a 5'11", clean-cut guy in a suit. But it worked like a charm, rallying the college students to their feet and captivating their attention, including Jen's.

"You're alright," she had said to me with a sly look as the dance party got underway.

"Alright enough to get your number?"

"I think we probably can work that out."

"How about alright enough to let me come to Pensacola and take you out for dinner sometime?" Travel benefits were then, and still are, some of the best perks of working for an airline. And they particularly came in handy while trying to woo a woman who lived several states away from me.

"Maaaaaaybe," she said, tucking her chin down and grinning. "But you're pushing it!"

A few weeks later, I flew from my home at the time in Dallas/Fort Worth to see her. And as I was waiting in the Pensacola airport terminal for her to pick me up, I received a call offering me a pilot interview at Continental Airlines.

"You must be my lucky penny," I told her as I slid into the front seat of her Ford Escort.

"Oh, really?" she asked. "Why's that?"

"Because a few minutes ago I got a call to interview for my dream job."

"Whoa!" Jen exclaimed. "That sounds like big news. Congratulations!"

But despite her excitement, I knew she didn't fully understand the significance of that call. Then again, how could she? She didn't know the airline business. She didn't realize that securing the earliest possible hire date was absolutely critical to a pilot's long-term success, since it was the hire date that largely determined a pilot's seniority number. She wasn't aware that absolutely everything about a pilot's career depends on that seniority number—from the types of airplanes and routes the pilot flies to the monthly schedules and annual vacations he or she receives. In fact, seniority is the only factor used to determine whether a pilot is promoted or demoted. Nothing else matters.

Jen didn't know any of this. But I did. And that's why I had pushed so hard for the seven years leading up to that call, making my life's focus accumulating the education and flight experience I would need to stand out from the other 15,000 or more applicants I suspected would be angling to get hired as a pilot at a major airline. It was why I started taking flying lessons as a seventeen-year-old in between my junior and senior years of high school in my hometown of Chambersburg, Pennsylvania. It was why I had packed my Embry-Riddle course load and taken summer classes at the Daytona Beach campus to facilitate an early graduation. It was why I'd happily moved to Washington, D.C. and Houston, Texas, for unpaid internships that might give me an in with both a regional and a major airline. It was why I had accepted a job as a flight instructor in Lynchburg, Virginia that paid a whopping $14,000 annual salary—my first job after college, the one where I imagined my high school teacher shaking his head at me for making such a silly career choice. It was why I spent countless early mornings and late nights building flight time as a flight instructor while my friends were out having fun. It was why I was ecstatic to move back to Texas in 2004 for a job as an airline pilot for American Eagle Airlines making barely over $20,000 a year.

Jen didn't know any of that. But I did. It was all I had thought about. It had consumed every moment of my life. And finally that call had come. Finally, the realization of my childhood dream was tantalizingly close. And there was no way I could wait a few hours, let alone a day or two, to share my news with my family and closest pilot friends.

Rightly so, Jen seemed on the edge of annoyance as she drove us to dinner while I chatted away on my phone beside her, almost as though she were my personal chauffeur. Yet somehow she refrained from kicking me to the curb right then and there. Her incredible display of patience was just one more thing proving to me how amazing Jen really was.

The two of us dated off and on the next few years. Once, we took a pause when life got crazy as Jen finished her master's degree and I relocated to Pennsylvania to be closer to Continental's Newark hub. A while later, Jen moved to Syracuse, New York, to be closer to her family, and we started dating again. But we ended up taking another pause when I stupidly got cold feet after things started getting serious.

Almost immediately, I regretted the decision. There was no one else like Jen. There was just something about her—a spark and confidence that made me come alive inside. And no other woman I dated came close to measuring up to her in my eyes.

It took a lot of convincing—well, groveling really—but Jen eventually agreed to give me one final chance. Thankfully, the third time proved, in fact, to be the charm. I proposed on a bitterly cold and windy January night along the Brooklyn Heights Promenade overlooking Manhattan's classic skyline. And ten months later, in November of 2010, we were married.

We had taken a rather circuitous path to the altar, but our winding road and all its twists and turns eventually got us where we needed to be. Neither of us knew where that road would lead us next—Chicago, it turns out—but we knew we'd get there together. After all, we were more than just partners or best friends. We were Husband and Wife—two terms that seemed appropriate, if not overly obvious, nicknames we could adopt for one another. And so we did just that.

Now, almost four years after saying "I do," Jen and I reach the next small staircase at the Houston training center, and I guide her down to the boarding platform for two more mammoth flight simulators. One of the machines isn't in use, resting instead on its fully-compressed stilt-legs. Its narrow entry door is open, and a white metal drawbridge connects the Box to the platform where we are standing.

Jen points to a thick bundle of wires dropping from the base of the machine. "What are all those cables?"

"Those connect the Box with the server room handling the millions of complicated calculations that are necessary to actually make the simulator work. I can't even imagine how powerful the processors need to be to run this thing."

"Seriously," she says.

"Let's hop in and take a look for a minute."

I open the gate at the start of the loading bridge, which is about ten feet above the floor of the bay, and the two of us head toward the simulator. "B-777" is written above the entry door in Boeing's signature font, signifying that this simulator is for the much larger jet United uses for its ultra-long-haul flights, such as Newark to Hong Kong.

As we step inside, we notice the sound of fans whirring to keep the electronics cool. Jen gazes around the tiny room, focusing on the cockpit cutout in the front. "How similar is this to the real thing?"

"If it's not identical, it's pretty darned close," I say. "It's almost like the simulator manufacturer went to Boeing's assembly line and stole the entire nose section of a plane already in production— avionics, buttons, switches, displays...everything. All the way down to the cup holders and window cranks. And everything works the same as it would on the real plane, with only a few minor exceptions here and there."

"That's crazy," she says as she lets her eyes drift around the room, eventually settling on the computer station with several large touchscreen displays behind the left pilot seat. "What's that?"

"That's the instructor's station. From there, the instructor programs the simulator's location and the various weather scenarios and aircraft system failures the crew will face."

"It looks complicated."

"Fortunately—and unfortunately—for us, there are definitely a lot of options, that's for sure. We can practice or recreate almost anything in here, which is why the simulators provide such good training. They are truly technological marvels."

I point out the two additional observer seats, which are mounted to rails in the floor, and then motion toward the left seat with my arm. "Go ahead and take a seat," I suggest.

She looks at me a bit hesitantly and then smiles as she maneuvers around the wide center console covered in buttons and slides into the tall-backed captain's chair. She grabs onto the control wheel with her left hand and rests her right hand on the thick throttle quadrant, peeking over her shoulder and giving one of those endless smiles I love so much.

"Captain Jen," I say. "I've gotta get a picture of this!" Jen isn't amused, but she reluctantly smiles as I pull out my iPhone to snap a pic.

"The visuals look so real!"

"Judging from the terminal buildings, it's Paris." Having been there many times, I assure her it looks exactly the same in person. "Can you see the ramper?" I ask.

Jen pushes up on the armrests to cast her view over the dashboard. A synthetically generated person stands stoically on the ground, holding two orange wands above his head in an X—the command for the crew to stop the jet and set the parking brake. "Amazingly, his arms never get tired," I joke.

Jen rolls her eyes. "I just can't get over how realistic this is."

"Wife, I'm not kidding when I say you can forget you're flying a simulator. You feel a small thump when they simulate closing the cabin door. During taxi, you feel little bumps as you pass over seams in the concrete. And when you're flying, it feels very close to the real thing—even the simulated turbulence the instructors like to throw in just for fun."

"Is it scary?"

"I wouldn't say scary. But your adrenaline definitely pumps while working through challenging situations and complicated procedures. But that realism is why it's such great training. I mean, in here we can safely practice engine failures, fires of all sorts, flight control jams, hydraulic leaks, and a host of other critical system malfunctions that would be far too dangerous to practice on a real airplane. And we can practice them again and again if necessary. That way, if we face the issue in real life, we're ready. The same thing goes for unbelievably foggy conditions or extreme crosswind landings at the limits of the airplane's capabilities. We wouldn't want to deal with any of those for the first time when hundreds of people's lives depend on us nailing it. Hands down, the Box is one of the biggest reasons flying is safer than crossing the street."

"Just crazy," she says.

"Want to fire it up and take it for a spin?"

"No way, Jose!" Jen exclaims. "I'll leave the flying to you!"

I chuckle, suggesting, "Well then, I guess we should get moving. If we're late for dinner, Kurt and Kim will never let us live it down."

"Truth!"

Red wine cascades over the bottle's lip, sloshing about as it pools together along the bottom of Kurt's tall glass.

"Rioja," he says to us as he swirls the glass's ruby contents and lifts it toward his nose for a quick sniff and a small taste. Turning to the waitress, he says, "This will be great." She quickly goes about filling the empty glasses for Kurt, his wife Kim, Jen, and me before taking our meal orders.

Dinner is at Jasper's, a self-proclaimed "gourmet backyard"

restaurant near Kurt and Kim's home in The Woodlands, Texas. The kitchen's giant indoor grills cast the rich summertime scent of charcoal throughout every nook and cranny of the trendy dining room. To me, Jasper's seems much more city-chic than backyard bash, especially with the exposed wooden beams in the ceiling that are painted black and which give the room a distinctly loft-like feel.

The four of us sit around a wooden table that is polished to a glassy sheen. A single overhead light, which is perfectly centered above us, bathes the table with a warm glow and casts small shadows across our faces.

I play with the stem of my wine glass, grinning as I lean back into my chair.

"What's so funny?" Kurt asks.

"Nothing, really," I say. "It's just that Rioja makes me think about all those trips we used to do to Madrid and Barcelona," I tell him, referring to the years that he and I spent flying the Boeing 757 and 767 for Continental Airlines.

"Oh, yes," he agrees. "It's hard to beat tapas in the Plaza Mayor."

"Or paella along the Med."

We both smile, letting a slight nostalgic pause fill the air.

"Those were some good times," Kurt continues.

"I'd call that the understatement of the night." Both of us fully understand the uniqueness and good fortune of our opportunity as first officers to travel to Europe several hundred times before reaching the age of 30. "I know international is a lot more tiring than the mostly domestic flying we're doing now, but there's just something about crossing an ocean that makes it seem more..."

"More exotic?" Kurt offers.

"I was going to say impactful. But yes, exotic, too."

"Why impactful?" Jen asks.

"So many reasons," I reply, pulling a dinner roll from the basket on the table. "For starters, it's not like you're going to hop in your car and drive to Rome. I mean the only other way to get there is to spend two weeks on a boat. And who really does that anymore?"

"Retirees on cruise ships?" Kim asks, tucking a few strands of her long blond hair behind her ear.

I laugh. "Fair point," I say, pulling apart my roll. "But cruisers aside, I just think a long international flight feels more like a big event instead of mere transportation."

"And that's before you even take off," Kurt says.

"Exactly," I say, spreading some butter across my roll. "And once you do, the next thing you know you're looking down upon the entire hook of Cape Cod and the rocky cliffs of coastal Maine and eastern Canada. Then the sun sets and you head out over the Atlantic Ocean, where the darkness of night and the blackness of the water combine to create this unbelievable setting for the most spectacular stargazing you can imagine." I notice Jen smiling. "I'm talking about stars like you've never seen. Thousands of them. All of them completely unobstructed by manmade lights, speckling the highest points of the sky," I say, lifting my hand and my eyes upward to emphasize my point, "all the way down to the ocean's horizon line."

"Oh, wow!" Jen exclaims. "Sounds beautiful."

"It's spellbinding," I say, taking a bite of my roll.

"I always loved seeing that," Kurt says. "Although, I'd often wonder if it was as enjoyable for the Pan Am guys who made those crossings on the flying boats," he says, referring to the iconic Boeing 314 Clippers.

I chuckle. "Probably not." Truthfully, I can't even imagine what it was like to fly such routes without the accurate weather radar, precise navigation equipment, or reliable long-distance communication systems we have today.

"But it sure would have been a great adventure," Kurt says with a smile.

"Something like that," I say, although I know he's right. "Anyway, next thing you know, the sun rises and the accents of the air traffic controllers change, almost like an audible map of your progress across Europe." I take a sip of wine. "First the Irish and the Scots, then the French, and finally the Italians. Soon you're stepping out of the crew van in front of the hotel, looking at this beautiful architecture, listening to locals chattering around you in Italian, and it hits home that you're actually in Rome!"

"With twenty-four hours to go see the sights," Kurt says, giving us his characteristic grin. "And to grab a good meal, of course." And as if on cue, our salads arrive.

"The best part," I say, "is that since it's likely you'll be back again, there isn't the pressure most tourists have to try and see everything during that one trip. You can actually take your time." I slice into my wedge salad, which is covered by blue cheese and thick chunks of bacon. "In fact, I'd say some of my favorite layovers were the ones where all I did was grab a bite to eat at a small café and then camp out on a park bench, reading a book as if I were a local."

"Remind me again why you don't take me to fun places like Rome?" Jen asks somewhat sarcastically, but somewhat not, as she takes a bite of her wedge salad, too.

"Because I need to make sure you have something to look forward to," I say. "And because I was too busy taking you with me on other trips to London, Shannon, and Oslo."

"Yeeeessssss," she says, slowly and drawn out as she sets her fork down and dabs the corners of her mouth with her napkin. "Oslo. The trip when you tried to leave me in Norway!"

"Sadly," I say, "it's not trying if it actually happens." I can still vividly remember Jen standing by the terminal windows in Oslo, looking on with disquietude, as I waved to her from the right seat of the 757 while our plane pushed back from the gate without her.

"I just needed there to be one more seat!" she exclaims.

Kurt laughs. "Oh, the joys of space-available travel."

"It's great when it works, and not so great when it doesn't work," Kim adds, taking a sip of wine. "We've all been there."

"Besides, it builds character," I joke. "And now you've got a good story to tell about your great Norwegian adventure."

Jen rolls her eyes. "I'm just relieved I made the direct flight home the next day and didn't need to attempt the ridiculous Plan B you and Kurt had devised for me."

"Wait, wait, wait," Kurt interrupts, leaning forward and grinning from ear-to-ear. "The flights to the U.S. from all over Europe were full for days. We didn't *want* you to have to get home the long way, but—"

Jen cuts him off. "You say the long way. I say a train to the smaller Oslo airport, a flight to Dublin, an all-night bus across Ireland, and then a flight from Shannon to Newark is way more than just the long way."

"That's right," I interject. "It's called the scenic route."

Jen rolls her eyes again.

"I just wish we could have figured out how to get you on a ferryboat," Kurt adds, reveling in the replay of the night the two of us plotted out Jen's elaborate backup plan. "That way you could have hit all the major forms of transportation."

"You're such a helper, Kurt," she chuckles, shaking her head. "Both of you are."

"Now *that's* the truth," Kim pipes in with her refined Texas drawl. "Leave these two alone for too long, there's no telling what sort of trouble they'll get you into."

"I think you mean good times," I suggest.

"Exactly," Kurt agrees, laughing. "Ahhhh, man. We've definitely done a lot of cool things over the years. You even managed to loosen up a bit compared to the first time I met you, which, quite honestly, I didn't expect."

Jen chuckles. "Oh really? Why's that?"

"He hasn't told you the story?"

Jen shakes her head.

Kurt looks back at me and asks, "We were, what, maybe three or four days into freshman year at Embry-Riddle?"

"Something like that," I say sheepishly, knowing where the story is going.

"Mr. President over there was hoping to get a jump start on his political career. So—"

"It wasn't a political career," I interrupt, "just a—"

"—so he knocks on my door, hands me a flier with his campaign talking points, and asks for my vote for this organization I'd never heard of."

"The Embry-Riddle Resident Student Association," I cut in again, trying to explain my logic. "I figured it would help me become one of the residence hall resident advisors later that year," which I understood was viewed favorably by the airlines offering internships.

Kurt plows ahead with his story. "But I'm barely even listening because all I can think about is how this kid is as formal as they come." Jen laughs, knowing his description of me is spot on. "Pressed khakis, button-down, penny loafers. Carefully practiced stump speech. The whole thing. So I'm like, 'Dude, it's Florida, remember?'"

"Kurt definitely remembered," I jump in. "I'm not sure you brought anything other than shorts and flip flops to Daytona."

"And yet somehow, I became an RA, too."

"Which is one of life's great mysteries," Kim chimes in, even though the truth is that Kurt is a lot more driven than his carefree, ready-to-party, west-coast demeanor would suggest.

"Well, we all have our own paths," I say, taking another bite of salad. "I just wanted to make sure mine had the i's dotted and the t's crossed."

"It really is ironic how similar those paths have been for you guys," Jen says. "The two of you along with Paul and Dianna," two friends who had also been in our group of new-hire RAs at Embry-Riddle.

Like us, Paul and Dianna were both highly motivated aspiring pilots. Paul hailed from New Jersey and sported the thin gold chain and somewhat-softened accent to prove it. And for her part, Dianna was a prim and proper, Volvo-driving southern belle from Virginia...who excelled in not-so-prim-and-proper sports such as target shooting. Yet despite the differences in our backgrounds, or perhaps because of them, the four of us became fast friends.

"Very ironic," I say. "It seems like we have been chasing each other around the country since the day we all met."

It wasn't far from the truth. The four of us had all cycled through the same internships while at Embry-Riddle, including the one with Continental Airlines. Then, after graduation, we trekked around to various flying jobs, such as the one Dianna helped me land in Lynchburg, Virginia, where I worked with her as a flight instructor and charter pilot. After building our flight time credentials, the four of us each moved up the airline pilot career ladder by getting hired in rapid succession by American Eagle Airlines, then the primary regional airline for American Airlines. It was during our time with that company that Kurt and I decided to save money and become roommates in Dallas, Texas, which, it so happened, was how he met Kim, who was one of my church-league softball teammates. And finally, the four of us continued on to Continental Airlines, joining the company only a few months apart in 2006 and 2007. Kurt, Paul, and I even ended up purchasing our first homes just a few miles from one another in eastern Pennsylvania after we were assigned to fleets based out of the airline's Newark, New Jersey, hub.

"At least we were chasing each other around the country until you two bailed on us and moved to Chicago," Kurt says, pointing at Jen and me.

The Chicago move had come about after the management team of the new United made changes to the structure of the combined airline. They had determined significant synergies could be realized by more efficiently deploying the new United's aircraft assets across its worldwide route network, irrespective of which livery—Continental's or United's—was painted on the sides of the planes. The logistics of executing such a plan, however, were complicated by many factors, not the least of which were union rules prohibiting pilots from one airline from flying the planes of the other until the two seniority lists were fully integrated. But integrating the seniority lists was an incredibly complicated process that wasn't scheduled to conclude until the fall of 2013. And so the short-term workaround was to staff a small number of pilots from Continental Airlines in the hub airports of United Airlines and to staff a small number of pilots from United Airlines in the hub airports of Continental Airlines. The Continental 737 pilot base in Chicago was one such base, and I had been instantly intrigued the moment the base was announced in mid-2012.

At the time, Jen and I were living in the eastern Pennsylvania city of Bethlehem. Jen was job searching after her employer downsized, and I had a freshly minted MBA from Penn State University that I was eager to put to work. Given that Chicago had always been one of my favorite cities, that I loved the idea of the two of us spending a season of our lives experiencing city living before we started a family of our own, and that the new United's corporate headquarters were in downtown's Willis (a.k.a. Sears) Tower, a move to Chicago seemed to me like a great life adventure for the two of us to undertake, not to mention an opportunity for me to possibly land a job in the airline's Flight Operations management ranks. Jen wasn't immediately excited by the prospect of moving to a big city several states away from friends and family, but she eventually warmed to the idea—particularly after she landed a job at the University of Chicago's Booth School of Business only a few weeks later. Before we knew it, my transfer to the O'Hare 737 base as a first officer had gone through, we put our house on the market, and we headed west toward our new city life.

"You know," I say to Kurt, "if memory serves me, you left Pennsylvania for Texas even before we left for Chicago."

Kurt chuckles, "Actually, I think you're right," he admits, his tone more somber. "Either way, our moves have definitely made these get-togethers a lot less frequent."

"And we need to work on that," I say.

"Yes, we do," he agrees.

The waitress returns, placing delectable-looking plates of baby back ribs and grilled pork tenderloin in front of us. "Enjoy," she tells us.

"So how *are* you liking Chicago?" Kim asks, looking at Jen as she takes her first bite.

"It's great!" she exclaims. "Very different than our home on Country Lane, but so far I like it a lot more than I ever expected, which is really saying something since I never considered myself much of a city girl. You'll have to come visit!"

"I'm not sure your little apartment will fit the four of us and our two kids," Kurt says.

"Ah, come on," I say. "There's plenty of space."

"You say that now. Just wait until you have kids of your own and you see the mountain of gear that comes with them."

"Mmhmm," Kim agrees.

"Well, thankfully, we've still got some time before then," I say in between bites of ribs. "At least a few months."

Kim looks up, her interest piqued.

Jen jumps in, saying, "We've been talking about starting a family for a while. I know there's no perfect time, but right now I'm training for another marathon, so we're thinking maybe after that."

"Really????" Kim asks, her eyebrows raised and her smile beaming. "How exciting!"

"Sounds like the clock's ticking, my friend," Kurt chides.

I nod, saying, "Tick-tock, tick-tock," to which Kurt lets loose one of his signature rapid-fire laughs.

"Ohhhhh, man," Kurt says. "Korry Franke, a dad. Never thought we'd see the day."

And now I'm the one rolling my eyes.

Kim looks to Jen. "You two will make great parents."

"Thanks, Kim! That means a lot, coming from you," Jen says. "We're getting really excited about it."

"It's a lot of change, but it's worth it," Kim replies. "Raising kids is the toughest and most rewarding thing you'll ever do." She pauses for a moment and then adds another, "How exciting!"

"So, Korry," Kurt says, clearly ready to redirect the conversation back to shoptalk. "How are you enjoying being based in Chicago?"

"Overall, it's been great," I respond. "I like taking the train to work—"

"Although I'm not so fond of him riding it in the middle of the night," Jen interjects.

"It's not that bad, Wife." I look to Kurt. "All part of the city experience, right?"

"Riiiiiight," Kurt says, laughing. He knows all too well how interesting public transit can be late at night thanks to his short stint living in New York City's East Village years ago.

Kim asks, "Is your subway stop close to your apartment?"

"Yeah. Just a few blocks away. Not bad at all, really."

"Nice," she says.

"And what about the crews at O'Hare?" Kurt asks.

"They've been a lot of fun," I say. "Midwestern nice."

Kurt nods.

"O'Hare doesn't have quite as much variety in the 737 trips as Newark did, but there's still a good mix of destinations."

"Well, it's hard to top Newark's flying on just about any fleet,"

Kurt says. "Europe or Asia, California or the Caribbean, there are good options for everyone."

"No doubt about it," I emphatically agree. "Granted, I could probably do without Chicago's winter weather, especially on the days when the wind rips off Lake Michigan." I pick up my wine glass. "Throw in a little snow and O'Hare landings can get a bit sporty." I take a sip. "Then again, my flying skills have never been sharper."

"I bet," Kurt says.

"Honestly, the only part of O'Hare that I'm not too fond of is the dynamics of the crew room. It's just contentious given all that's going on. And it sure doesn't help that we're still wearing differently colored uniforms."

"Why's that matter?" Kim asks, cutting a bite of tenderloin.

"Because the Continental pilots make up such a small percentage of the O'Hare base. It's like a sea of navy blue United uniforms with a few specks of black and gold sprinkled in here and there." I take a sip from my glass. "Makes it pretty obvious which 'team' a pilot is on."

"I see," Kim says.

"And I'm sure the United pilots who are now flying out of Continental hubs like Houston and Newark probably experience the same thing, only with the uniform colors reversed. The bottom line is the new uniform can't come fast enough."

"Same for the integrated seniority list," Kurt suggests.

"And that, my friend, is truly the giant elephant in the room. Until that's done, it will be nearly impossible for anyone to move beyond the us-versus-them stuff and embrace our new *united* team. Right now, emotions are simply too high."

"That's because there's so much at stake," Kurt says. "That list controls everything. It's why you got the captain upgrade and I didn't: your number was up."

"Precisely," I say. "So it is what it is. Nothing's gonna change until that list comes out."

"And maybe for a while after that," Kurt adds. "But it's going to make for some interesting times for you in the left seat."

"Interesting…and challenging," I say.

"Why challenging?" Kim asks.

"Because of the furloughees. And my age. And a lot of things."

"Why your age?" Kim probes.

"Oh, come on, Kim. Look at that baby face!" Kurt chides.

"What?" Kim asks with a laugh. "I see a little peach fuzz on those cheeks."

"Yeah, and it took him a week to grow it," Jen pipes up.

"Thanks, Wife."

"Just saying," she responds, taking another bite.

"Maybe that will be good when I'm fifty. But at thirty-one it's going to make it obvious that I'm substantially younger than most of these pilots, potentially by a lot. So you combine all those factors—the furloughs, the contention around the seniority list, my age—and I just suspect it's going to make for a tough dynamic."

"Ahhhh, buddy," Kurt says as he polishes off the last of his ribs. "I really do feel for you. But don't forget that at the end of the day, they still know you're the captain. It's not like you'll be hiding the four stripes on your shoulders."

"I know," I say, picking up the last of my Brussels sprouts. "I just never want to use the 'Do this because I'm the captain' line. I sort of feel that if I have to say that, then I've failed as a leader."

"I can see that," Kurt says. "Well, I'm excited to see how it goes for you. And honestly, I think you'll do really well."

"Thanks, Kurt."

"I'd be lying if I said I wasn't just a little bit envious of you getting the upgrade, but my number will be up soon enough."

"That it will," I respond. "And you'll have the benefit of learning from all my missteps along the way."

"I expect you to take good notes!" he tells me.

I laugh, saying, "I'll do my best!"

Kurt raises his glass, offering a toast. "To Captain Franke. Congratulations, buddy. It's going to be one hell of a ride."

"I'll toast to that!" I exclaim.

And the four of us clink our glasses together.

The weekend passes much too quickly, and soon I'm waving good-bye to Jen as she boards her flight home to Chicago.

Fun's over, I think. *There's work to be done.*

I walk back to my room at the airport Marriott, my home for the training cycle, and sit down on the desk chair beside the paper cockpit mockup I have stuck to the wall. With my flight manual open on my lap, I study procedures and review the callouts I'll need for simulator session number one the next morning. My alarm is set for 2:45 AM. There is no time to waste.

CHAPTER 3

Muscle Memory

"It's not the will to win that matters.
Everyone has that. It's the will to
prepare to win that matters most."
- Paul "Bear" Bryant

Houston, Texas – Late June 2013

*H*ow is it that something so familiar can look so different, I think as I
look up at the 737 simulator's overhead panel for the first time
from the stiff gray captain's seat.

But it does look different. In fact, it looks *very* different, almost
like every single switch on the complicated panel has been moved,
although I know that's not the case. But from three feet to the left
of the seat I used to occupy—a seat I spent several thousand flying
hours in as a first officer—my perspective is completely different. And
something inside me says this won't be the last time my perception of
my surroundings shifts.

I jump into my preflight flow, letting my hands dance across
the panel, flipping the switches that control various aircraft systems
into their correct positions for flight, including some that were
intentionally misplaced by my instructor as a test. I tune navigation
instruments and check that Chris, my partner for this simulated
flight, has correctly loaded the flight management computer with
the performance information and routing we will need during our

session. I pull out the appropriate navigation charts for the lesson and clip them to the base of the window beside me. And finally, I plug in the headset I will use during our "flight," which is the last step for "making my nest," as I call it, each time I crawl into another airplane.

I hear the simulator's entry door smack closed behind me, immediately turning the inside of the Box dark as night. Only the soft instrumentation backlighting and a few moveable overhead lights above Chris and me cast any glow into the replicated flight deck.

"Okay, fellas," the tall, mustached man says in a thick Texan accent as he plops down onto his chair next to the simulator control station, both of which are directly behind my seat. "Chris, you did a really nice job. Now it's Korry's turn in the hot seat."

"And I *definitely* appreciate him setting the bar so high," I say.

Chris chuckles.

Since the two of us are captain upgrades, each of our four-hour simulator sessions will be split into two equal parts. Each day, we will alternate who starts out as captain. Then, after a short break in the middle, we will swap seats and do the whole lesson again. On this day, our first session in the Box, Chris has drawn the short straw, and so he starts us out. I'm not disappointed, since this lets me ease back into the hyper-aware simulator mindset that is necessary in the Box. It also gives me the opportunity to watch Chris manage all the day's issues before I must face them myself—a welcome warm-up for my first day playing captain. Chris sets a strong example for me to follow, and it's obvious that his previous experience as a regional airline captain will prove invaluable to him now.

"Motion's coming on," the instructor tells us. I feel a small jiggle in my seat as the Box comes to life, stretching its hydraulic stilt legs and moving into its neutral position. Concurrently, I hear the instructor's fingers tapping away on his control screen behind me, likely programming the weather and initial system faults that Chris and I will soon encounter.

It's about to get real, I think to myself. My heart beats a little faster as my first taste of nervousness sets in. I buckle my seat belt across my waist and pull the two shoulder harnesses down from behind my head. Then I rest my right hand on the center console thrust levers, awaiting the instructor's signal that it's time to begin.

As I do, the thought strikes me that the carefully refined muscle memory I've developed over ten years of flying in the right seat will need to be completely relearned because everything is now backwards. Instead of tweaking the throttles with my left hand, I'll now use my right. And instead of moving the control wheel with my right hand, now I'll use my left. Flying the 737, I suspect, will feel like throwing a baseball with my non-dominant arm, or perhaps more appropriately, like driving a manual transmission car from the passenger's seat.

But there is an even greater challenge awaiting me in the left seat than simply relearning muscle memory: changing my flight-deck mindset from being tactically oriented as a first officer to being strategically focused as a captain. As a first officer, I *did* a lot of things to assist the captain, such as setting up the flight deck, loading the flight computer, checking the exterior of the airplane, and sharing flying duties. But as the captain, I will be tasked with more leading than doing. Now, I'll focus on the big picture. I'll evaluate the flight plan and fuel load. I'll brief the flight attendants, coordinate with mechanics, and set expectations for the entire team. Most of all, I'll dictate the pacing of all flight-related activities and make any final decisions for issues that arise during a flight. I once had a captain at American Eagle refer to these captain duties as "orchestrating the dance," and it really is a fitting analogy. The captain, after all, isn't the dancer; rather, the captain is the conductor who brings the dance to life by effectively tapping and directing the talents of those who dance. And on this day, it's about time for me to grab the baton and start the show!

"Fellas, I believe I'm all set back here," the instructor says. "So whenever you're ready, I'm ready."

I look to Chris, who nods, and then I launch into a preflight briefing with him that is intended to set the tone and my expectations for our flight. The two of us discuss our plan for taxiing from the gate to the runway and departing, as well as our strategy for handling any challenges we may face on departure—such as an engine failure during takeoff, which is faaaaaar more likely to occur in the Box than in real life.

"Any questions or additions, Chris?" I ask after finishing the briefing.

"Nope. That all sounds good to me, boss," he replies in his slow and relaxed way.

"Well, then, *Preflight Checklist*, please." A smile creeps across my face; calling for that checklist is a captain's duty.

"Coming right up," Chris says, slapping his hand on the top of the dashboard and pulling out the folded white laminated card from its slot. He springs into the back-and-forth, call-and-response cadence that guides us through the fifteen or so items that are of the utmost importance to check before flight, concluding with, "Preflight checklist complete."

"Captain, are you ready to go?" the instructor asks, now posing as the gate agent as he hands me our flight's final paperwork.

"Yes, indeed," I respond.

"Okay, gentlemen. Have a safe flight," the instructor replies, just as any gate agent would normally say.

A moment later I feel a small thump as the simulator recreates the cabin door closing. I take a deep breath, knowing our lesson has begun. From now on, every word I say and every action I take is being graded and evaluated. The pressure is on.

Coordinating with the pushback tug driver on our ramp crew

through the intercom, another role played by our instructor, we push back from the gate and begin starting our engines.

The first motor spools up perfectly. The second one, however, proves more problematic. Midway through its start, I notice a gauge indicating the engine is overheating rapidly.

"Hot start!" I declare, shutting down the motor. If not caught quickly, a hot start could melt the engine's core and turn the multi-million dollar turbine into a congealed mass of junk. "*Engine Start – Aborted Start* checklist," I call to Chris.

He grabs the thick spiral-bound emergency checklist by his knee, and the two of us work swiftly through the short procedure.

"Nicely done, fellas," the instructor says. "If you'd just set the start lever to IDLE, I'll go ahead and spin up that engine for you to save time." And with the press of a button on one of his simulator control screens, we immediately have two motors turning normally as if nothing has happened. The simulator saves bundles of time that way.

Soon we receive our taxi instructions from ground control, who is played by...you guessed it...the instructor. "United One-Two-Three, Houston Ground. Taxi to Runway One-Five-Left[6] via a left turn on November-Bravo[7], left on November-Romeo, and right on Whiskey-Whiskey."

---

[6] Runways are named for their magnetic alignment, rounded to the nearest 10 degrees. Additionally, if two parallel runways exist at an airport, the runways are given the designation Left / Right, or, in the case of three parallel runways, Left / Center / Right. In this instance, Runway 15L is the left runway of two parallel runways that are aligned toward roughly 150-degrees, or approximately south-south-east. Of course, as viewed from the opposite end of each runway, the magnetic alignment is reciprocal. Thus, the same runway that is named Runway 15L when departing and arriving to the south-south-east is also Runway 33R when departing and arriving to the north-north-west.

[7] The International Civil Aviation Organization dictates that taxiways are named with letters. To ensure clarity, pilots and controllers use a standardized phonetic alphabet when referencing letters over the radio. Therefore the appropriate phraseology for taxiway name "N" is November, "B" is Bravo, and as is the case in Houston, "NB" is "November-Bravo."

I trace my finger along the paper airport diagram clipped to my window as Chris reads back the clearance in aviation lingo that perfectly corresponds to the assigned taxiways we will follow to the runway.

"Clear left," I affirm, looking out my side window to make sure nothing is obstructing our path, like a rogue fuel truck or another airplane that has been placed there—lovingly, of course—by our instructor. In the simulator, no detail is too small to be left out.

"Clear right," Chris replies after likewise checking his side of the jet.

It's time to taxi. My left hand falls to the wheel-like steering lever called a "tiller," which is mounted along the left-hand wall of the cockpit. Unlike the rudder pedals, which can only command turns of a few degrees left or right, such as those required for staying on the runway during takeoff and landing, the tiller can swivel the nose wheel almost 80 degrees to either side. But with only one tiller installed on most airliners, including the 737, taxiing is exclusively the duty of the captain—a duty that I have never before accomplished.

The tiller feels cool to the touch as I wrap my fingers around its scalloped grip. With my right hand, I inch the thrust levers forward, spooling up the engines just enough to get us moving. Our seats quiver as the Box rocks slightly to simulate our forward movement across the tarmac.

Approaching our first turn, I remind myself that since the 737 is roughly the size of a small house, and since its main wheels are far behind my perch up front, I need to slightly overshoot my turns, somewhat like a truck driver pulling a long trailer. At just the right time, I firmly squeeze the tiller and rotate it backwards to command my first big turn. The nose jerks hard to the left.

Wow, that's touchy! I think, surprised by the sensitivity of the tiller. *You've gotta be smooth, Korry,* I scold myself, knowing that in real life I'll have a team of flight attendants standing in the aisle for their preflight safety demonstration.

We creep down the taxiway, and after a few more turns and yet another checklist, we arrive at the runway's end.

"United One-Two-Three, Houston Tower, Runway One-Five-Left cleared for takeoff," the instructor says.

Chris reads back the clearance, and I reach up just above the front window and flip on the jet's landing lights on the overhead panel as we crest across the runway's threshold. I pull the tiller backwards again, turning the jet to line up with the long runway and its thick white centerline stripes.

I look to my right. "Shall we?"

"We shall," Chris says.

Smoothly, I push the throttles forward and command, "Check thrust." The simulated engine noise grows louder as the engines reach takeoff power, and the Box shimmies as the plane begins accelerating.

"Thrust set, ninety-five percent[8]," Chris announces, which is just what we expect.

I feel a consistent push against the small of my back as the Box rocks further and further back on its haunches to provide the sensation of acceleration. I focus my eyes down the long runway, occasionally peeking at the engine gauges on the center dashboard to ensure all indications are normal. I press down gently on the rudder pedals, using only the tips of my toes to subtly tweak the plane's path left and right to stay perfectly overtop the white dashed centerline.

"One hundred knots," Chris calls. The lights lining the edge of the runway zip past us in a blur. We are now in the "high speed

---

[8] Takeoff power is routinely set to less than 100% thrust in order to reduce engine wear, limit the chance of mechanical malfunction, and improve fuel efficiency. Many factors go into calculating takeoff thrust, including a runway's length, its condition (dry, wet, snow, etc.), the aircraft's weight, and the outside air temperature and winds, all of which affect an aircraft's acceleration rate. In general, the longer the runway or the lighter the aircraft's weight at takeoff, the lower the calculated thrust setting is.

regime," or what is more commonly considered "the go zone." Above 100 knots, we will abort the takeoff only for something catastrophic, such as an engine failure, a fire, or some other event that we believe may render our craft un-flyable.

Faster and faster we race, and the jiggling in our seats intensifies. "Vee-one," Chris states at our "decision speed" of approximately 175 miles per hour. Now, we are going flying no matter what—engine failure or otherwise—because the risks of attempting to stop on the ever-shortening runway far exceed those of taking off and handling the issue in the air. To confirm this decision, I pull my right hand away from the throttles and place it on the control wheel.

"Rotate," Chris says.

It is time to go "flying!" I pull back on the control wheel and watch as the simulated images projected onto the curved screen in front of our windows show the nose rising off the runway. The white runway stripes disappear beneath us, and a moment later, the jiggling stops altogether as the simulator calculates that all our landing gear wheels have lifted off the runway's surface into the smooth "air."

"Positive rate, gear up," I say. Chris grabs the long handle with the wheel on its end from the center dashboard, pulling it outwards and then up to command the hydraulic actuators to push the gear into the wheel wells. Without the drag of the gear hanging in the air, the plane accelerates quickly.

"Flaps to one," I say.

Chris moves the flap lever on the right side of the throttle quadrant up two notches, and the large metal pieces along the backside of the wings begin retracting inward, further reducing drag and helping us speed up even more.

"Flaps up. *After Takeoff Checklist,*" I command.

Chris flips a series of switches and then reads from the white laminated card to double-check that all the items are complete.

We keep climbing, just as expected, all the way up to cruising altitude. But the normalcy doesn't last long.

BOOOOOM!!!

The simulator jerks hard, almost as though our "plane" has been punched on its right rear side. The sudden jolt startles me, as does the loud bell that starts ringing continuously. Concurrently, a bright red light illuminates near the base of the throttles, indicating a fire in the rear cargo compartment located in the belly of the jet. Making matters worse, the fire appears to be accompanied by an almost instantaneous loss of cabin pressure. Of course, the simulator can't actually change the pressure in our ears, but it does sound a separate beeping noise and illuminate yet another red light that reads, "CABIN ALTITUDE."

Must have been some sort of explosion, I think.

Chris and I immediately grab our oxygen masks and place them over our heads. The masks heavily distort our voices, making us sound like Darth Vader, especially when either of us takes a breath with the intercom mic turned on and a *Kroooohhh! Paaahhhh!* sound is heard. The arduousness of communication makes it easy to see how confusion could creep in.

Admittedly, part of me feels a bit silly going through all the motions because I know we are at no risk of succumbing to high-altitude hypoxia or burning up from the cargo fire despite the visual and auditory signals suggesting otherwise. But that is what the procedure calls for, and we know we'll perform in the real world like we practice in the Box, so we don the masks and play the game.

"Declare an emergency and request lower immediately," I command in my heavily modified Vader-voice.

"Roger that, Korry. *Kroooohhh! Paaahhhh!*" Turning to air traffic control, also known as ATC, Chris commands, "Mayday! Mayday! Mayday! *Kroooohhh! Paaahhhh!* Houston Center, United One-Two-Three declaring an emergency. *Kroooohhh! Paaahhhh!* We've lost pressurization and request an immediate descent to 10,000 feet," which is where the air will be thick enough that we won't need our oxygen masks.

The instructor . . . I mean, ATC . . . grants our request without question. I pull the thrust levers to idle, pitch the nose of the plane down, and extend the speed brakes to assist with our rapid descent.

"I've got the airplane and the radios," I tell Chris. "*Kroooohhh! Paaahhhh!* You run the checklist."

Chris flips through the large tabs of the 300-page spiral-bound emergency checklist book to locate the appropriate procedure. Then he methodically works through the various steps of the procedure, reading each one aloud to keep me in the loop. Some steps require my confirmation, such as when Chris needs to press certain buttons to arm and discharge the fire suppression agent into the purportedly fire-filled cargo bin. And of course, the execution of the procedure is interspersed numerous times with *Kroooohhh! Paaahhhh!* for good measure.

"End of procedure," Chris says after finishing the checklist.

A few moments later, we level off at 10,000 feet where we both take off our masks.

"Oh, thank God," I say as I set my mask on top of its storage case beside me. "You've got the radios again," I tell Chris. "Request direct Houston." With no additional fire protection for that bin and no confirmation that the fire is out, we need to get on the ground ASAP.

"You got it, Korry."

The instructor, still in the role of the air traffic controller, clears us directly to the Houston airport for landing. I swiftly set up our navigation instruments while Chris relays to air traffic control the precise nature of our emergency, including how much fuel we have remaining, what type of assistance we require on the ground, and the number of "souls" on board, which is the official way of referring to the total number of passengers and crewmembers aboard our plane.

Then I pick up the flight deck interphone to call one of the flight attendants, who again sounds strangely similar to the instructor.

"Hey, this is Jimmy in the back," the instructor says in yet another different accent as he pretends to answer the interphone call.

"Jimmy, this is Korry. We've had an indication of a cargo fire along with a decompression. Are you all okay?"

"Yeah, we're fine and so are the passengers. Figured something was up when I saw the rubber jungle drop down," he says, referring in slang to the passenger oxygen masks and tubes that would have extended down from the cabin's ceiling during the decompression.

"Great. We're returning to Houston and are only five minutes from landing. Airport crash, fire, and rescue personnel will be waiting for us. Be ready for an evacuation in case they tell us the fire hasn't been fully contained."

"I'll pass the word along. I knew I should have called in sick today."

I roll my eyes. Instructors always seem to love being comedians when role-playing in the simulator.

Without missing a beat, the instructor, again acting as air traffic control, pipes up, "United One-Twenty-Three, Houston Approach. Report the field in sight."

"Wilco," Chris says in aviation lingo for "Will Comply."

The thick simulated cloud deck begins to separate, leaving only a few puffy clouds around us. In between them, we see the 3-D satellite imagery of the Houston area. And soon, the airport comes into view.

"United One-Twenty-Three has the field in sight," Chris reports.

"United One-Twenty-Three, thank you. You're cleared for the visual approach to Runway Two-Seven. Contact Houston Tower on frequency one-three-five-decimal-one-five. They are aware of your emergency."

Chris changes to the tower frequency and checks in as requested.

"United One-Twenty-Three, Houston Tower. You're cleared to land Runway Two-Seven. Fire trucks are standing by."

"Cleared to land, Runway Two-Seven, United One-Twenty-Three," Chris confirms.

The only thing left is to finish flying the plane. We slow down, extend the landing flaps, lower the gear, and fly the last five miles as we would any other approach.

As we near the runway, the airplane's automated voice tells us, "Fifty…forty…thirty…twenty…ten."

The Box shifts upward on its stilt legs to create the sensation of our wheels touching down. Inside the Box, I pull up on the thrust levers to initiate reverse thrust and press firmly on the brake pedals to bring the jet to a stop, all the while feeling the Box leaning forward in a recreation of the stopping sensation.

As we reach a complete stop, the instructor jumps into his next role, this time as one of the airport firefighters. "United One-Two-Three, it appears you have a significant amount of smoke and possibly flame coming from your aft cargo bin."

I turn to Chris, saying, "Notify ATC we'll be evacuating on the runway."

We leap into yet another emergency checklist, this one to ensure we correctly shut down our engines and secure other potentially hazardous systems prior to commanding the passengers to exit the jet. When the checklist is complete, I grab the public address microphone on the back of the center console in the cockpit and announce to my imagined passengers and flight attendants, "Release your seatbelts and get out!"

Immediately—and deadpan—the instructor interjects in his real voice, "Okay, fellas, nice job. The sim's on pause. Let's set up again for the I-L-S to Runway Two-Seven so we can do some low visibility approaches," which would be necessary, for example, when landing in the fog. "I'm repositioning you now."

It's as though the chaotic scene never even happened. I can almost hear the instructor going through the lesson plan in his head: Engine start abnormal…check. Normal takeoff…check. Cargo fire…check. Depressurization…check. Evacuation…check. And that's exactly how each lesson in the simulator is supposed to be—packed full. The sessions are mentally exhausting and physically draining, which is why most pilots—including me—find our normal once-a-year visits to the schoolhouse for recurrent training to be more than enough time in the Box.

An hour later, all the day's items are complete. As the instructor brings the Box "off motion," a beeping similar to a truck's back-up siren is heard, signaling that the narrow boarding bridge is lowering into place. Day one is in the books.

We pack up our things, and meet the instructor back in the briefing room we used earlier in the morning. Once there, he peppers us with questions about every aspect of our performance. What did we do well? What could we have done better? How did we work together as a crew? Did we follow procedures appropriately? Did we forget anything? Every event is discussed. Every line-item receives a grade.

"For your first day, fellas, I'd say you did very well," he tells us.

The accolades are nice to hear, although I know I made a few mistakes here and there, giving me plenty to work on before tomorrow's simulator event.

"If there aren't any more questions, that's it for today," the instructor concludes. "I'll see you back here tomorrow. Same place, same time."

As we leave the briefing room, Chris asks if I want to grab a bite to eat.

"That sounds fantastic, actually," I tell him. Since my 2:45 AM wakeup call, I have subsisted completely on coffee and Snickers bars, which aren't the most robust provisions.

"Great," he says. "I know just the spot."

The waitress lowers a nearly overflowing plate of food onto our booth's laminate tabletop. "Western omelet with French toast for you," she says, looking at me. "And huevos rancheros for you," she tells Chris. "Can I get you anything else?"

"I think we're all set," Chris says. "Thank you."

"Well, then," she says, glancing over at our little coffee mugs and finding them freshly refilled, "enjoy your breakfast."

Chris sees me eyeing up my food. It looks and smells fantastic, which I admittedly find somewhat surprising given my first impressions of the diner. The Hot Biscuit had looked to me like a low-budget Denny's, and I'd wondered if the lack of patrons was because of the time of day or because its greasy spoon was, perhaps, a bit too greasy. Remembering that airline crews are unrivaled pros at sniffing out cheap and tasty fare in cities all around the world, I realize why Chris chose this place. Despite its outward appearance, he knows that the Hot Biscuit delivers.

"I can't believe you doubted me," Chris chides, picking up his fork.

"My wife tells me that all the time," I joke, doing the same.

"It may be a little rough around the edges, but it's good."

"I just hope it's still good a few hours from now, too."

Chris chuckles. "Now, I know better than to make any guarantees about that!"

I laugh as the two of us tear into our meals, consequences be damned, before turning our conversation to our day's performance in the Box.

"Chris, I can't tell you how much I appreciate your help today."

"Same for you," he says, still chewing. "Training is so much easier with a good partner."

"For sure," I say, sipping my coffee. "It's easy to tell you've got prior experience in the left seat. You seem so at ease. Like you're riding a bike."

"Maybe a very old and rusty bike," he quips, taking another bite of his eggs. "All things considered, I'd say we both did well today."

"I totally agree. Plenty to work on, but for day one, I'll take it."

"Yep."

I drizzle some syrup over my French toast. "It does bug me that I forgot to make an announcement to the passengers after the cargo fire and depressurization. That's basic stuff."

"Nah, don't sweat it, Korry. We were busy. You do what you can and move on." He picks up his coffee cup. "The flight attendants would have made an announcement anyway." He takes a sip. "Besides, you know how this works; it all comes together by the end of training."

"That's true," I agree, setting the syrup down. "There's just a lot on the line now. The forgotten announcement was a little mistake. But what if it's something bigger next time? I'm aiming to get everything."

"Well, you can aim all you want, Korry, and most of the time you'll get it. But sometimes you won't. That's why there's two of us on the flight deck."

"Oh, I know," I say, cutting off a bite of my French toast.

"And a checklist. Lots of checklists," he says, laughing.

"I'm just a perfectionist, that's all."

"We all are." Chris sets down his fork and dabs the corners of his mouth with his napkin. "But perfection is an impossible goal, Korry. For never having sat in the left seat, I'd say you did really well."

"Thanks, Chris," I say, feeling my spirits lift with his reassurance and confidence.

A big smile creeps across his face. "It sure is a hell of a lot of fun to sit over there and call the shots though, isn't it?" He takes another bite.

I nod, grinning. "Oh, yeah. Stressful, but a lot of fun. And a lot different than being an F-O," I say, using the shorthand for a first officer.

"You'll get used to it real quick," he says, taking another sip of coffee to wash down his sauce-covered eggs. "And then you'll never want to go back to the right seat again."

I laugh. "Don't doubt that in the least."

"No more being a chameleon. No more walkarounds in the rain. Now it's just you. And you can run your ship however you want to run your ship."

"That'll be very nice," I agree.

"I just hope we keep our seats after this seniority list comes out."

"I really think we will," I say, "but I guess that depends on how the company changes staffing numbers for each base once the new list is out and they have more flexibility to put pilots wherever they like."

"Which is what scares me," Chris says. "The uncertainty. It's all out of our hands."

"Completely," I reply.

We both take another bite.

"Do you think the arbitrators give much thought to how much their decision will affect our lives?" Chris asks.

"I don't know," I say, picking up my coffee. "I'm sure they think about it. They know the stakes." I take a sip. "But they're looking at it from a big picture perspective. Broad strokes, not the pilot-by-pilot reality of the award."

"It's just maddening to have no control."

"Oh, I agree. But that's how it always is."

"Yep."

"And that's been one of the biggest eye openers for me as I've read the seniority arbitration hearing transcripts."

Chris looks up, puzzled. "I'm not tracking with you," he says.

"I mean that all through the years, management teams for both airlines made decisions they believed were in the best strategic interests of their companies. Sometimes those decisions benefited pilots, such as when planes were purchased and bases were opened. And sometimes those decisions did not, such as when fleets were parked and bases were closed. But not once," I say, leaning forward and holding one finger up, "did the pilots really have a say about those long-term strategic decisions." I sit back. "They were just along for the ride, through good times and bad, benefiting when those management decisions grew the pilot ranks, and bearing the brunt of the decisions or circumstances that shrank them."

"You know," Chris says, nodding his head contemplatively, "I never really thought about it like that."

"I hadn't, either." I cut off a bite of my omelet. "And yet the irony is we are now asking these three arbitrators to pick sides and combine our two lists based on the various pros and cons of each airline. But those very pros and cons exist because of decisions that pilots on both sides had little or nothing to do with."

"That's true."

"And when the arbitrators eventually create the new list, they'll do so independently and without any direct pilot input. And that list will undoubtedly benefit some pilots more than others, for every aspect of our airline lives, for the rest of our careers."

He picks up his coffee. "At least until our next merger." And takes a sip.

I look sternly at Chris. "Don't even joke about that. One merger is enough."

He laughs.

"Makes you wonder how much our success in this industry depends on luck and timing," I say.

"Probably a fair amount," Chris suggests.

"I'm afraid you're right," I say. "And if that's the case, is there any way we can control that?"

Chris lets out a long sigh. "Other than making the best decisions we can in the moment, I'm not sure we can."

"I'm not sure we can, either."

"Just see what cards you're dealt, play your hand the best you can, and then hold on and see what happens."

"Hold on tight," I chuckle, knowing Chris is right.

He pauses for a moment before raising his coffee mug up for a toast. "Well, buddy, here's to luck being on our side."

"I'll toast to that!" I exclaim, grinning as I lift my mug up to clink with his.

After our meals are finished, we split the bill and head back to Chris's truck. He drives me to the airport Marriott and drops me off under its main portico.

As I step out of the truck, Chris asks, "Dark and early again tomorrow?"

"And the day after that. And the one after that. And the..."

Chris laughs as my voice trails off. "Well, I'll see you then. Get some rest."

"You, too," I reply, closing the truck's door and offering a small wave as Chris beeps his horn and pulls away.

Training continues, and Chris and I follow the same basic pattern for the rest of our course: wake up at 2:45 AM, brief for the simulator at 4:00 AM, jump in the Box for a four-hour session at 6:00 AM, debrief with our instructor, eat breakfast at the diner, take a nap, and prepare for the next day's events. Again and again.

With each new session, our skills improve. Each of us grows more comfortable in the left seat, and we become more decisive and at ease with orchestrating the dance. We work through all sorts of complicated mechanical malfunctions. We practice dozens of low-visibility approaches and train for crosswind landing after crosswind landing at the most extreme limits of the airplane.

Interspersed with our training days are clusters of days off, and I take each chance I get to zip home to Chicago to see Jen. The visits provide a fantastic opportunity for the two of us to catch up and for me to relax and recharge from the busy and stressful days at the training center. Some days we take long walks along the city's peaceful lakeshore paths. Other days we spend hours on our 37th-floor balcony, gazing onto the immersive urban landscape of Chicago's Financial District while we sip wine and chat about our plans for the future.

Eventually, I return to the Houston Training Center for one final set of simulator events. But this time it isn't training; it's our final evaluations, or "checkrides" as we call them.

Chris and I both feel the weighty pressure of the rides. Everything we've worked toward during training—not to mention our professional lives—comes down to passing these two checkrides as a team. And we know they won't be easy.

CHAPTER 4

The Window Test

*"Whether you think you can
or you can't, you're right."*
- Henry Ford

Houston, Texas – Late July 2013

I'm sitting in the left seat, waiting patiently—albeit nervously—for the instructor to clear us for takeoff. The simulated fog is so thick that there's no way Chris and I can tell we are purportedly in Los Angeles. In fact, the only things we can see out our windows are a handful of white runway lights extending into the gray abyss in front of us along with a massive "25R" painted in white on the runway. My five-point seatbelt harness is tight against my chest, which only exacerbates my heavy breathing. I wait for the instructor's call with my right hand resting atop the throttles and my left hand loosely gripping the control wheel.

And then the instructor's call comes. "United Eleven-Eleven, Los Angeles Tower. Runway Two-Five-Right cleared for takeoff."

Chris reads back the takeoff clearance as I flip on the landing lights at the base of the overhead panel. Slowly but steadily, I push the thrust levers forward and call, "Check thrust."

The simulator jiggles as the jet begins its takeoff roll.

"Thrust set, ninety-eight percent," Chris replies as the engine noise increases within the Box.

The runway lights move past us, whizzing faster and faster each second. My eyes focus on the white centerline stripe and its embedded lights. I tweak the rudder pedals slightly left and right to ensure the jet stays perfectly centered above them.

"One-hundred knots," Chris says. We are back in the high-speed regime and go-oriented.

My breathing quickens even more, and my gaze darts from the runway to the air speed indicator. Then back to the runway and then to the engine indications. Everything appears normal, so we press on as the jet keeps accelerating. The runway edge lights are a near-constant blur as we accelerate through 120 knots and then 140. The faster we go, the closer the fog seems to creep toward the jet. In fact, we can only see a few runway stripes at all before they disappear into the thick simulated cloudbank.

"Vee-one," Chris announces. We are past decision speed, so I move my right hand away from the thrust levers and place it on the control wheel to ensure we continue the takeoff no matter what.

Almost instantaneously, we hear a violent *BANG!*, and the airplane jerks hard to the left.

"ENGINE FAILURE!" Chris cries out.

I press hard on the right rudder pedal to keep the jet from veering off the runway centerline as we continue accelerating to rotation speed. My adrenaline pumps almost as fast as the runway lights zipping past us, undoubtedly because I know that there is not a worse place for an engine to fail than right after decision speed on the takeoff roll.

"Rotate," Chris commands.

I pull back on the control wheel and ease the 737's nose off the ground. A moment later, a small click indicates the wheels have lifted off the pavement.

"Positive rate, gear up," I say.

Chris pulls the lever from the center dashboard and moves it upward. And a few seconds later, the simulated wind noise decreases dramatically.

With only one engine operating, our jet has lost half its power and 80% of its performance. Only by flying with the utmost precision will I be able to accelerate and climb. But piloting the 737 with such precision can be a significant challenge given the instability caused by the intense asymmetrical thrust. The jet constantly fights my control inputs, wanting desperately to roll and list to the left. But I won't let it. I keep the right rudder pedal pressed nearly to the floor, and I twist the control wheel to level the wings.

What I wouldn't give for a horizon line, I think to myself, knowing that such a visual reference would make the task of flying on one engine all that much easier. But instead, I must use only my flight instruments, specifically the small attitude indicator, the magnetic heading indicator, the altimeter, and the vertical speed indicator, the last of which shows the craft's rate of climb or descent.

My eyes move quickly in a well-rehearsed pattern to scan the gauges: attitude, airspeed, attitude, altitude, attitude, heading. Again and again, tweaking and adjusting the control wheel and rudder pedals to stay on course. Yet without visual queues, the plane's subtle gyrations often provide false sensations of turning, so I must concentrate intently and ignore those illusory feelings. The gauges are all that matter.

"Los Angeles Tower, United Eleven-Eleven experienced an engine failure on takeoff and is declaring an emergency. Request straight out departure. Standby the rest," radios Chris.

"United Eleven-Eleven, Los Angeles Tower, approved as requested. When able, request souls on board, fuel remaining, and intentions," the instructor responds as air traffic control.

"Roger, standby."

I glance at the indicators for the left engine, which show that the engine has completely seized.

So much for trying to restart it, I think.

"Heading select," I call. Chris reaches up to the center control panel and presses a button that will help guide me in flying a specific heading.

Seconds tick by as our plane limps ahead. We have been airborne nearly a minute by the time we finally reach a safe height above the ground to accelerate from takeoff speed. "Flaps one," I say. Chris moves the flap lever, which is just to the right of the throttles, up two notches, and the 737 begins to pick up speed. A few seconds later, I call, "Flaps up," and Chris moves the flap lever to its full upward position.

Finally, as the jet reaches its best single-engine climb speed, I instruct, "Set max continuous thrust, engine failure checklist. Autopilot A is coming on." I breathe a small sigh of relief as I hand over the task of flying the jet to the autopilot; however, I know that with one engine failed, even the autopilot requires some assistance from me to keep the plane flying well.

Chris pulls out the emergency checklist. "Okay, let's see," he says as he flips the pages of the spiral-bound book to the Engines tab. *"Engine Failure or Shutdown,* I've got it here. Condition: one of these has occurred," he says, reading from the checklist. "An engine failure...yes." Qualification met, he moves on to the next part. "If severe damage is suspected—"

"And it is, since we aren't getting any N-1 rotation," I interject, referring to the name of the main fan blades at the front of the giant motor.

"—go to the *Engine Fire or Engine Severe Damage or Separation* checklist." Chris flips a few more pages to find that checklist. He holds the book carefully, using his right thumb to mark his place throughout each step of the lengthy procedure. "Autothrottle, disengage," he says, reciting the next step. He reaches up to the center panel and flips off the autothrottle's control switch.

"United Eleven-Eleven, this is Los Angeles Tower. Do you have those souls and fuel on board figures?" the instructor asks.

"I've got the jet and the radio," I tell Chris. "You work the problem." Then to air traffic control I respond, "One hundred seventy minutes of fuel, and one hundred sixty-two souls on board," even though I know there are clearly only three people in the Box that day. "Any change to the weather on the field?" I ask the instructor/controller.

"United Eleven-Eleven, the fog is slowly lifting. Ceiling is now two-hundred feet overcast, and the winds are calm."

That's right at our single-engine minimums, I think. *How convenient.* But in truth, I expect nothing else in the Box, where the worst case is almost always the usual case.

"Los Angeles Tower, United Eleven-Eleven," I say, "we'd like to return to L-A-X for landing at this time."

"Roger that, United Eleven-Eleven. Contact SoCal approach on one-twenty-four-decimal-five."

I read back the frequency as I dial it into our radio panel. After checking in with the new approach controller, we are given a variety of turns to set us up for a westbound landing in Los Angeles.

Meanwhile, Chris continues to work through the complicated checklist. "Thrust lever affected engine, confirm," Chris says, almost as a question to me. He places his fingers on the left thrust lever and waits until I look down to ensure he is touching the correct lever.

"Confirm," I verify.

"Close," Chris says while moving the lever backwards. I see him move his right thumb another line lower on the checklist before continuing, "Engine start lever, affected engine, confirm."

This time, Chris places his hand on a small gray switch at the left base of the throttle quadrant. I look down and make sure Chris is touching the correct switch, since moving the wrong one will shut down the only operating engine. Obviously, that would be catastrophic. For safekeeping, I move my hand to the operating engine's start lever so as to guard it from being inadvertently shut down. When I am absolutely sure we are ready, I say, "Confirm."

"Cutoff," Chris announces as he moves the left switch down, shutting off fuel to the left engine. Since nothing happens, we know for sure that Chris has moved the correct lever. Once again, Chris moves his right thumb down another line and reads from the checklist. "If the engine fire switch or 'ENG OVERHEAT' light stays illuminated —," he pauses, glancing down to the center console where those switches are located. "They're out now, so I'll continue."

"Okay," I acknowledge, doing my best to watch his work closely as I monitor and assist the autopilot as needed.

Chris works methodically through the checklist for several more minutes. Each step along the way, I verify his actions as we secure hydraulic systems and air systems and turn on our auxiliary power unit to provide additional electrical power to the airplane. Eventually, the arduous checklist is complete.

"Chris, I'd like to transfer control of the jet and the radios to you so I can send a text message to the dispatcher and brief the flight attendants and passengers about what is going on."

"You bet, Korry. I see we are at 4,000 feet in Heading Select and Altitude Hold," Chris says, referring to the respective lateral and vertical autopilot modes that are presently engaged. "I have the aircraft."

"You have the aircraft," I confirm.

Using the flight computer's keypad, I send a text message to our flight's dispatcher, who plans and monitors hundreds of United flights from the company's sprawling 52,000-square-foot Network Operations Center, which consumes the entire 27th floor of the Willis (a.k.a. Sears) Tower in downtown Chicago. Aside from planning our flights, the dispatcher also serves as our best point of contact for coordinating any and all resources United has at its disposal. Of course, in the Box, my message goes to the instructor sitting behind me. But once again, things play out just as they would in real life.

The same is true for my update to the lead flight attendant, whom I call using the cockpit interphone.

"Hi, this is Sarah," the instructor says in a rather forced, high-pitched voice.

"Sarah, it's Korry on the flight deck. Our left engine failed on takeoff, and we're in the process of returning to Los Angeles."

"Oh, wow!"

I roll my eyes at the instructor's feigned incredulousness. "You've probably got about five to ten minutes until we land. Emergency equipment will be meeting us on the runway, but I don't anticipate an evacuation at this time. Is there anything else you need from us?"

"No, sir. We'll get the cabin ready."

"Great. I'm gonna make one quick announcement to the folks and then the P.A. is all yours."

"Thanks, Korry."

I place the interphone in its cradle and pick up the P.A. microphone. "Ladies and gentlemen, this is Captain Franke." I hear the announcement reverberate through the speakers in the Box, and I wonder if people outside our particular simulator can hear it, too. "We've had a problem with our left engine, and we're returning to Los Angeles for landing. We should be on the ground in a few minutes. The flight attendants are going to walk you through some important safety information, so please pay close attention to them. I want you all to know that we train regularly for events like this," I say, the irony of my words not lost on me, "and I have no reason to believe this landing will be much different than a normal one, except for the fire trucks you may notice approaching the plane once we're safely on the ground. We'll have more instructions for you at that time. Thank you."

Announcement finished, I place the microphone on the center

console. "Okay, I'm back," I tell Chris. "Flight attendants are up to speed and the passengers are briefed. I'm going to us set up for the approach. Do you have it on your side?"

"Yep. Sure do," he says.

"Okay, great." I dial in frequencies for the navigation aids we will be using. I pull out the emergency checklist to confirm our expected landing distance given the single engine. And then I talk Chris through my plan for our approach and landing. "If that all sounds good to you, I'll take the airplane back and ask you to continue with the *One Engine Inoperative Approach Descent Checklist.* I see we're now at 4,000 feet in Heading Select and Altitude Hold. I have the aircraft."

"You have the aircraft," he confirms before completing the next checklist.

"United Eleven-Eleven, SoCal Approach, turn left to heading two-eight-zero and descend to one-thousand nine-hundred feet," directs the controller. "You're ten miles from LIMMA, cleared for the I-L-S Two-Five-Left approach."

"Left to two-eight-zero to join the localizer, descend to nineteen-hundred, and cleared I-L-S Two-Five-Left, United Eleven-Eleven," Chris replies.

"United Eleven-Eleven, contact Los Angeles Tower one-two-zero-decimal-niner-five. Twenty-ninety-five. They are aware of your situation."

"Two-zero-nine-five, United Eleven-Eleven," says Chris, changing the radio frequency on the center panel and then dialing 1,900 feet into the altitude window of the autopilot. He checks in with the tower, and the instructor/controller clears us to land.

"Korry, I need to see you hand fly this approach, okay?" the instructor says to me…as himself.

"Sure thing." I disconnect the autopilot and announce, "Autopilot is off." The airplane is now completely in my hands.

Moments later I turn the jet to align with the electronic "localizer" that provides lateral guidance to the runway. As a diamond-shaped indicator begins moving down the side of my display, I say, "There's the glideslope," referencing the electronic path that will guide our plane vertically to the runway. "Gear down, flaps 15, *One Engine Inoperative Landing Checklist*, please."

Chris moves the gear lever down, extends the flaps, and reads from the checklist as I slow the jet and begin the shallow descent, tracking the invisible beam through the clouds to the runway's threshold all the while. "*One Engine Inoperative Landing Checklist*. Speed brake, armed. Gear, down and three green," he says.

"Down, three green," I confirm, pointing to the three green lights on the dashboard indicating all our landing gear are down and locked.

"Flaps 15, green light," Chris continues. "*One Engine Inoperative Landing Checklist* complete."

We drift closer and closer to the ground, still enveloped in the thick gray clouds. I fight the desire to make large inputs to counteract the asymmetric thrust. *Easy does it*, I tell myself, knowing that small corrections will be needed to keep the jet on the proper path, particularly since the sensitivity of the localizer and glide slope that guide us will increase as we get closer and closer to the ground.

"One thousand," Chris says.

"Set missed-approach altitude."

As we drift down the glide path, my eyes zip from one flight instrument to the next in a carefully practiced scan to monitor the jet's position. I grimace slightly as I tweak the controls left and right almost constantly. There's little room for error.

"Five hundred," Chris announces. We are now roughly the same height above the ground as the apex of the Washington Monument.

I slowly increase the power on the operating engine to keep our speed on point. We are right on the path, but not yet out of the clouds.

"Approaching minimums," Chris calls as we descend from 300 feet above the ground. If we do not see at least some part of the runway's approach lights in the next 100 feet, we will have to go around.

Come on!! I plead silently to myself. *Show me those lights!!*

My eyes are glued to my altimeter as it ticks downwards to our 200-foot minimums: first 280....then 260....240....And then through the gray haze, two parallel rows of white runway edge lights extend before us—just in the nick of time!

"Landing!" I call out forcefully. The runway lights seem partially obscured by the foggy drizzle, but there is no mistaking them for something else. I can even see the flashing lights of airport fire trucks spaced along the far end of the runway as they await our arrival.

The 737's wings rock as I make final corrections while cresting over the runway's threshold. The automated voice of the airplane then calls out, "Fifty...forty...thirty...twenty...ten." I jostle the controls left and right and pull back to raise the jet's nose for the landing flare.

Ba-bump! We are down!

I guide the nose wheels down onto the runway and shift my feet up to the tops of the pedals to apply the brakes.

"80 knots," Chris calls as the plane continues to slow.

When the 737 comes to a stop, the simulator rocks back to its neutral position. Behind me, I hear the instructor tapping his finger on the computer screen at his station. "Okay. If you would bring the start lever back up and get the rest of the switches into position, I'll set us up for the next event."

Vee-one cut...check! I think. *Just a few more maneuvers until this first checkride is over.*

Checkride number two, the Line Oriented Evaluation, or LOE, commences the next day—in the afternoon, thankfully, instead of the early-morning sessions that have been our norm. Admittedly, Chris and I both believe the harder of the two checkrides is behind us, since the first one—the maneuvers validation—tends to be the most frantic, stressful, and jam-packed test of all the required flight maneuvers and procedures we must prove we have mastered. The LOE, on the other hand, is designed to test how we handle some combination of issues relating to aircraft performance, weather, mechanical malfunctions, and passenger concerns during a simulated real-time flight between two cities.

In our case, we will fly from Dallas/Fort Worth to Houston and then back again. But unlike the maneuvers validation where we are hammered by one issue after the next, on the LOE we will likely face only a few issues, although the effects of them are often compounding. Since we are encouraged to fly the LOE as we would "on the line"[9], we take our time and are very methodical about addressing the issues that do come our way. That slower pace tends to lower our stress levels substantially. But perhaps best of all, we know there is no single correct answer for how the various issues on the LOE should be managed. In fact, if we land safely, work well together as a crew, and don't violate any rules or regulations unnecessarily, we pass, even if we make choices that are different from those other pilots might make. If at any point, however, the safety of the flight is in doubt, we fail.

Chris and I meet our evaluator, Doug, in one of the tiny preflight briefing rooms as usual. His white close-cropped hair bespeaks that

---

[9] "On the line" and similar "line" phrases such as "flying the line" or "lineholder" (or even air*line* itself) are routine airline-isms, the origin of which is fodder for great debate. Some say the "line" term shares nautical origins with ships that traversed the oceans. Others believe it refers to the railroad similarities. My vote, however, is that the line in airline refers to the lines on early air carrier route maps. With airplanes of that era incapable of flying direct long-distance coast-to-coast flights, air carriers operated between distant cities using a series of shorter point-to-point flights. One such route was United's "Main Line," which connected New York and San Francisco via stops in cities such as Cleveland, Chicago, Omaha, Denver, and Salt Lake City along the way. For a pilot to be out "on the line" or out "flying the line" would mean that he or she was flying somewhere along that route, literally on the line. Accordingly, a pilot with a regular schedule of flights on a particular segment of a given route would be referred to as a "lineholder. " And an air carrier with a collection of routes could reasonably be considered an air*line*. Today, the term "line" refers to the actual operation of the airline.

he is likely nearing the mandatory pilot retirement age of 65, which isn't surprising since both Chris and I have heard that Doug is the most senior evaluator on the 737 fleet. We have also heard that he is one of the toughest, and his gruff demeanor seems to buttress that reputation.

Our pre-simulator briefing isn't much of a briefing. Instead, it feels more like a fireside chat with a member of the old guard. It's part testing our knowledge of aircraft limitations and procedures and part passing along wisdom Doug has gained over the years, particularly with respect to the role of the captain.

As the two-hour briefing nears its end, Doug becomes more serious. "Gentlemen," he says in his heavy Texas drawl. "There is no more important task for an evaluator at this airline than to make sure we get the captain LOEs right. And do you know why?" he asks rhetorically, letting his gaze burn deep into us. "Because the company is asking us to certify that you are ready to be entrusted with the keys to their hundred-million-dollar airplanes and the lives of their passengers." Doug leans back into his chair. "Now that is one hell of a tall order, fellas. Don't you agree?"

Chris and I both nod.

"So what I need you to do today is prove to me beyond a shadow of a doubt that you're ready for this kind of responsibility. And the standard I'm going to use is that I need to know I have absolutely no reason to worry about putting my own family on one of your flights. Now, can you do that for me? Can you prove to me that you're ready and deserving of wearing four stripes on your shoulders?"

His question hangs silently over the room for a moment before I respond, "I believe we can," hoping Chris and I will perform to his exacting standards.

"Good," Doug says. "I believe you can, too, or you wouldn't be here right now. Then again, there's only one way to find out. So I guess it's time for us to go fly."

Doug pulls our flight paperwork from his leather satchel and plops the packet on the table. Then he reaches into his pocket and grabs a quarter, sliding it across the table. "The coin is to decide who flies the first leg," he tells us. As it happens, I win the toss, although because our LOE is graded as a crew, it really doesn't matter who flies which leg. The onus of ensuring our flight's safety is on both of us for this checkride, just as it would be in the real world.

We take a short break and then head to the Box. For the next four hours, Chris and I manage our respective flights as we work through predictable procedural tests like programming runway changes and flying through foggy weather in both simulated cities. I'm tasked with managing a minor mechanical malfunction en route during leg one, which doesn't lead to any major complications. But Chris is put to the test on leg two with a difficult mechanical malfunction.

Maneuvering for landing in Dallas, Chris calls for me to extend the landing flaps. Doug, however, has programmed one side of our flaps to jam almost immediately. This flap asymmetry scenario involves carefully working through a highly complicated checklist. The end result is a landing at a much faster speed than normal—nearly 210 miles per hour, which is faster than a NASCAR race car at full speed! The faster speed means we use considerably more runway and brake energy than normal to stop, putting us at risk of a potential brake overheat or fire if we aren't careful. Once again, decision-making, teamwork, and leadership are front and center. And once again, the two of us seem to be at the top of our game.

When we finally pull into the gate and park at the Dallas/Fort Worth airport, I feel certain we have passed, even though Doug hasn't said a word other than to instruct us to meet him back in the tiny briefing room in a few minutes. Nonetheless, I breathe a sigh of relief as the two of us pack up our things, knowing that we couldn't have asked for our LOE to have gone more smoothly.

When Chris and I enter the briefing room, Doug is already busy filling out paperwork we will need to sign. As with every other simulator debrief, Doug asks us how we think the flights have gone, and he seems to agree that the checkride has gone quite well. "I am completely confident I could send my family with you and not think twice about it," he tells us. I feel myself beaming at what I imagine is as good a compliment as Doug offers.

He slides the paperwork across the table, and Chris and I scribble our signatures in a few different spots.

"Congratulations, gentlemen," he says, reaching across the table to shake our hands. "I think you're gonna really like being captains. And I think you'll both do a very nice job out there."

"Thanks, Doug," Chris says. "It's exciting."

"It sure is," he tells us. "Hopefully you feel your time at the training center has given you a few more tools and techniques to combine with your existing experience." Doug picks up our paperwork and slides the folders back in his satchel. "But remember this was just training. Soon, the situations will be real. The choices will be real. And most of all, the consequences of those choices will be real." Doug pauses, staring both of us in the eyes. Then he leans forward. "You know, fellas, for quite some time now, both of you have been used to sitting in the right seat. And when issues arose on the flight deck, you'd make some suggestions and then you'd look to your left and ask the captain, 'So what do you want to do?'" He pauses momentarily. "Well, gentlemen, now the first officer is gonna be looking at you. And you're gonna look to your left as you always have, and the only thing you're gonna see is your reflection in the window." He leans back in his chair. "Because you're the decider now," he says, pointing his index finger back and forth at both of us. "And I implore you to decide wisely."

Doug's words hit me every bit as hard as I suspect he intends. I have been the first officer asking that very question many times. I can easily imagine that question being asked of me many times over the next year and beyond. And I can already imagine how strange it will feel to now be the one who has to make those calls. Doug's "window test," as I call it, is a perfect finish to training and a strong reminder of what the role of the captain really is.

Chris and I celebrate our success with a round of drinks at the pub down the street from the training center. I thank him for his help and for being so patient with me, and Chris thanks me for doing the same for him. We haven't known each other very long, but I can tell that this experience will lead us to become friends for years to come.

After Chris drops me off at the Marriott, I decide to go for a walk through the airport terminal, since my flight home to Chicago isn't until the next day. I walk for a long time, down one concourse and then the next, smiling and excited about finishing training and achieving this major personal and professional milestone. But I'm also feeling nervous as I contemplate the magnitude of the responsibility about to be laid upon my shoulders.

Everywhere I look, I see people hustling to catch their next flight: families heading on vacation, business people dashing off to check on a factory or to develop relationships with new clients, military service members reporting to new duty stations, love-struck newlyweds jetting off to their honeymoons, and more. As I watch the travelers, I imagine people like them boarding one of my flights, and in so doing, entrusting their lives to me. They don't know me, but they trust I will get them to their destinations safely. They probably don't understand the true dynamic between a captain and the crew, but I do. They probably don't realize that I'll be making the final calls on issues affecting their flights, but I do. And they probably haven't given much consideration to the fact that how well I perform my job may very well determine their fates…but I have. In fact, I can't stop thinking about it.

Being a captain is a huge responsibility, whether that's for a 31-year-old like me or a pilot nearing the mandatory retirement age of 65. Part of me wonders if I'm truly ready or if I'm too young—something I'm sure others may wonder about me, too. But deep down

I know that age is just a number, not an indication of ability. I believe in myself and know I will rise to this challenge—even the challenge of proving myself to the formerly furloughed United pilots who will undoubtedly make up the lion's share of my first officers in Chicago. And despite the slight nervousness I feel, I can't wait to get started.

There is just one final hurdle to jump before I'm completely signed off as a new captain: initial operating experience.

CHAPTER 5

Training Wheels

"Confidence is a very fragile thing."
- Joe Montana

Chicago, Illinois – Late July 2013

I slide my Windsor-knotted tie into position at the base of my neck before taking a brief moment to study my freshly pressed uniform in the bathroom mirror of our Chicago apartment. The four stripes of the epaulets on my shoulders grab my attention. So do the captain wings affixed above my left breast pocket.

You look like a captain, I tell myself. *Now it's time to perform like one, too.*

Only a few minutes earlier, I had removed the captain wings from the congratulatory card given to me by United during the *Role of the Captain* course more than a month ago. And now, with simulator training behind me, it's time to fly a real 737 with real passengers on board. It's time for what's called Initial Operating Experience, or IOE.

I walk over to my black, heavy-duty crew bag in the corner of my closet and stuff my leather Penn State toiletry case inside its cavernous belly before pulling its zipper closed. Then I grab the crew bag's nylon handle, which is embroidered with "K. FRANKE" in royal blue font, and set the bag upright.

That bag—"the Tank" as I call it—has accompanied me all around the world throughout my nine-year airline career. And unfortunately for the Tank, it bears the scars to prove it. Its exposed metal frame, which has been rebuilt several times by the factory, is nonetheless dented and scratched from climbing over thousands of cement curbs and into more hotel vans than I can count. Only half of the Tank's main handle locks into place, and even then it bows ever so slightly—a permanent reminder of the strain caused by the heavy leather navigation chart bag that hooks to its front. Its right side pocket is torn near the bottom thanks to a sharp tab that protrudes in the back of every 737 flight deck luggage compartment. And yet despite its flaws—or maybe because of them—I've come to view the Tank more like a trusty sidekick than a piece of luggage.

Break's over, I tell the Tank as I slide my laptop bag over its handle. *The road is calling.*

Jen lies in bed, and I give her a quick kiss before wheeling the Tank and its accoutrements out of the apartment and onto one of the building's high-speed elevators. Thirty-seven floors later, we arrive at street level of a just-awakening Chicago.

The light is dim, the streets are quiet, and the sidewalks are empty as the Tank and I venture into the magnificent glass and steel canyon of the city's financial district. We zig and zag along the canyon's base for four blocks, ultimately reaching the Blue Line's Jackson stop as the rays of the rising sun begin to glisten against the canyon's imposing rim.

I grunt as I hoist the Tank off the ground to schlep it down the subway's stone staircase and through its entry turnstile. Standing on the deserted boarding platform, the Tank and I wait patiently for the L train to rumble into the station. When it does, I take my usual seat—a single one—near the emergency exit at the side of the car. An hour later, the train arrives at the end of the line: O'Hare.

It's show time, I think. From here on out, I know people will be staring at me and sizing me up—especially my pilot colleagues. And as expected, the inquisition begins as soon as I enter the concourse.

The stares of my fellow pilots seem to follow the same pattern. First, they notice my black uniform. Then its four gold stripes. Next, their eyes dart to the pilot wings pinned above my left breast pocket, presumably to ascertain if I work for United mainline—the air carrier that operates flights on actual United Airlines aircraft with actual United Airlines employees—or one of its independent regional partners that are contracted to operate shorter flights on smaller aircraft painted with the United livery. Given my youthful appearance, my thought is that most of them suspect the latter.

It's in your head, Korry, I try to remind myself, knowing that even if the other pilots are judging me, nothing constructive will come from entertaining such thoughts or worries. Still, the barrage of stares leaves me on edge by the time I arrive at United's operations area underneath O'Hare's Terminal C—a feeling that only intensifies as I walk down the long cinderblock hallway lined with luggage racks and enter the spacious pilot crew room.

I offer forced smiles and polite nods to the pilots I pass on my way to one of the dozen or so computers in the middle of the large room. Along the edges, I notice several clusters of legacy United pilots wearing blue uniforms and one cluster of legacy Continental pilots wearing black uniforms. But nowhere in the room do I see a single cluster containing pilots wearing both black *and* blue uniforms.

Not exactly a united United, I think. Officially, we all play for the same new United team, but it's obvious that the names of our former employers loom large over our relationship at this point. *Maybe someday,* I muse.

After printing a copy of my trip's itinerary and reviewing the weather and flight plan created by the dispatcher on the 27th floor, I take a seat at one of the small briefing tables lining the edge of the room to wait for Jack, my IOE check airman. He saunters in a few minutes later, offering me a wave as he heads to the computer to check the flight plan for himself.

As it happens, Jack and I have flown together in the past, although that was long before he was designated a member of United's corps of Line Check Airmen[10], or LCAs, who are responsible for providing final in-flight training and routine evaluations—both scheduled and impromptu—for all captains and first officers. Tall and thin, with brown hair featuring a wavy part, a big smile, and a distance runner's build, Jack definitely looks the part of an airline pilot. Best of all for me, his laid-back personality reassures me I couldn't have asked for a more pleasant check airman to fly with.

Jack drops the 25-page flight plan packet on the table as he sits down across from me. "Well, congratulations, first of all," he says with a big grin and a firm handshake. "Are you excited?"

"I am," I reply, smiling.

"And a bit nervous?"

I chuckle. "That easy to tell?"

Jack grins. "Just a little. But trust me; we've all been there. You'll do fine."

"Hope so."

He leans in. "Look, Korry. You already know the 737. IOE is about polishing the rough edges from training."

"I know."

"It's captain training wheels, that's all." He sits back. "So for the next several days, I want you to do everything you would as if you were a captain on your own, okay?"

I nod.

"You set the pace. You run the show. And I'll be right beside you the whole way."

Right beside me and ready to step in, I think, knowing that I won't officially be a captain until I accumulate at least twenty-five flying hours of IOE and pass two in-flight observations—one by the FAA

---

[10] The term Line Check Airman is not gender specific. Many female pilots proudly serve as LCAs.

and one by United. Until then, Jack is the captain, even though I'll be sitting in the left seat. He'll do his best to make me feel like I'm the captain, but in the back of my head, I'll know he can override my decisions at any moment. It is, after all, still his ship.

After reviewing the routing to Florida, the two of us grab our bags and head for the plane. We meet our four flight attendants just inside the 737's entry door. One stands in the forward galley, prepping her carts for the flight. The others are relaxing and chit-chatting in the leather first-class seats while the team of aircraft cleaners scurries about, vacuuming the carpet and refreshing the jet's cabin.

Jack and I make small talk with the flight attendants for a minute or two before I launch into my crew briefing, which I have practiced many times in my head. I rattle off the flight time, expected turbulence areas on our route, and a slew of other important items. But all throughout the briefing, the flight attendants seem confused as to why I'm the one conducting the briefing. And apparently Jack senses this, too.

"This is Korry's captain IOE," he tells them as I finish. "First leg, actually."

The lightbulbs click on, and the crew showers me with rounds of congratulations.

I find their kind words and apparent lack of concern about their green quasi-captain quite comforting.

"So if you need anything," Jack continues, "Korry's your guy."

Briefing complete, Jack and I stow our bags in the cockpit luggage compartment and take our seats—mine three feet to the left this time.

Jack commends me for my briefing as his hand glides along the overhead panel, flipping switches. "You set a nice open tone back there with the flight attendants. That's gonna be critical. This cockpit door can be one hell of a barrier at times."

I smile. "Thanks, Jack."

A short while later, after the passengers have boarded and our preflight routines are complete, the gate agent steps into the flight deck with the final flight paperwork, asking, "Captain, are you ready to go?" She extends the paperwork my way but then stops. Her eyes dart around, looking at me in the left seat, then at my four stripes, then at the check airman in the right seat and his four stripes, then back at me again. Then she turns sharply toward Jack, saying, "Here you go."

Jack holds his palms up, laughing. "I don't want that." He points to me, offering, "He's the captain!"

The agent covers her mouth with her hand. "Oh my gosh, I'm so sorry about that!"

"No worries," I reply, completely unsurprised that my age has caught the agent off guard.

"You just look too young with that baby face!"

I smile. "Something tells me I'm going to get this a lot!"

"I suspect so! Can I ask how old you are?"

Jack chuckles as I reply, "I'm 31."

"31? What were you when you started flying? 12??"

"17."

"Wow. Well, good for you," she says. "Youngest captain I've seen around here in a long time!"

"Thank you," I say, keeping to myself that I'm actually the youngest captain currently flying at the airline. "Anyway, if the flight attendants are ready, then we're ready to go."

"Okay, fellas. Have a safe trip!"

As the main entry door closes, we feel a thump behind us, just like in the Box. I reach halfway up on the overhead panel and flip on the seatbelt sign before calling for the *Before Push Checklist*.

Checklist complete, Jack obtains clearance for us to push back, and I relay the instructions through the intercom to the tug driver. "Flight deck to ramp, the brakes are released. You're cleared to push, tail north."

"Roger that, tail north," the driver replies.

The tug's motor revs to life, and our craft inches backwards.

Here we go! I think.

"Cleared to start engines," the driver tells us.

"Roger that."

Moments later, we're parked in the alley and disconnected from the tug with both engines running. After completing yet another checklist and obtaining our taxi clearance, I ask Jack if he's ready.

"Yep. Clear right," he says, peering over his shoulder.

"Clear left," I respond, likewise twisting to see as far as I can behind us.

My right hand pushes the thrust levers up enough to power us ahead at a snail's pace. My left hand grips the steering tiller along the left sidewall so fiercely that it's on the verge of cramping up as I rotate it forward to turn the jet hard to the right.

Just relax, Korry, I tell myself. I release some of the pressure on the tiller, but my hand loosens too much. The sensitive tiller jolts back to its central spring-loaded position, jerking the nose of the jet along with the passengers and flight attendants, too.

Note to self, I think, *easy on the tiller.*

The nose of the jet bobs ever so slightly as we pass over the seams in the well-worn pavement. Ahead of us, an employee bus whizzes by on a marked access road crossing our taxiway. With all the potential obstructions, my feet quiver atop the brake pedals. As a catering truck races past our left wing, I nearly slam the pedals to the floor.

"Good grief," I say.

"It looks closer than it is," Jack assures me. "You'll get used to the parallax."[11]

---

[11] Parallax refers to the difficulty in judging the precise location of an object — for example, the wingtip — in relation to other nearby objects because of the viewpoint of the observer. For pilots, the parallax stemming from viewing the wingtip from the cockpit often makes it seem that the wingtip sticks much farther out than it actually does.

"Hope so," I reply. Given the sly smile on Jack's face, I'm certain he's getting a kick out of my elevated stress level. But I'm not, because the taxi obstacles continue unabated. First it's the fuel trucks and baggage carts careening around the parked jets. Then it's the other airplanes on the taxiways, all of which seem much closer than ever before—an illusion my mind has so nicely created for the occasion. I feel like my head is constantly swiveling left and right, and my feet are ready to hit the brakes at a moment's notice.

Finally, after 10 nerve-wracking minutes of taxiing around O'Hare's sprawling terminal complex, across a bridge above an airport entry road, and through several sets of left and right turns, Jack and I find ourselves stopped just before two yellow "hold short" lines that are painted across the taxiway, just shy of the start of Runway 22L.

The air traffic controller chatters away as we wait patiently for our takeoff clearance. The frequency seems less congested than I'd expect for the morning bank of flights at one of the world's busiest airports, but then again, some days are like that.

Jack and I watch as an airborne jet passes in front of us and lands on an intersecting runway. A second one lands a minute later. And then another one after that.

Funny, I think. *I don't recall hearing any of them get a landing clearance.*

I look down to the center console's radio control panel, and a sinking feeling overwhelms me as I see 121.75 in the active frequency window.

"We're still with ground control!" I shout to Jack as I press the button to flip radio frequencies to O'Hare Tower.

I no sooner press the button than I hear the tower controller shouting, "UNITED TWELVE-FORTY-FIVE, HELLLLLLLO?!?!"

Jack and I look at each other like two kids about to get scolded.

"United Twelve-Forty-Five is up now," Jack says, a bit timidly.

"Therrrre you are," the controller replies. "And are you ready to go, or would you prefer a few more minutes to admire the arrivals on Two-Eight-Center?"

Jack and I roll our eyes at the controller's sarcasm, but neither of us are surprised by his retort. O'Hare controllers are renowned the world over for "pushing tin" at a feverish pace with incredible precision. Equally well known, however, is the ire awaiting any pilot who breaks an O'Hare controller's rhythm, say, by stopping unnecessarily on a taxiway as we have done. In fact, such remarks might even be considered a rite of passage for pilots new to O'Hare.

But Jack and I aren't O'Hare rookies, and that's probably why Jack takes the comment in stride and quips right back. "You know, I suspect we could sit here all day and not see a more graceful landing than the one a moment ago. So whenever it suits you, United Twelve-Forty-Five is ready for takeoff."

"An outstanding choice," the controller says, his tone hinting that he may have even enjoyed Jack's quick rejoinder. "United Twelve-Forty-Five, Runway Two-Two-Left, cleared for immediate takeoff. And next time, don't forget to flip the switch from ground control, okay?"

"Will do. Two-Two-Left, cleared for takeoff. United Twelve-Forty-Five."

With that, I push the throttles forward to get us moving. Once aligned with the runway's centerline, I set full power to send us racing down the runway and into the sky.

"Positive rate, gear up," I call after hearing the familiar click that indicates our wheels are off the ground.

Jack moves the landing gear lever up, and shortly thereafter, I bank the plane into a left turn to the southeast. We zoom over residential neighborhoods, climbing at a frantic pace. Chicago's skyline shimmers against Lake Michigan in the morning sun. We are Florida-bound.

Passing through 10,000 feet, I press a button on the center dashboard and tell Jack, "Autopilot A is on."

"Roger that," he responds.

And in the quiet of the morning, as we climb higher and higher into the sky, I breathe deeply and begin to relax for the first time all day.

It's also then that I start to reflect on the radio frequency mistake at O'Hare. I know it was a simple mistake, one with no impact on flight safety whatsoever, since, as with everything in aviation, there are multiple backups to every system, including the controller-to-pilot communication link. For example, the controller could have contacted us on "guard," the standard backup frequency all flights are supposed to monitor on their second radio. And if for some reason that didn't work, there's a process in place for controllers to reach us through our onboard text message system. Nonetheless, I know that as the captain I'm responsible for everything that happens on the jet, even things like radio communications on the ground, which are usually first-officer duties. This incident drives home that I need to develop better habits and routines to ensure I catch even the tiniest of errors. I'm not sure how to do that just yet, but I commit to figuring out a way, because next time, the error might be much more consequential.

Lesson number one of IOE, I think.

"United Twelve-Forty-Five," the air traffic controller radios to us, "contact Indianapolis Center on frequency one-three-three-decimal-four-two."

"One-three-three-decimal-four-two, United Twelve-Forty-Five," Jack responds, dialing the frequency into the radio.

He checks in with the next controller and the two of us fly onward. Flat checkerboard farmland turns into rolling tree-covered hills as we swap from air traffic controllers working Indianapolis Center to the ones working airspace around Memphis and Atlanta.

Along the way, Jack peppers me with "What would you do if..." questions, and he details his view on the role of the captain. We discuss my pacing of the pre-flight preparations in Chicago, my thought process for evaluating the flight plan and fuel load, and Jack's techniques for even smoother taxiing.

Eventually we check in with Jacksonville Center, which indicates that our descent to Sarasota is imminent. Our flight path brings us directly overtop the western coastline of Florida, and the clear morning makes it easy to see all the way across the marshy lake-dotted state to the Atlantic Ocean. By the time we pass Tampa and its signature bridges set low and flat against the bay, Sarasota has come into sight.

With the runway directly ahead of us, I turn off the autopilot and hand fly the last five minutes of the flight. I notice the muscle-memory deficiency right away. I tweak the controls, but it's clear to me that the tiny movements are not as refined as they were from the right seat. But I trust I will adapt quickly.

"Gear down," I tell Jack as he receives our landing clearance.

The air seems perfectly calm as we near the runway, which I appreciate for my first real-life landing from the left seat. Still, my nerves have me jiggling the controls, rocking the wings back and forth.

"One hundred," calls Jack as we cross onto airport property. I tiptoe the throttles up and down to stay perfectly on speed, trying my best to make only smooth corrections to the control wheel.

"Fifty," reports the computerized voice over the flight deck speakers as we crest the long runway's threshold. "Forty…thirty… twenty…"

I pull back on the control wheel to pitch the nose up for landing. "…ten…"

The jet's main wheels perfectly straddle the white centerline stripes as the tires plop onto the runway's surface—a bit firmer than I had hoped, but for leg one in the left seat, I will take it!

The autobrakes kick in and start slowing the jet.

"Eighty knots," Jack calls.

As the plane nears taxi speed, I drop my left hand onto the nose wheel tiller and steer us off the runway. It takes no time at all to taxi to our gate, which is easy to spot at the small terminal thanks to several ground marshalers wearing orange vests who are in position to guide us in.

"You can shut down engine number two," I tell Jack as we approach the gate. The marshaler in front of us holds his two orange wands upright and makes forward and back motions to instruct me to keep moving straight ahead. As we approach the stopping point, he moves the wands down to his sides and then raises them up in the same motion as a jumping jack, only more slowly, until he crosses them above his head.

I press on the brakes, and the jet rocks back after coming to a stop. I set the parking brake and shut the left engine down. Leg one of IOE is complete.

A few minutes later, I stand at a computer inside the spartan confines of United's Sarasota operations office, scanning the return flight plan to O'Hare. With all company hands on deck to assist with the cleaning, catering, and loading of the jet, I find myself alone in ops until the aircraft fueler wanders in.

"How's the fuel, Cap?" he asks.

"I think it's fine, but let me double-check," I tell him as the scent of jet fuel, which clings to his uniform, wafts over me. I take a quick look at the weather and our planned fuel over destination figure to determine if I'm satisfied with the dispatcher's plan or if I'd prefer to add some extra fuel. "Yep. We're good to go," I confirm. "Plenty of gas for my comfort level."

"Okie dokie. Makes my job easy."

I print the paperwork and return to the jet, where boarding passengers already line the jetway. I update the lead flight attendant on the return flight's details and ask her to pass the word to the rest of the crew. Then I crawl back into the left seat.

"Here's the paperwork," I tell Jack. "It all looks okay to me."

"Great."

With another round of preflight checks, briefings, and checklists behind us, all that's left is my welcome-aboard announcement to the passengers. I pick up the microphone to my left, press the push-to-talk button, and begin the announcement I have rehearsed many times.

"Well, good morning, ladies and gentlemen, from the flight deck. My name is Korry Franke, and it's my privilege to fly you to Chicago." I cover the flight time, our routing for the day, and a few other odds and ends before concluding, "On behalf of myself and our entire team, thanks so much for flying United. Welcome aboard."

I nailed it! I think as I set the microphone back into its slot to my left. And once again, a sinking feeling hits me, because the microphone to the left is the one for air traffic control, not the PA system! Immediately, a flurry of snarky pilots who are listening to Sarasota Ground begin piping in.

"Superb," one says.

"Best PA I've heard all day," offers another.

"You're on Sarasota Ground," says the controller, sans snarkiness.

"Enjoy Chi-town," chides another pilot.

I see Jack chuckling again. He points to the mic on the center console. "Might want to use this one," he says.

I roll my eyes. "Thanks for the tip."

"You bet."

I pick up the correct microphone, pausing to collect my thoughts for take two. Looking to Jack, I say, "I just wanted a little practice, that's all."

He laughs.

"I even got some good feedback."

"You sure did," Jack says.

Once again I key the mic, and once again I feel like I nail my PA.

With all our tasks complete on the flight deck, I scan the switches and gauges in search of anything we may have missed. When I come to the fuel gauges, I'm surprised to find them indicating the same quantity we had after landing.

"Jack, do you see a fueler out your window?"

He twists around to look toward the 737's fueling port on the right wing. "No, I sure don't, Korry." He looks back at the gauges. "But we are definitely going to need more than what we've got in the tanks to get to Chicago."

"No doubt about it."

"I'll call ops and see what the story is."

I listen as Jack inquires with ops.

A few moments later, the woman in the office responds, "The fueler claims the captain told him you were good to go."

Jack looks to me, and my head falls back against the headrest as it dawns on me what has happened.

"He asked me how the fuel was while I was in ops," I say to Jack. "I thought he meant the fuel load on the paperwork, so I said we were good to go. He must have interpreted that as meaning we were good to go with the fuel we had on board the plane."

"Ahhh," Jack says. "I bet that's it."

"Sorry, Jack."

Jack waves his hand, saying, "Don't worry about it. Easy fix. We'll just be a little late, that's all."

Yeah, I think. *A little late…because of me.*

I'm embarrassed as I make a PA fessing up to the passengers—with the correct microphone, thankfully. I know it's an honest mistake—a simple miscommunication—but I know this particular mistake has repercussions. Maybe our twenty-minute delay will result in a passenger being late for an important business meeting or family event. Or maybe it will cause someone to miss a tight connecting flight at O'Hare. All because I failed to communicate clearly.

Thankfully, in the end, I get lucky. We receive a few en route shortcuts from air traffic control, and we end up landing on O'Hare's

Runway 27L, which makes for a super short taxi to our gate. And as I set the parking brake and shut down our engines, I notice we've arrived basically on time after all.

Of course, that isn't the point; the point is that words matter. *Lesson number two of IOE,* I tell myself. Sure, the miscommunication with the fueler is a small issue, as is Jack forgetting to switch the radio frequencies earlier in the day. But the same type of miscommunication could happen with a first officer or flight attendant during a major emergency if I'm not careful. And I know I can't let that happen.

Jack and I have a three-hour break in O'Hare before our last flight of the day. I grab dinner in the food court and call Jen to update her on how things are going. I can tell she's excited for me, and I can also tell she senses my frustration about the little mistakes.

"Don't worry, Husband. You've got this," she reassures me.

And after things start clicking on our flight to Washington Dulles—a flight without any surprises, gotchas, or mistakes—part of me starts to believe her confidence is well-placed.

But then Denver happens.

I think we're almost done boarding," I say to Jack the next day after twisting around in the left seat to look down the long aisle of the 737. "Looks like just a handful of people still loading bags into the overhead bins."

"Great."

I prop my left foot up on the lower dashboard footrest and lean my head against the top of the captain's chair, letting my eyes drift around the cockpit in search of anything we may have missed on the preflight. "Plenty of gas this time, too," I joke.

"See? It's all coming together."

And it really feels like it is. Our flight from Washington Dulles to Denver had gone as smoothly as I could hope for. And Jack even had hinted that if the trend continues over the next couple days, he'll be comfortable scheduling my FAA observation ride and United company line check—the last two hurdles to traverse before being completely signed off as a United captain.

"Knock, knock," a fellow pilot named Brian says, tapping his knuckles against the open flight deck door and interrupting my gaze at the Rocky Mountain foothills some thirty miles west of the airport. "Any chance I can ride your jumpseat to Chicago?"

I spin around and see Brian smiling with his hand outstretched, proffering his United ID as well as his pilot and medical certificates for my review. Showing the captain of a flight these documents is standard operating procedure for pilots hoping to ride to or from work on the extra cockpit jumpseat when all the cabin seats are full.

"You bet," I say, scanning Brian's documents before remembering that, technically, Jack is the captain and the one who *owns* the jumpseat, so I hand the documents to him.

"We're doing IOE," Jack says.

"Ahhhh," Brian responds. Then he turns to me asking, "You get the left seat on the last bid?"

"I did," I say, noticing Brian's blue uniform pants, which identify him as a legacy United pilot.

"Well," he says, pausing for a moment, "congrats."

The words seem a bit forced, and they immediately put me on edge given the controversy surrounding Bid 14-02.

Bid 14-02 had been open only to legacy Continental pilots, and it was to be the last such bid prior to the publication of the arbitrated joint seniority list. Pilot contractual agreements stipulated that all subsequent bids be open to all pilots from both sides of the new airline, using the new seniority numbers of the integrated seniority list to determine bid awards. Many pilots on the legacy United side of the airline had openly acknowledged frustration over not being permitted to bid on the 14-02 captain slots, such as the one I had secured. They had argued that awarding those positions prior to the publication of the new seniority list could lock in captain slots for people whose new seniority numbers might or might not be senior enough to hold those positions. They suggested it would be cleaner and fairer to simply withhold the bid until the new list was published. Unfortunately, given the lengthy amount of time from when a pilot is awarded a new position to when that pilot actually completes training and is staffed in his or her new position, the reality of waiting to award those positions would have made it incredibly difficult at best for United to meet its short-term pilot staffing demands. And so despite the inevitability of controversy, United management opened Bid 14-02 to the legacy Continental pilots as scheduled. And unsurprisingly, the results of Bid 14-02 became an issue of contention between the two pilot groups.

It doesn't matter, Korry. That's not your fight. Just focus.

I try to change the topic. "So what airplane are you on?"

"The fifty-seven," Brian says, referring to the Boeing 757. "I used to be a solid lineholder here in Denver," using the term that refers to pilots with set schedules as opposed to "reserve," which is the term for pilots who are on call to cover flights for pilots who misconnect, call in sick, or are out of position for a variety of other reasons. "But they've moved so much of the 757 flying to other bases that I'm back commuting to Chicago."

"Oh, man," I say, sensing the tension rise even more. Many pilots choose to commute to their bases from homes all across the country. It's a great perk to be able to live anywhere. But feeling forced to commute is a whole different ballgame.

"Wouldn't think that would be necessary with fifteen years on property," Brian adds, "but it is what it is."

And now I definitely sense tension in the air. I've been with the airline a little over half the time Brian has. And I can't shake the feeling that Brian may be judging my performance on the flight, not because of me, but because of whom I represent: a young Continental pilot who got a captain upgrade on Bid 14-02. I worry he will interpret my performance as being representative of *all* Continental pilots or *all* younger captains. And instantly I feel additional pressure because I don't want to let my colleagues down. I've got to prove I'm worthy—and that my fellow Continental colleagues are worthy—of sitting in the left seat. And yet another part of me knows it's silly even to think this way.

Maybe Brian doesn't even care about Bid 14-02 or the fact I'm a captain and he's not, I think. *And even if he does, what difference does it make? It's just another flight. Focus!*

But it's next to impossible to block out the feeling I'm being judged when Brian is sitting two feet behind me on the fold-down cockpit jumpseat. I convince myself that he's staring over my shoulder, watching everything I do, and listening to every word I say, ready to pounce on any error I may make. Granted, I have no idea if my worries are legitimate or not, real or imagined. But I do know the pressure I feel seems greater than ever before.

The cockpit goes silent for a bit. A few moments later, the gate agent arrives with the final flight paperwork and closes the cabin door. I call for the *Before Push Checklist* as I reach up to the overhead panel to flip the seatbelt sign on. Jack grabs the laminated card and rattles through its various items. Checklist complete, he calls Denver Ramp Control for pushback.

"United Twelve-Fifty, good afternoon. Your pushback from Bravo Twenty is approved. Call for taxi," instructs the ramp controller.

I toggle the mic switch on the control wheel to talk with the pushback crew on the tug attached to the nose gear. "Cockpit to ramp, you are cleared to push."

"Cleared to push. Here we go," the ramper replies.

I gaze out my left window toward the picturesque mountains in the distance as the tug revs its motor. But we don't move. I notice the tug's motor ramping up even more. A second or two passes. Then out of nowhere we hear a loud *BANG!!!!* followed immediately by a thud we feel just below our feet.

My mouth gapes as I turn to Jack as though I've seen a ghost. I'm afraid to look at the center console, fearing I already know what has happened. Slowly, my eyes shift downward. They don't even make it to the console before I notice the searing red light beside the throttle quadrant, confirming the worst of my suspicions: I never released the parking brakes!

My heart sinks as I contemplate what type of damage my mistake has caused. Is the nose gear okay? What about the tow bar or the tug?

Feebly, I key the mic and ask the ramper, "What was that?"

"Couldn't get the plane to move," the ramper says. "Guessing the shear pin failed."

The shear pin. Dear God, let it be the shear pin, I think, knowing the shear pin connects the tow bar to the nose gear and is designed to break first so as to prevent any damage to the nose gear itself. I pray it has worked as designed!

"Does it look okay? Any damage?"

"Just checking on that now. Give us a second."

"Roger that," I say, hating that I don't have an immediate answer.

I'm beyond embarrassed by my mistake; I'm mortified. We haven't even left the gate, and I figure the chances are good Brian already thinks I have no business sitting in the left seat.

I look to Jack and ask if I should make a PA to the passengers, which he agrees is a good idea. I take a moment to compose my thoughts. Then I grab the PA microphone to 'fess up.

And then the three of us sit silently in the cockpit as the ramp crew evaluates the situation. With the steady hum of avionics cooling fans offering white noise, my mind drifts to the worst-case scenario: damage to the nose gear. I wonder what on earth that will cost to fix. Then I imagine an aircraft swap and annoyed passengers who will miss connections, meetings, and events in Chicago—all because I failed to be mindful of the details…again.

"Ramp to flight deck," I hear through my headphones.

"Flight deck to ramp. Go ahead."

"Yeah, Cap. Definitely the shear pin. Everything else looks fine."

My eyes close and I breathe a sigh of relief.

"We got lucky," the ramper continues.

"You can say that again," I reply, rubbing my forehead.

"Just gonna need to find another tow bar, that's all. Give us a few minutes."

"We'll be here."

A short while later, we are racing above the prairie toward Chicago. Fortunately, there is no more excitement on the flight. The three of us even enjoy good conversation the whole way, which I hope means my fears about Brian judging me were imagined. To top it all off, I make my best landing yet from the left seat. But with the parking brake debacle still fresh in my mind, my confidence is badly shaken nonetheless.

Late that night, Jack and I depart for Pittsburgh, and when we do, we find the radios so quiet it feels like we are the only plane in the sky. The crisp grid of Chicago's streets, which are bathed in an orange glow from thousands of tiny streetlamps, extends in front of us, building in intensity until the skyscrapers of downtown meet the blackness of Lake Michigan. I marvel at how from only a few thousand feet off the ground I can see the urbanized coastline continuing south of Chicago, beyond the steel plants of Gary, Indiana, all the way around to the western edge of Michigan's lower peninsula. It's a spectacular sight; our reward for a long and trying day.

Reaching cruise altitude, Jack holds up his packet full of IOE questions and asks, "You good if we cover the rest of these tomorrow?"

I smile, relieved. "I think that's a great idea."

The two of us press on for Pennsylvania, savoring the serenity of the cockpit and admiring the beauty of the nocturnal landscape. Beneath us, dimly lit towns and cities speckle the ground all the way to the horizon. Connecting them are a series of meandering highway arteries made visible by the headlights and taillights of thousands of terrestrial travelers.

As I watch the scenery out my window and the miles remaining to Pittsburgh ticking down on our flight computer, I find myself reflecting on the events of the past two days—particularly my mistakes. The common link seems to be a lack of discipline, and such mistakes are unacceptable for any leader—particularly one responsible for the lives of hundreds of people. I know I can and must do better, and I commit to doing just that, starting with improving my mental toughness. It's not enough to simply keep track of the big picture; I also must become an expert at sifting through the mountain of minute details so I can ensure our team is focusing on the ones that really matter. I need to communicate clearly and succinctly. And I need to never again let someone else's opinions—whether real or imagined—affect the quality of my work. *Lesson number three of IOE*, I think. After all, such distractions will never end. In fact, those types of challenges will only intensify after IOE is over, since then I'll be flying with pilots who are new to United or returning from a years-long furlough—not experienced check airmen like Jack.

Only discipline will keep you and your passengers safe, I tell myself. *I can accept nothing less.*

I promise myself that I'll strive to attain that lofty standard, but I know that no pilot is perfect. That is, after all, why there are two of us up front to begin with (not to mention the checklists and numerous other backup mechanisms that accompany us).

But I have to stop the errors and catch the easy mistakes. Because as my favorite aviation adage says, every pilot starts with two bags: one full of luck, and the other empty of experience. The trick is to fill the bag of experience before emptying the bag of luck.

Thankfully, I know my bag of experience is far from empty. Unfortunately, I also know my bag of luck won't last forever.

I wake up in Pittsburgh, convinced that the previous day had been a significant turning point in my captain IOE. And as Jack and I criss-cross the country over the course of the next several flights, I'm able to prove it to him, too. He notices my resolve to catch the little things. And with each takeoff, each landing, and each mile in between, Jack senses my emerging confidence and sees me growing into my new role as a captain.

Sitting in the cockpit as we pack up our things in O'Hare after the last flight of our trip, Jack says to me, "I'm thinking it's time we pull off the training wheels."

I stop and look at him, my unplugged headset in my hands. "Are you sure?"

"I am," he says confidently. "Tomorrow, I'll get your fed ride and line check scheduled," he says, referring to the FAA and company observation flights, which represent the true end of training and the final blessing by the U.S. government and the airline itself of a new captain's preparedness to lead. "You're ready to be a captain, Korry. I have no doubt about it. You've come a long way in just a few short days."

"Thanks, Jack," I say, smiling with equal parts excitement and nervousness, particularly since the two observation flights are all that stand between me and my attainment of the appellation I've chased for 14 years.

Two days later, I fly back to Pittsburgh, this time with Brent, a tall and paternal FAA examiner, squished into the flight deck jumpseat to observe me. He carefully checks my pilot credentials, listens as I brief the flight attendants, and asks a few random questions here and there before we even push off the gate in Chicago. I know he's probably just making conversation, but I'm on edge. I remind myself to breathe, but relaxing is difficult since I hear the tip of Brent's pen tapping constantly against his clipboard as he makes notes. A number of challenges crop up during the taxi out to the runway, including a rogue catering truck that fails to stop at an intersection and a change in departure runways that requires reprogramming of the flight computer. But once we're off the ground, the rest of the flight proceeds flawlessly. And as we touch down in Pittsburgh, I know I have passed.

Later that week, United completes its own observation of one of my flights, this time from Phoenix to Chicago. The line check goes well, with few if any hiccups the whole way...except for my rather firm landing at O'Hare, which earns me a few backhanded compliments from exiting passengers.

But the comments don't even phase me. Not on this day. Not in this moment. Because my dream is at hand. And a few minutes after the passengers have finished deplaning, I sit with the check airman at one of the little tables in the crew room, signing forms that finalize the completion of my captain IOE and certify that I am now free to command one of United's jets without supervision!

"Congratulations, Captain Franke," the check airman says while shaking my hand when the signing is complete. "You'll do well out there" he assures me.

"Thank you," I reply with cautious confidence.

And I truly hope he's right. Because there are no more simulations and no more captain training wheels. Now, it's just me. On my own. Starting with a flight the next morning to San Diego.

CHAPTER 6

Day One

"The buck stops here!"
- Harry S. Truman

Chicago, Illinois – August 6, 2013

The rear hatch of our black SUV closes with a thud.

"Is my tie straight?" I ask Jen, standing curbside at O'Hare around 6:00 AM on the morning of August 6, 2013.

"Yep! You look good," she tells me, smiling as she brushes her hands over the four-stripe epaulets on my shoulders. "My husband, the captain!"

I'm thrilled to see her beaming with pride, and so appreciative of her steadfast support of me.

"Thanks, Wife," I say. "It's just a little flight to San Diego, right? I've done this dozens of times. How hard could this be?"

"Would you please stop doubting yourself? You've got this."

I nod as another car pulls in behind us. "I'll work on that."

"Good."

"After I land safely in San Diego."

Jen shakes her head.

"Okay, I've gotta go," I say, leaning in to give her a kiss. "I love you."

"Love you, too, Husband. Fly safe!"

As Jen gets into the SUV, I grab the Tank by its handle and pull it over the curb, adding yet another scrape to its metal frame. Reaching the terminal's entry doors, I turn and wave to Jen. She blows me a kiss, offers a final wave, and then drives away.

Here we go, buddy, I tell the Tank. *It's show time once again.*

The two of us enter the airport, clear security, and walk swiftly through the towering glass and steel terminal to the United crew room at the end of the rainbow-colored tunnel connecting concourses B and C.

The crew room bustles as pilots, including me, prepare for the morning bank of flights. Standing at one of the computers in the middle of the room, I review the dispatcher's plan, and I'm pleased to find everything completely copacetic. In fact, I doubt we will encounter a single cloud on the four-hour flight.

Couldn't have picked a better day to fly, I tell myself.

I grin as I click the checkbox on the computer screen to accept the flight release—my first time doing so as a captain. It's now official: I'm completely responsible for the plane, its crew, and its passengers.

After printing a copy of the paperwork, the Tank and I reverse course and make our way to gate B-2 at the far end of the concourse. We find the gate area teeming with passengers, 121 of whom will be joining us on our flight. I offer multiple "good morning" greetings as I dodge and weave my way through the sea of passengers toward the jetway entry door, where a trio of flight attendants stand waiting.

"I'm Korry," I say with a smile and an outstretched hand as I reach the crew. "Korry with a K. You working San Diego, I presume?"

"You got it, Korry with a K. I'm Andrea," says the young flight attendant with her blond hair pulled back. She smiles. "With an A." She laughs a bit at her own joke—and so do I—as we shake hands.

"Well then, it looks like I'm in the right place. Nice to meet you, Andrea with an A."

"Likewise," she says.

Standing beside Andrea are two other flight attendants: Carrie, a brunette in her late twenties, and Timothy, a forty-something man with salt and pepper hair.

As I shake his hand, he cocks his head and asks, "Four stripes this time?"

"Amazing the difference a few months can make," I joke, recalling that we had last flown together only a few weeks before I started captain training.

"I guess so," he says. "Congratulations."

Soon, another pilot joins us after picking his way through the crowd.

"And I'm guessing you must be Kent," I say.

"An excellent guess," he replies, shaking my hand.

Kent stands several inches shorter than me. His light brown hair is barely long enough to accommodate the part on the side, and it's starting to recede up front and gray along the edges—subtle hints that reveal Kent is several years older than me despite his being junior to me on the Continental pilots' seniority list.

"So when did scheduling tag you with this trip?" Kent asks.

"Early last night. Maybe six-ish," I reply.

"Sounds about right. The captain I'd been flying with was reassigned to cover something else, although I'm not sure where they sent him."

"Who knows," I say, wondering what intricate puzzle the crew schedulers on the 27th floor had been trying to solve that time.

"So are you with me the next three days?"

"Nope," I say, "Just today." I notice a few stares from nearby passengers, but slough them off and look back to Kent. "I deadhead back here as soon as we land."

"Ahhh. Easy enough," Kent says. "Hope they gave you a good seat."

I smile. "12A. I always go for the window."

Kent chuckles. "Guess I'll probably get a new captain for each leg of this trip."

"Maybe so," I say, thinking, *But probably not as new as me.*

The gate agent steps up to our small gaggle of pilots and flight attendants and asks if we're ready to head down. After I nod that we are, she opens the jetway door and checks our IDs. Then the five of us meander toward the awaiting 737-700. And with every step I take down the jetway, I feel my heart thump harder.

"Tell you what," I say to Kent as we approach the jet. "I'll kick the tires."

"You sure?" he asks, knowing the exterior walkaround is usually a first officer duty.

"It's your lucky day," I reply, figuring the fresh air might help calm my growing nerves.

Kent laughs.

I put in my earplugs, enter the code for the door leading outside, and hustle down the jetway's narrow metal staircase to the tarmac. From there, I begin a meticulous visual inspection of the jet's exterior, checking the lights, tires, and brakes, looking for fluid leaks or dents, and marveling along the way at the size and scale of United's smallest mainline jet. Its tires reach my waistline. Its wings span forty yards from tip to tip. Its tail rises taller than a two-story house. And from nose to tail, the baby 737 stretches fifteen feet beyond the hoop-to-hoop length of an NBA basketball court.

A pretty big baby, I think. *And it's my responsibility to get it to San Diego in one piece.*

Walkaround complete, I scamper back up the metal steps, grab the Tank, and pull it into the jet.

"The outside looks good, sir," I tell Kent as I crouch down beside the cockpit door to stuff the Tank into the flight deck's luggage compartment. "Two wings, two engines, six wheels. It flew in, so it'll fly out."

"Roger that," he chuckles at my bad joke while pecking away at the flight computer to load our routing.

"Korry, we're ready for the crew briefing whenever you want," Carrie says, leaning into the flight deck from the forward galley.

"Great. Be there in a second," I say before asking Kent if he minds joining us.

The two of us make our way back to the empty first class cabin, where the flight attendants are already seated. Kent plops down into an open seat beside one of them, and I nervously play with my hands as I launch into my standard preflight briefing of the flight time, weather, turbulence, and other items. Once they're covered, I say, "There's also one other piece I'd like to share with you today: this is my very first flight as a captain." I pause, expecting gasps, but instead see only smiles from the crew. "Honestly, the fact that none of you jumped up and ran off the plane means a lot to me." The crew laughs at what Jen would refer to as one of my "dad jokes." But I'm not kidding; their cool confidence in me is humbling. "Of course, I'd appreciate if we keep this fact between us. No need to worry the passengers, okay?"

Everyone nods.

"Now, I'm telling you this for two reasons: first, because I genuinely want your feedback—good, bad or indifferent. Without it, I'll never know how I can become a better captain for you and your colleagues."

More nods.

"And second, I'm telling you because this is a very special day for me. Only once in a lifetime does a pilot take command of an airliner for the first time. And by random chance, you're here to experience it with me. And so as a memento of the occasion," I say, reaching into my pocket, "and because I'm a sucker for sentimentality, I've written each of you a short note to say thank you for being a part of my inaugural captain flight."

I pull the notecards from my pocket and hand them out, receiving smiles, handshakes, and congratulatory wishes as I do. Several of the crewmembers open the envelopes right away. On the front of the card, they find a quote from Gandhi: "In a gentle way you can shake the world." Given the tumultuous times of our mega-merger, the quote seemed particularly apropos to me. Change is everywhere. And as frontline employees, it is easy to feel powerless and to think our individual efforts don't make a difference. But I believe differently. While we can't determine the strategic direction of our new airline, I know we can shape its success by doing our small parts exceptionally well. We just have to work together—all 80,000 of us—from the C-suite to the crew rooms, from the ops center in Chicago to every outstation around the globe. And if we do that, I believe our collective efforts will prove powerful enough to launch our combined airline to great heights.

Inside the card, the crew members find the following message:

"Many years ago, I dreamed of one day becoming a major airline captain. Our flight this morning marks the end of that personal quest, as well as the beginning of a newer and even more important one—that of becoming a captain that earns the respect of his coworkers, company and passengers by his example, teamwork and leadership, not just his seniority.

I realize this journey will take some time, and I thank you in advance for your patience! Nonetheless, I promise to strive each and every day toward that goal, and I'm confident that with your help, we can indeed shake our world here at United for the better...if only in a small way.

I'm honored to serve as your captain. I'm proud of the work you do. And I'm excited to share the sky with you today.

So let's go flying!"

Not long after sliding back into the left seat, it's time to do just that. The gate agent hands me the final flight paperwork. The cabin door closes. The preflight checklist is completed. And Kent calls ramp control for pushback clearance.

Clearance received, I toggle the push-to-talk switch on the control wheel and say, "Flight deck to ramp." I pause, staring at the bright red parking brake light that shines beside my right knee. *Not this time*, I think. *Not ever again.* I press my toes on the tops of the rudder pedals, releasing the parking brake and extinguishing the light. "The brakes are released. You are cleared to push into the alley."

"Roger that, fellas," the ramper replies. "Here we go."

With the tug disconnected and our engines spinning, Kent radios for clearance to taxi. My breathing quickens and my palms sweat as I push the throttles forward to start the jet rolling. I swear every airplane seems even closer than during IOE, and every baggage cart and catering truck seems more likely to veer in front of me without notice. Being the captain puts my senses on high alert, even though it's just another routine day in Chicago.

I make a left turn. Then a right. Then a long swooping curve around the terminals. My head swivels at a frantic pace. I am not about to make a mistake on day one.

Approaching the runway, I glance down at the radio panel, and I'm relieved to see the correct frequency loaded for O'Hare Tower.

"United Ten-Sixty, O'Hare Tower. Runway Two-Two-Left, cleared for takeoff."

"Cleared for takeoff, Runway Two-Two-Left, United Ten-Sixty," Kent answers.

I flip on the landing lights and maneuver the jet onto the runway, swinging the nose around to align perfectly with the thick runway centerline stripes.

"Well," I say, looking at Kent. "Let's go to San Diego."

I advance the thrust levers smoothly, and the high-pitched whine of the engines grows louder and more pronounced.

"Check thrust," I say.

"Thrust set, ninety-eight percent."

A runway stripe disappears beneath us. Then another. And another. The jet's nose bobs slightly as it springs across seams in the pavement. And the elevated runway lights along the edges whiz by.

"One hundred knots," Kent says as we pick up speed and momentum.

My eyes glance at the engine gauges; everything looks great. Then they switch to the end of the runway, and the tips of my toes shift with the deftness of an expert dancer atop the rudder pedals, all to keep the jet perfectly centered on the runway. My peripheral vision is completely blurred as we race past 120 knots. Then 140.

"Vee-one," Kent calls. I move my right hand away from the throttles and back onto the control wheel. "Rotate."

Here we go! I think.

I pull back on the yoke, lifting the jet's nose off the runway, above the treeline in the distance, and into the air.

Click! The wheels come off the ground. And in that instant, before I even have a chance to say, "Gear up," time stands still as an eerie—and strangely familiar—feeling creeps over me. It presses down heavily upon my shoulders, stealing my breath, just like it did fourteen years earlier.

Hagerstown, Maryland – July 12, 1999

I have never noticed the small slit in the vinyl seat beside me. Then again, the 17-year-old-me has also never seen that seat empty. But it is now. And I'm alone—perhaps more alone than I've ever felt in my entire life.

I watch my flight instructor walk away from me. He turns around before entering the nearby building to give me a thumbs up and a smile.

He is crazy, I think. *Completely nuts.*

I use the back of my hand to wipe the beads of sweat from my brow. But it's useless; the humidity is stifling inside the tiny two-seat Cessna 150—even with my left elbow pressing the hinged side window open.

And you'll sit in this 100-degree oven until you are absolutely ready, I tell myself. *There is too much at stake.*

So I sit in silence, trying to calm my nerves by listening to the steady rhythm of my heavy breathing and the subtle sloshing of the fuel in the wing tanks above my head.

Who am I kidding? I'll never be completely ready. So just do it, Korry. Rip the Band-Aid off and get on with it.

I grab the white laminated card and begin working through the checklist. Flight instruments—check. Altimeter—set. Mixture—rich. Throttle—cracked. Master switch—on. This last item sends electricity pulsing through the plane's instruments, and a steady hum emanates into the air.

I set the checklist down while taking another deep breath. I look around the tiny plane and yell, "CLEAR PROP!!!" out my window.

Hearing no reply, I press hard upon the brake pedals, a task made more difficult by the nervous twitching of my legs, and twist the ignition key with my left hand. The engine coughs and sputters as the two-bladed propeller begins twisting in front of me. Finally, the engine fires up with a hearty *barrrrrrummpppp!*

I flip on radios, check the flight controls, and complete still more checklists. Finally, I request permission to taxi.

"Cessna One-Seven-Niner-Three-Quebec, Hagerstown Ground," the controller responds. "Taxi to Runway Two-Zero."

"Taxi to Runway Two-Zero, Cessna One-Seven-Niner-Three-Quebec," I reply.

I glance once more around the plane; the area is clear. I push the throttle in, adding more power than necessary to start the taxi. My shaky legs release the brakes, jerking the plane ahead.

It's a short taxi to the runway's end. Once there, I do the same pre-departure engine check I've done with my instructor many times before.

And then I wait, staring at the cockpit, searching for something I may have missed. Scared to take the next step.

Let's go, Korry. Stop delaying. You're ready. Just do it!

Feebly, I key the microphone and say, "Hagerstown Tower, Cessna Niner-Three-Quebec is ready for takeoff, Runway Two-Zero."

"Cessna Niner-Three-Quebec, Runway Two-Zero, cleared for takeoff."

"Cleared for takeoff on Runway Two-Zero, Cessna Niner-Three-Quebec," I confirm.

I push the throttle in and the plane begins to move. I taxi across the runway's threshold and turn the plane to align with the slightly downward-sloping asphalt. I press the brakes, and the plane rocks back as it comes to a momentary stop. My heart feels like it's going to burst out of my chest.

Through the arc of the rapidly spinning propeller, I see my future ahead of me. It's waiting for me to come get it and the myriad opportunities and adventures it holds—most of which I cannot even fathom at this moment. And to start me on my way, all I have to do is this one thing. And yet doubt fills my soul. It paralyzes me with fear—of the unknown, that I'm not good enough, that it's too risky.

Oh, to hell with doubt, Korry. Let's go!!!

I release the brakes and shove the throttle forward until the

100-horsepower engine is giving all it can. Its roar is deafening, even beneath my bulky green headset. The propeller bites hard on the air, pulling the plane down the runway. My speed increases, and at just the right moment, I haul back on the control wheel. The nose gear shimmies, shaking the lightweight plane and startling its novice pilot. And a nanosecond later, the main wheels come off the pavement. I am airborne—flying solo for the first time in my life! And a massive smile spreads across my face.

But then I notice the empty seat to my right, and its reality hits me: this time, there is no flight instructor to step in. There is no one to correct my mistakes. There is no one to offer tips or suggestions. It is just me. Me versus the plane.

Yet there is no time for nerves. No time for wishing I am magically back on the ground. No time for feeling scared, and definitely no time to panic. There is only time to act. Because one way or another, this plane will eventually return to the ground, and only I can ensure that happens safely. My life, quite literally, depends on it.

So I keep breathing, concentrating on flying the plane as my instructor has taught me. It lumbers into the thick summer air, and with every foot of altitude it gains, my fears, nerves, and insecurities threaten to bubble over. Each time they do, I force myself to shove them away. I must focus on moving forward, because forward is all that matters.

Returning to the runway requires me to fly a rectangular racetrack pattern in the air. At 500 feet above the ground, I make my first 90-degree left turn. A few seconds later, I make my second turn to parallel the runway. Leveling off at 1,000 feet above the ground, I look out my left window. The runway seems to move beside me. And at its halfway point, I say to air traffic control, "Hagerstown Tower, Cessna Niner-Three-Quebec is midfield left downwind Runway Two-Zero."

"Cessna Niner-Three-Quebec, Hagerstown Tower. Runway Two-Zero cleared to land," the controller instructs.

"Cleared to land, Runway Two-Zero, Cessna Niner-Three-Quebec."

I pull the throttle out a touch, letting the airplane drift downward at a gentle pace. I extend the flaps on the trailing edge of the wings, just like I've practiced, and when I see the runway behind my left shoulder, I bank the plane into yet another 90-degree left turn. Moments later, I begin the final turn, watching as the ground angles across my windshield. I see the runway again, and I attempt to time my turn so as to roll my wings level with the narrow strip of blacktop directly in front of me. I'm mostly successful, and staying on the correct glidepath requires only a few slight corrections. I jiggle the controls, rocking the wings left and right. I feel the dampness of my clammy hands upon the control wheel. And the plane drifts closer to the ground.

Keep focusing, Korry, I tell myself. *You're almost there.*

I keep the nose aimed right at the giant "20" painted on the runway's threshold. Nearby trees and buildings seem close enough to touch as I crest across the airport's perimeter fence, less than 100 feet above the ground.

This is it, Korry!

Left and right. Left and right. Power in a bit. Power out a bit.

And now I'm above the runway's pavement. I pull the throttle to idle and pitch the nose up, hoping to ease the plane onto the runway as my instructor has taught me to do. But I flare too high! I'm floating down the runway a few feet off the ground, wiggling the controls at a feverish pace, attempting to settle the plane's tires onto the asphalt. But there is to be no settling.

WHHHAAAAMMMMMM!

The plane slams onto all three of its wheels, bouncing immediately back into the air. The ferocity of my "landing" fills me with terror. I pull back on the controls again, trying to wrestle the craft back onto the runway. But so doing allows precious bits of airspeed to slip away, and the plane drops again. It meets the runway with another forceful *WHAM!* before bobbling from one wheel to another for several frightful seconds in a game of airplane hot potato. And then, mercifully, the craft finds its footing and remains planted on the ground.

I press the brakes, slowing the Cessna's pace to a fast walk before turning off the runway. Finally, the bird comes to a complete stop. My legs pulse and twitch from adrenaline.

YESSSS!!!! I shout to myself. *I'M ALIVE!!!! I DID IT!!!! I LANDED THE PLANE BY MYSELF!!!!*

It wasn't pretty, but I landed. Twice. And the most amazing sense of freedom floods over me.

I have faced my fears and anxieties. I have pushed myself. I have risen to this challenge. And most of all, I have done it on my own.

From now on, I will practice, and I will improve. I will respect my fear and nervousness, but I will not let fickle emotions control me... or my destiny. Nothing will keep me grounded; instead, I will fly to great heights—in airplanes, and in life.

This, I tell myself, *is just the beginning.*

And so is this. The wheels are off the ground in Chicago, and the responsibility for getting our plane safely to San Diego is mine. I feel twinges of fear and nervousness within me, but I know they are unfounded. I am an experienced pilot. I believe in myself, as does United and the FAA. And unlike my first solo, this time I'm not alone. This time, I have an incredibly capable first officer at my side. I have a team of experienced flight attendants in the cabin. And I have hundreds of people at United's Network Operations Center on the 27th floor of the Willis Tower just a phone patch away if I need them. I just need to keep focused on moving forward. I need to trust my training and experience, and remember that the fear and nervousness exists only because this is a new experience. The only way my leadership muscle can grow is by stretching myself. And while that may feel uncomfortable at times, if I respect my limits, I know I will not fail. I will rise to meet this challenge as I have done many times in the past.

I breathe deeply, letting air return to my lungs. And once again, time starts moving.

"United Ten-Sixty, contact departure on one-two-five-decimal-four," instructs the O'Hare tower controller.

"One-two-five-decimal-four, United Ten-Sixty. So long," Kent says.

So long, indeed. So long to the life I have known before this moment. So long to my life as a co-pilot. I am a captain now. I'm moving up, moving on, and moving forward...one mile at a time.

Several hours—and more than 1,700 miles—later, Kent and I descend over large clusters of dusty mountains. The giant boulders studding the hillsides create the appearance of evening stubble upon the mountain faces. And in the distance, we see San Diego's modern skyline glimmering against the deep blue Pacific Ocean. Within a few minutes, we find ourselves above dense residential neighborhoods within the city limits.

"Gear down, *Landing Checklist*," I command.

Kent moves the big lever out and down. "Speed brake, armed. Gear down, three green," he says, pointing to the three green lights, indicating the gear are down and locked.

"Down, three green," I respond, glancing at the lights before returning my gaze to the runway a few miles ahead of us.

"Flaps to go," Kent says.

"Set speed one-sixty."

Kent rotates the speed knob on the center dashboard to 160.

"Flaps twenty-five," I say. And as the speed drops further, I continue, "Flaps thirty, set target."

Kent moves the flap lever one final time, and he rotates the speed knob again. "Flaps thirty, green light," he says. "*Landing Checklist complete.*"

Just focus, Korry. You've got this.

The light winds and clear skies make for perfect landing conditions. And after zipping past the tops of downtown skyscrapers, we are over San Diego's airport property.

"One-hundred," Kent calls out.

Then the computerized voice takes over: "Fifty…forty…thirty…"

I jostle the controls.

"…twenty…ten."

I pull the throttles back and pitch the nose up for the flare.

Chirp-chirp. Our main gear wheels are down, and the nose wheel follows soon after. I pull up on the reverse thrust levers and engage the brakes, smiling with satisfaction as we slow, because I know this landing is a heck of a lot better than that of my first solo.

"Eighty knots," Kent offers.

I continue slowing as I steer the 737 off the runway and onto an adjacent taxiway that leads to the terminal ramp.

Reaching taxi speed, Kent says, "I'd say that was a pretty nice first landing…*Captain!*"

The way he emphasizes the last word tells me Kent has been waiting for just the right moment to make his comment. I smile with satisfaction; it is the first time a fellow pilot has referred to me in earnest as Captain. And that feels really, really good. After all, I haven't just arrived in San Diego; I have arrived professionally.

Like my first solo, it's a moment to savor—one I will not soon forget. But I know this flight is just a warm up; future ones will likely involve more challenging weather, passengers, and perhaps even crewmembers. And I can't help but wonder if those factors will combine two days later when I depart for a city whose chilly climate seems like it could be an omen for things to come: Anchorage.

CHAPTER 7

The Day Line

"The real voyage of discovery consists not in seeking new landscapes but in having new eyes."
- Marcel Proust

Chicago, Illinois – August 7, 2013

H is name is Clint," I tell Jen as we sit on our 37th-floor balcony, gazing out at the city on a warm August evening. I hand my iPhone to her so she can see Clint's picture, which I've pulled up on United's employee website.

"He looks nice," she says. "But he needs to lose the comb-over."

"I'll be sure to tell him the moment I meet him."

Jen chuckles. "Or maybe not."

"That's probably a better idea," I say as Jen hands the phone back to me. "Anyway, he's a double furloughee, so we'll see how that goes."

"Husband, you're so worried about the furloughees. Why does it matter?"

I pause to consider how best to explain it. "Well, take Kent the other day," I begin. "I didn't have to worry about what he thought about my holding the captain seat, since he was junior to me on the Continental seniority list."

"Okay."

"But I don't know what Clint or the other furloughees will think." I shift in my seat and turn toward her. "Clint was probably hired back in the late 'nineties, possibly even before I started taking flight lessons. And then September 11 happened. And the Great Recession. And boom—two furloughs." I look back at the skyline. "Combine that with the merger, contention over Bid 14-02, the looming seniority list integration, and my being close to ten years younger than him, and, well, I'm just expecting pushback, that's all."

Jen nods slowly. "I get that they've had a rocky road," she says. "But why does your age matter?"

I look back at her. "Because the power dynamic will feel all wrong."

"How so?"

"All my life I've reported to people who were older than me, and now they're reporting to me. Will Clint be resentful about that? Will he push back and try to act as the captain from the right seat? And if he does, how will I control that?" I ask with my hand out and my palms up.

"But Husband," she says, reaching over to grab my outstretched hand, "you can't control what he thinks or how he acts."

The look on my face softens. "I know, Wife."

She laces her fingers together with mine. "So why even worry about it?"

I sigh. "Because I'm supposed to be the captain. I'm supposed to be in control. That's my new job. And if the guy sitting next to me is mad about how things have turned out for him—"

"—which in fairness to Clint, you don't know will be the case."

"That's true. But if—"

"So why not give him the benefit of the doubt until proven otherwise?"

"Well," I pause, "I guess you have a point. But if he *is* mad," I say, trying to skirt around her question, "how do I keep control when the power dynamic is flip-flopped? When I'm still trying to get used to my new role as captain?"

Jen pauses for a moment, contemplating my question. "Maybe

there's a way to use your inexperience in the left seat to your advantage."

"I'm listening," I say.

"What if you just put it out there? 'Fess up. Engage them. See if they'll give you tips or advice."

I wobble my head back and forth. "I don't know, Wife. Could be a slippery slope."

"So don't slide down the hill," she says. "But give them a chance to prove their years of experience count for something. Put that experience to use."

I rub my chin as I think about her suggestion.

"And listen to their stories."

"Their stories?"

"Yes," she says, nodding. "You say people love to talk about themselves. Take, for example, Exhibit A." She motions to me, and I roll my eyes, even though I know she's right. "Let them tell you where they've been." She pauses. "And actually *listen*."

"I'm sorry, what?" I ask, joking.

Jen shakes her head, grinning. "My point exactly."

I smile. "No, I know," I sigh. "And I hear you. It's a good idea."

"And do it without thinking about your immediate rebuttal."

I look toward her. "You say that as though I always have a rebuttal."

She drops her head and smirks. "Husband, you just gave a rebuttal."

"Oh," I say. "Right."

She grabs my hand again. "I just think you may be surprised by what they tell you. If you listen."

I nod. "Yeah. Maybe so."

"And if you're saying you suspect they may be resentful of your being in control, then are there ways you could give them some of that control? Decisions they could make about things that don't really need to be made by the captain?"

"Probably," I say. "Although again, it's a slippery slope."

"But isn't it an even slipperier slope if you try to steamroll them?"

"Probably."

"Because no one wants that. Especially from a young punk like you," she says, joking—I think—about the last part.

I roll my eyes and look out at the skyline and a United jet cresting the shoreline on its way to O'Hare.

"So, what do you have to lose by trying? By giving them the benefit of the doubt until you're proven otherwise? By trusting their abilities and valuing their opinions?"

I look toward her. "Probably not much."

"So then do it already!"

"But what if that doesn't work? What if they still push back?"

"Well, dude," she says. "You're the captain. You've gotta figure some of this out on your own. I can't go around giving you all the answers."

I laugh, shaking my head. "You're a mess, you know that?"

"Besides, it's like you tell me: Maybe those challenges will teach you something."

"You know," I say, shaking my finger, "I see what you're doing."

"What I'm doing?"

"Yes. Throwing my words back at me like that."

Jen grins. "I'm just saying it's worth a shot."

I turn away, gazing onto the city. "I suspect you're right."

Jen leans toward me. "I'm sorry. What was that?" she asks, holding her hand up to her ear. "I didn't quite catch it."

I toss her some side-eye. "You heard me."

"I'm not sure, though. Can you say it again? I'm what?"

"Mmhmm."

Jen lets out a deep laugh. "No, really. Say it. Please."

Another roll of my eyes. And slowly I tell her, "I said, 'You're right.'"

A huge smile radiates across her face. "Thank you very much!"

I watch her gleaming in her chair. "You really are ridiculous, you know that?"

"Yep! And I'm completely okay with it," she says as both of us laugh.

"Well, I'll give it a shot tomorrow morning, and we'll see how it goes."

"Good," she replies. "And tell him about the comb-over. Seriously. It's got to go."

I chuckle. "That's definitely something I'll consider."

Jen laughs. "You're such a dork."

I pull the seatbelt straps down from behind my shoulders, snapping them into the five-point harness at my waist.

"Starting down," I say to Clint as I press a button on the flight computer to command the 737 to pitch downward and begin its descent into Anchorage.

"Roger that, boss," he replies. His folksy drawl is surprisingly disarming, but I'm still on edge and cannot entirely determine if there's an element of passive aggressiveness in the way he says "boss."

Slightly more than five hours have passed since we left Chicago and headed northwest for Anchorage—the longest 737 flight in United's network. The dense Chicagoland suburbs are but a distant memory now. So, too, are the wide-open Wisconsin farmlands that we climbed above on our way up to our 36,000-foot cruise altitude. From those crystal clear skies, Minnesota's ten thousand lakes appeared as tiny blue dots upon a verdant, tree-covered landscape. And as we continued barreling through the sky at the rate of about one mile every seven seconds, the dark greens had quickly become the light browns of russet wheat fields stretching as far as we could see across the North

Dakotan countryside. Only after passing into Canadian airspace and cresting above a blanket of low-lying clouds did the sightseeing become monotonous. And that's when we turned to conversation to pass the time between our flight's enroute checkpoints, which were spaced about fifteen minutes apart during the 2,842-mile trip.

With our feet propped up on the little rubber footrests at the base of the dashboard, we reclined in our seats, and with our elbows resting on the leather armrests, we explored the usual topics of enroute chit-chat. First up were our flying resumes and the latest company rumors—especially those about upcoming bids, airplane orders, or potential destinations we might be starting to service. Next came a review of the layover hotel for that night, including the quality of its beds, its gym, and any nearby restaurants of note. Finally was a cursory review of our families, hobbies, and favorite sports. With some pilots, the last part of this routine expands into more free flowing conversation. But more often than not, a lull eventually develops. And when the conversation peters out, one of the pilots will suggest it is time for a bathroom break or a call to the flight attendants about the status of our crew meals.

Sometimes, I envy the more robust relationships developed by Jen or my friends with traditional jobs. Over time, they learn the subtle nuances of their coworkers. They throw parties for their colleagues to celebrate birthdays, weddings, and holidays. They are missed if they call in sick, take a vacation, or accept a job in a different department. They are a team in every sense of the word.

But pilots—and flight attendants for that matter—are far too nomadic for that type of close-knit working relationship. We live all across the country, regardless of the hub airport to which we are assigned. And while it's common for pilots—or flight attendants—to remain paired together for the duration of a three- or four-day trip, it's a rarity to keep the same pilot *and* flight attendant teams paired together for more than one or two flights at a time. If we call in sick or go on vacation, it's doubtful anyone—except possibly crew scheduling—even realizes we are gone. It's as though we are independent contractors hired by United to work specific flights. Or, to steal a line from Edward Norton's character in the movie *Fight Club*, it's as though we are single-serving friends who, for a period of a few days, walk through airports together, share long hours on the flight deck together, dine together on layovers, and then shake hands at the conclusion of the trip, saying, "Great flying with you," while secretly hoping we will still remember each other's name if we cross paths six months later.

But now, starting into the descent for Anchorage, those thoughts are far from my mind. Instead, I'm thinking about the mountains hidden by the clouds and the windy conditions I expect to encounter upon landing.

"Anchorage Center, United Fourteen-Ninety-Two is leaving flight level three-six-zero," Clint reports as the nose of the airplane drops below the horizon and the throttles automatically retard to their idle position.

"Roger, United Fourteen-Ninety-Two," the controller replies.

A few minutes later, we zip through the cloud deck's puffy rounded tops and enter what looks like a narrow fjord with undulating marshmallow walls along the sides. Then we submerge into the cloud itself. It swallows us whole and turns the view from our windows an opaque white. Eventually, we drop out the cloud's bottom into a separate tunnel comprised of white and gray clouds. Its cloudy floor is thin and wispy, and beneath that gauzy layer, I believe I see the mighty Chugach Mountains. But I can't tell for sure. They remain elusive, darting in and out of view until the thin cloud layer suddenly disappears, creating a stunning grand reveal of the majestic mountains.

"Oh wow," I say, mesmerized by the rocky cliffs that jut endlessly across our cockpit's panorama. "That's spectacular!"

"It sure is," Clint agrees.

We lean forward in our seats, pressing our faces against the thick, heated windows. Even in early August, most of the mountain peaks are capped with pristine, white snow. And draped around their pointy white necks are blue glacial scarves that slide gracefully down the hillsides until they spill into long, narrow turquoise lakes.

In the distance, we see the city of Anchorage. It's nestled against the mountains on one side and the Turnagain Arm Bay on the other. A few midrise office buildings stretch toward the sky from downtown. But the rest of the city appears more like a small town, despite being home to half the state's population.

Air traffic control circles us north of the city before turning us toward the airfield for a landing to the southeast on Runway 15. And as we make the final turn to the runway, I feel the turbulent winds pick up substantially.

"Gear down," I command while disconnecting the autopilot with the button on my control wheel.

Clint lowers the gear lever and completes the landing checklist.

I wrestle the controls back and forth as one gust after another thumps against the jet. They aren't the strongest gusts I've ever felt, but I can see from the ripples on the bay that the wind is howling—thankfully straight down the runway, since a crosswind makes any landing far more challenging. Even so, my adrenaline pumps as I guide the jet down the glidepath to the runway, which starts just beyond the water's edge.

"One hundred," Clint calls as we cross the marshy shoreline onto airport grounds.

The runway grows nearer and nearer, filling the window in front of me. And I jiggle the controls, back and forth, back and forth.

"Fifty...forty...thirty..."

I start my landing flare by easing back on the control wheel.

Almost immediately, the speed falls away unexpectedly as a strong gust dies off.

"Twenty…"

I shove the throttles forward aggressively, hoping to regain some of the disappearing airspeed and reduce the quickening descent rate.

"Ten…"

But I'm too late, and the plane plops onto the runway with a thud.

Well, we're here, I think. *Safe and sound, but definitely no greaser* — the Holy Grail of landings, one so smooth that it's impossible to tell that the wheels have returned to the ground.

I pull up on the reverse thrust levers and apply the brakes to slow the jet to taxi speed. Several minutes later we park at the gate and shut down the engines.

By the time I gather up my things and slide the Tank out from its cubby, the plane is nearly empty. I stand in the cockpit doorway, resting my hand on the Tank's extended handle, offering goodbyes to the last few exiting passengers.

As the last passenger steps into the jetway, the flight attendant in the forward galley says, "That's it. You boys enjoy your layover."

"Thanks," I reply. "And you enjoy your flight to San Francisco. Although I can't say I envy you; that's a long day."

"Gotta get my hours in."

I smile. "Definitely no money to be made sitting on the ground," I joke, referring to how it is that pilots and flight attendants get paid only from the time the cabin door closes and the plane pushes back in one city until it parks at the gate and opens the cabin door in another. "Well, thanks again," I say with a wave as I grab the Tank's handle and begin making my way up the jetway.

The hotel van is waiting for Clint and me as we exit the terminal into the almost fall-like Alaskan air. The driver opens the van's side door and scoops up our luggage. Clint sits in the front row, and I crawl into the one behind him.

After buckling my seatbelt, I turn on my cellphone, and almost immediately my phone buzzes with a text message.

JEN: Yay landed!!

It's the same message I receive from her after almost every flight, and it makes me smile every time. Jen loves tracking my flights, often keeping the flight's map from United's website open on her laptop as she works from her windowless office at the University of Chicago.

Another text comes in.

JEN: How did it go? How is your FO?

I text back as our van pulls away from the terminal.

ME: Good flight. Gorgeous arrival. FO very nice.

As I await Jen's reply, I look out my window and notice the large seaplane base at the lake beside the international airport, part of the invaluable general aviation infrastructure that keeps remote Alaskan communities both supplied and connected. My phone vibrates.

JEN: Oh, that's good.

JEN: What about the comb over?

I look up from my phone and see Clint scrolling away on his, presumably texting and checking emails, too. I smile as I type my reply to Jen.

ME: First thing I mentioned.

Jen's response comes almost immediately.

JEN: SERIOUSLY?????

I let out a small laugh as I read her message.

ME: Of course not.

ME: And you're ridiculous. Just for the record.

JEN: Lol. Don't care.

Between texts, I glance at the houses and shops we pass along our way to the hotel. They're simple and unimpressive for the most part, nestled against the area's ubiquitous spruce, birch, and cottonwood trees. Almost all of them were likely built after the devastating 1964 earthquake wiped out most of the city, which makes it hard for me to imagine what it must have been like when my grandfather spent a short season of his life here in the 1940s working on the Alaskan Railroad. Of course, the mountains were probably just as impressive then as they are now, towering like an imposing castle wall around the city's eastern flank, with Denali, the tallest point in North America, standing watch from the north on clear days.

My phone vibrates again.

JEN: Did he give you any issues?

ME: Not a one.

ME: Almost weirds me out a bit. Expected at least a little pushback.

I look out the van's front window and think I see our hotel—a Sheraton—up ahead. *Buzzzzzz.*

JEN: Dude. It's in your head!

I text back.

ME: Starting to think that might be the case. Will see if it's the case tomorrow and on other flights.

The van pulls under the hotel's portico.

ME: At hotel. Gotta run. Will call you after dinner. Love you, bye!"

JEN: Sounds good, dude! Love you, bye!!"

Clint and I hop out, grab our bags, tip the driver, and walk into our home away from home to pick up our room keys from the front desk.

As we wait for one of the elevators to arrive, I ask Clint, "You like seafood?"

"I do," he responds.

The elevator doors open and we walk in. "Well there's a great spot I found online. Dinner's on me if you want to come. No worries either way."

"That sounds great actually."

"Excellent," I say as we arrive on our floor. "Meet in the lobby at five?"

"You got it, boss," he says.

"Great. See you then."

The fishermen stand almost shoulder-to-shoulder along the edge of the creek. Peering down on them from the dining room windows of Bridge Seafood, a restaurant whose structure forms a physical bridge over the creek, I wonder how they avoid bumping into one another while casting their lines.

"Do you fish?" I ask Clint. Like me, he's traded in his official pilot uniform for his unofficial overnight one—jeans, a polo shirt, and sneakers.

"Nah," he says. "You?"

"I used to. With my grandfather when I was a kid. But not much anymore." I pause for a moment, watching another fisherman cast his line into the creek. "In fact, I think the last time I went fishing was when I took a twelve-year-old kid I was hanging out with through Big Brothers Big Sisters." I chuckle. "But I'm not sure you can call that fishing, because we didn't catch a thing."

Clint grins. "He must have been very impressed with your skills."

"The kid or my grandfather?"

"The kid."

I shake my head. "Oh, I'm quite certain he was wholly unimpressed."

Clint laughs.

"Worst part was the whole time I kept thinking about how disappointed Papaw would have been about my performance—like I hadn't learned a thing from all his lessons."

"Well, sometimes the fish just don't bite."

"And sometimes it's the angler."

Clint laughs again.

"Either way," I say, noticing the waitress heading our way with two entrées balanced on her forearm, "this is a much easier way to catch a nice fish."

Clint sees the waitress now, too. "Easier. But not necessarily as rewarding."

"True."

"Okay," the waitress says as she arrives at our table. "King salmon for you," she says, setting the large plate in front of me. "And halibut for you, sir."

We both smile; our dishes smell fantastic.

"Anything else I can get for you?"

"Not right now," Clint says, "but thank you."

"Well then, enjoy!"

We take small bites of our perfectly prepared fish, savoring their buttery flavors as we continue watching the fishermen along the creek.

"There is definitely something intriguing about Alaska," Clint says.

"That's for sure."

"I'm not sure I could live up here, but I totally get why people love it."

"Me, too," I say, my fork easily pulling off another flaky salmon bite. "It's as though you're a million miles from anywhere."

"Because you basically are," Clint says. "Which has to be part of the allure."

I cover my mouth as I respond, "Probably so," while still chewing. A moment later I add, "I'm pretty sure that's why my grandfather moved up here—to get away."

"He lived here?" Clint asks, surprised.

I nod.

"How long?"

"A year or two, I believe. Maybe three." I dab my mouth with my napkin and take a sip of water. "It was back in the forties. He had moved from Pennsylvania to Washington state as a young man. Worked as a plumber at the shipyard in Bremerton. The story I've heard is that he wanted to be part of the war effort, and since he'd had polio as a child, the shipyard was as close as he could get to helping out." I grab another bite of salmon with my fork. "Somewhere along the way, an opportunity came up for him to work for the Alaska Railroad, although I'm not sure in what capacity. So he took the job and stayed a while before returning to P-A. And to this day, he still raves about his time living up here."

"That's really cool," Clint says, reaching for his dinner roll.

"I think so, too. And every time I'm here I wonder what it would have been like for him. Because I can totally see him fishing these very streams after work." I motion toward the fishermen beneath us. "Or camping under the stars, watching the northern lights."

"It was probably a lot different back then," Clint says.

"Anchorage, for sure. But the rest of Alaska? Maybe not. So much of it seems as untouched as ever."

"That's true."

"Anyway, I would have loved to have known him back then—a young man without a care in the world. Out here living some grand adventure."

Clint looks down at his plate. "Well, life's definitely a grand adventure, that's for sure."

The tone in Clint's response feels distinctly different from that of the other comments he has made. It seems to leave so much unsaid, and I find myself longing to know more about Clint's own grand adventure—more than the cursory overview he gave me during the flight. But I promised myself I would stay away from all topics relating to seniority and Clint's furloughs; there doesn't seem much good that can come from broaching those touchy subjects. And yet a question burns inside of me. I take another bite and stare out the window to buy time to contemplate whether to ask it or move on. Eventually, I think, *the hell with it,* and ask away.

"Do you mind if I ask you a personal question?"

Clint looks up from his plate, his guard heightened a bit. "Fire away."

"How do you do it?"

Clint offers me a confused look. "How do I do what?"

"How do you maintain such a positive attitude at work after all you've been through? The two furloughs, the ups and downs, the different companies, the hits to your seniority. All of that."

Clint cuts off another bite of halibut with his fork. "I don't know," he says. "You just do it. Left foot then right foot."

"But you seem to have taken it all with such grace."

Clint leans back in his chair, dabbing his mouth with his napkin. "Well, it's been really tough at times." He pauses again. "I mean, when I got hired by United, I thought I had it made. United was growing like crazy. Our union had negotiated an amazing contract. It seemed to be all upside—like I had won the lottery." He takes a sip of water. "And then September 11 happened and the whole damn industry came crashing down. No one saw that coming." He digs around in his veggies with his fork. "Soon, all the growth stopped. We took thirty-percent pay cuts to try and save our jobs. But even that didn't work." He takes a small bite. "At least not for me. And it wasn't long before I was furloughed and heading back to a regional airline again, where the pay was even worse than after our pay cuts at United."

I sit silently, listening intently.

"Some days I'd get really angry about it. And I mean *really* angry. I'd be flying along at the regional and find myself shaking as I thought about how wronged I'd been. About how I was losing all this seniority. About how my career was spinning backwards. And about how I couldn't control any of it."

I can feel the tension returning to him as he retells his story. I can see it in his face by the way his eyes close in and his lips tighten. And then the tension passes, as though he just shrugs it off.

"I'm sure you'll fly with some furloughees who still feel that way," he says.

"Which is sort of what I expected to find with all of you."

Clint shrugs. "Not all. But they're out there. Trust me. Still looking for the break that makes them whole for what they've lost."

"And you're not?" I ask, taking another bite.

"I used to be. But I'm not actively looking for it anymore. If it comes my way, I won't turn it down. But I've made my peace with this career."

"Made your peace?"

"Yeah," he says, leaning forward. "You see, I started thinking about the Pan Am guys I'd flown with early on in my career at United. When they got hired at Pan Am, they thought they'd won the lottery, too. And for a while, I guess they had. I mean, can you think of a more iconic airline to work for?"

"Not really."

"Me neither. That was the one. The best of the best."

"Yep."

"But here's the thing about lottery winnings," he says. "They have a way of drying up. And over time, and for a variety of reasons, Pan Am died a slow, painful death, eventually being gobbled up by United and Delta." He chews another bite. "Well, one day it hit me that just like those Pan Am guys, I was along for the ride. I had done my best to take advantage of opportunities as they'd come along. But after that, it was partially up to fate. Because none of us can predict the future, and in this business, so much of our careers is out of our control."

I think back to the conversation I'd had with Chris over breakfast during training about the looming seniority list integration. But it was one thing to consider the possibility of having our careers upended by no fault of our own, and another thing entirely to have lived that powerlessness.

Clint continues. "So I had to make a choice," he says, moving his hands up and down as though they are a scale, weighing the two options. "Either I could come to terms with my reality—my own grand adventure, if you will—or I could be consumed by it." Clint's words hang in the air as he reaches for his glass to take another sip. "And so I chose to accept my adventure for what it was—flaws and all."

I lean back into my chair. "But how do you actually—"

"Don't get me wrong, Korry; some days it's a lot easier said than done." He shifts in his seat. "I mean, would I have preferred for things to have turned out differently? Of course. Would I have preferred to be in the left seat at United by now? Absolutely. And does it sting a little when, quite honestly, I find myself pulling gear for someone like you who is so much younger than me and who doesn't seem to have hit the speed bumps I have? For sure."

I feel myself growing uncomfortable for broaching such a touchy subject.

"But that's not your fault," Clint says, "and it's not mine, either. It simply is what it is. So I come to work, do my best, and roll with whatever happens—good, bad or indifferent. Because at the end of the day, doing otherwise is just a waste of time and energy."

I set my fork down. "Clint, I...wow."

He turns to look out the window.

"Thank you for sharing that," I say.

He looks back to me and shrugs. "You asked."

Both of us turn back to stare out the window as well. After a few seconds I say, "Well, I'm really hopeful that if I'm ever tasked with overcoming challenges like you've faced that I'll do so with as much grace as you have."

"I hope you never have to find out, Korry," he says. "I hope it's smooth skies the whole way for you. But if it's not, if you hit some turbulence along the way, you'll have to choose for yourself to either accept things or be consumed by them. And I assure you that, in the moment, both choices can look appealing."

I nod, saying, "I believe that." Then I take another sip of my drink. "I am cautiously optimistic that smooth skies are ahead for all of us now."

"I hope you're right," Clint says. "But you know what?"

"It will be what it will be?"

"Exactly," he says, smiling. "Just a big grand adventure."

The check comes, and after I pay, the two of us walk back to our hotel. The sun still hangs above the horizon, as it will until nearly 11:00 PM that night.

"Gotta be honest," I say as we step into the elevator to head up to our rooms, "I'm dreading this redeye tomorrow night."

"Me, too, Korry. It's a long ride back to Chicago."

A few moments later, the elevator's doors open on our floor. "Sleep well, Clint."

"You, too, Korry."

I step around the 737's center console just before departure time the next night, and plop down onto its firm left seat. A long sigh escapes out of my mouth as I stare momentarily at the windshield, which is covered by tiny mist droplets that have pierced the nighttime Alaskan sky.

"What was that all about?" Clint asks as he pecks away at the flight computer, finalizing our routing and updating the flight's performance figures.

"Had to determine if a guy was okay to fly or not."

"And your answer was?"

"I think he'll be better tomorrow morning...after a good night's rest and a few Tylenol."

Clint chuckles. "And that's why they pay you the big bucks. Those calls are way above my pay grade."

"Something like that," I say, shaking my head as I reach behind my left shoulder to plug in my headset.

Out of the corner of my eye, I catch my reflection in the window, just as the examiner had predicted during my final simulator checkride. It's my first true "window test," and I'm thankful it has been an easy one to pass. After all, the federal aviation regulations are explicit and unequivocal when it comes to the carriage of intoxicated passengers; the captain cannot, under any circumstance, let them fly. Still, it's a great reminder that I must be ready for future window tests, because I'm sure others will be more difficult and less cut-and-dried.

"Anyway," Clint continues, "I think I've got us all set up. But please double check my work."

It takes a few minutes for me to review the airport's weather, our air traffic control clearance, and the rest of Clint's flight deck setup. But I quickly realize he hasn't missed a thing. In fact, he's even managed to bookmark the pages within my navigation chart binder that he expects I'll want to use for the flight—something he didn't have to do, but something that reminds me that, despite our differences, Clint is looking out for me as his teammate.

"This is perfect," I tell him. "Thank you."

"You bet, boss. Happy to help." And I know he means it.

A few minutes later, we race down the runway for takeoff and climb rapidly through the thin cloud layer hugging the surface into the pitch-black Alaskan sky. The magnificent Chugach Mountains are invisible in the darkness, but the pattern of red, yellow, and green dots on our terrain displays reminds us that the rock walls have not disappeared.

Given the hectic events that transpired on the ground, I appreciate the calmness and quiet of our nighttime flight. Clint seems to embrace the cockpit's solitude as well, and for a while, the two of us don't talk. Instead, we listen to the steady rush of air past our windows, and we watch a magnificent performance by the stunning northern lights.

Large swaths of neon green lights sweep across the moonless sky. Some sections glow brightly, featuring smooth curves and crisp edges that resemble brilliant emerald rivers flowing through the heavens. Other sections appear muted and subdued, as though an expert painter has used her fan brush to pull the viridian light across her expansive black canvas. Most astonishing, however, is the rapid pace with which the lights move and transform as they dance their mystifying waltz. At times they grow big and bold, and at others they shrink so small and subdued that I think the lights may disappear entirely. But then, as if on cue, they return again with more brilliance than ever, continuing their enthralling recital for close to an hour.

When the performance finally ends, Clint and I resume our inconsequential chitchat. Under dim cockpit lighting, we banter back and forth while sipping coffee and eating crew meals—activities we undertake to pass the time and remain alert as we monitor the long overnight flight's progress toward Chicago. And every few seconds, another mile ticks down. And every few minutes, the number of streetlights and small towns we see out our windows rises—a sign that Alaska's remoteness is farther and farther behind us.

With less than an hour of flight time remaining, the faint orange glow of Chicago appears nearly two hundred miles ahead of us along the easternmost horizon. Hanging in the black sky above the city lights is the twinkling bulb of Venus—the luminary that announces sunrise is imminent. Like clockwork, Venus climbs higher into the sky, pulling with it a dim arc of light. The arc starts out a dark blue color—almost black—but it steadily morphs, turning ever-lighter shades of blue as it expands, stretches, and arches higher and wider across the sky. This is the day line—the line where the sun's rays are no longer shadowed by the earth's curvature. It's a spectacular sight to behold, and it always leaves me feeling optimistic about the opportunities the new day may bring.

The farther east we fly, the more the arc's blues turn to reds, burnt oranges, and golden yellows. Soon, predawn light fills the entire sky, and the sun's backlighting causes the thin, wispy clouds of the upper atmosphere to appear purplish. Finally, the sun makes its grand ascent. It begins as a tiny pinprick of intense light on the horizon. But the pinprick swells rapidly. And without 35,000 feet of atmosphere to help filter it, the light's intensity is nearly blinding.

Clint and I reach for our sunglasses and the movable green translucent visors that are stowed in our side cubbies. We clip the visors to a single black railing that runs above all six cockpit windows, positioning them to block as much sunlight as possible.

"The sun really ruins the sunrise," Clint says.

"It's the worst," I chuckle.

Thankfully, the descent into O'Hare turns our focus away from the sun as we program the flight computers, manipulate the autopilot, and complete a few more checklists.

Soon, O'Hare is in sight, a sprawling open mass surrounded by dense Chicagoland suburbs. Beyond it, the skyscrapers of downtown form a jagged black silhouette against Lake Michigan and the colorful sky. We fly past the airport, and upon reaching the shoreline, air traffic control turns us around to land to the west. The steep bank angles of the turn allow us to peer out the right side windows directly onto the tops of the tall buildings and the just-awakening city streets, which are already bustling with commuters.

Just after 7:00 AM, we bring the plane safely back to earth. We meander around O'Hare's taxiways for a few minutes before parking at our gate. And as soon as I set the parking brake and complete the final checklist of the flight, I feel my eyelids become heavy; they sense the comfort of my bed is just a short train ride away.

I reach across the center console with my hand outstretched. "Thanks, Clint. Really enjoyed flying with you."

"Me, too," he says, shaking my hand.

"Hope we get to do this again soon."

"Agreed," he says. But we both know that's unlikely.

I pack up my things and pull the Tank from the luggage cubby.

I turn my cellphone on and stand in the flight deck doorway, saying goodbye to the remaining passengers. My phone buzzes against my leg, and during a gap in exiting passengers, I steal a look.

JEN: Yay landed!!

And then another one.

JEN: I'm in the cell phone lot. No train today. Call when you're ready and I'll come pick you up.

I smile and think, *What a wife!*

Jen pulls up to the curb at O'Hare at the same time I exit the terminal.

"Good morning, Husband," she says as she gets out of the car to give me a hug and a kiss. "Surprised?"

"I am!" I open the rear hatch of the SUV to put the Tank inside. "You're a good wife, you know that?"

Jen smiles. "I woke up early and figured, what the heck. After a long redeye, this is nicer for you than having to take the train."

"Much nicer!" I exclaim. "So, thank you. Like a lot."

Jen smiles. "Yeah, dude! It's good to have you home."

And I can't agree more; it *is* good to be home—at least for a few days, until my grand adventure continues with two international trips. And as I'll discover, one of them will leave me questioning if I really have what it takes to be a captain in more than name only.

CHAPTER 8

Border Crossings

*"No one is going to stick their head out
of the trenches for someone they don't
respect or trust. You can get shot doing that."*
- Gordon Bethune

36,000 Feet Above the Gulf of Mexico – Mid-August 2013

The sun races toward the western horizon line as Jeremy and I cruise above the popcorn-shaped clouds clinging to the surface of the Gulf of Mexico's deep blue waters. The two of us sit with our feet propped up on the dashboard footrests. Our seats are reclined slightly, our heads supported by the chairs' cushioned headrests. Our elbows pivot against the leather armrests and our forearms extend upwards in front of our faces, allowing both of us to tap the tips of our fingers together as we chat.

And yet our similarities don't end with the way we sit; Jeremy is the closest I've ever come to having an airline twin. We both are in our early 30s. We both are trim and clean cut, sporting polished shoes, starched uniforms, and civilianized high-and-tight haircuts that are spiked up in the front. We both live in downtown Chicago, and we both sold cherished BMWs when we moved there to open the Continental 737 sub-base after the merger. We both are foodies and enjoy a fine scotch from time to time. And perhaps most coincidentally of all, at least for a profession not requiring advanced degrees, we both hold MBAs, which is how our routine flight deck talk has turned to the deeper and more abstract topic of how the new United can foster a corporate culture that brings our two legacy workgroups closer together.

"We're three years past the merger, and in many ways, it still feels like we are two completely separate airlines," Jeremy bemoans.

"Oh, I agree one hundred percent."

"We use different crew schedulers and dispatchers. We fly airplanes specified for crews of one subsidiary or the other."

I roll my head toward Jeremy. "At least we'll finally get a common uniform in December. Then we'll at least look like we play for the same team."

"Which should help a lot. But people will still find a way to mark themselves as CAL pilots or United pilots."

"No doubt about it," I agree, grabbing the large water bottle beside me to take a swig.

"Even now, many of the furloughees who are flying on the CAL side wear red ID clips as a subtle way to identify themselves as United pilots while they're wearing the black Continental uniform."

"I've seen that, too," I say, setting the water bottle back down.

"So when does it end? When do we finally embrace our new company and move forward together?"

Jeremy's passion borders on desperation, a feeling I share. "It's gonna be a while, I'm afraid. Definitely not before the new integrated seniority list is published in a few weeks."

"But let's be honest; the new list probably won't help, either."

"Probably not in the short term," I agree, expecting the arbitrated award to be contentious, regardless of how the new list is built.

"Or even the long term," Jeremy laments. "I mean, I'm sure you've flown with many pilots over the years who are still bitter about the seniority list integration for the Continental, New York Air, PeoplExpress, and Frontier merger, right?"

"Oh, for sure," I say, noticing the white diamond on our navigation display that represents another aircraft. The screen's readout says the plane is 1,000 feet above and heading directly toward us. So I sit up, zoom in on the display's range, and begin scanning the horizon ahead of us for the traffic.

"United Fifteen-Sixty-Six," the Houston air traffic controller interjects with a lazy southern drawl. "You're ten miles northeast of AXEXO," which is the named latitude/longitude point defining the edge of Houston's airspace as well as that of the United States. "Contact Monterrey Center on frequency one-two-four-decimal-five."

"One-two-four-decimal-five for Monterrey, United Fifteen-Sixty-Six. G'day," Jeremy replies. Turning to me while he tunes the new frequency on the center console communication panel, he says, "And that merger was twenty-five years ago!" He keys his mic again and reports our position to the Mexican air traffic controller. "Monterrey, *buenas noches*. United One-Five-Six-Six approaching AXEXO, flight level three-six-zero."

Using sharp consonants and rolled R's, the controller replies, "United One-Five-Six-Six, Monterrey Center, radar contact. Maintain flight level three-six-zero. *Buenas noches.*"

"Maintain three-six-zero, United one-five-six-six."

And with that, the routine procedure for confirming radio contact with a new controller is complete.

I jump back into our conversation without missing a beat. "I think it all comes down to this: everyone longs for a sense of identity and belonging."

"No doubt about it."

I glance toward Jeremy. "And if you think about it, at our most basic level, humans are pack animals. And a pack is way more than just an animal's family; it's the animal's identity. It's who the animal is."

"Sure," Jeremy says.

I look back toward the horizon. "So an animal doesn't give up on his pack without a damn good reason for doing so."

"But isn't the merger a good reason?"

"It can be, but—"

"Look at all the opportunities we have now that we didn't have before. New bases. New fleets. New routes."

I notice a small but quickly growing speck just above the horizon line. "But that's all change, Jeremy. And when change is forced upon anyone—and I doubt any of us would say we had a choice about whether we were going to merge—it's human nature to resist that change."

"By turning to our packs?"

"Precisely," I say. "We turn to what we know—our original pack—because there's comfort and certainty there." I point ahead. "Traffic twelve-o'clock, slightly high."

Jeremy sits up and scans. "I got him," he says.

A few moments later, we watch a Delta Air Lines Airbus 320 zip past, almost directly above us. A short cloudy contrail extends behind it, and for a brief moment I watch the contrail twisting in tight counter-rotating cyclones—evidence of the powerful wake turbulence created by every jet as it speeds through the sky.

I lean back and return to the topic at hand. "Which is why some of the furloughees are wearing the red ID clips. It identifies their pack—the one with blue uniforms instead of black."

Jeremy nods. "I guess I can see that."

"And if the tables were turned, I guarantee the CAL pilots would have found some way to identify themselves, too. It's human nature."

Noticing a set of tall, billowing clouds far in the distance, I reach up to the dashboard's display control panel and press the "WX" button to turn on my weather radar. Moments later, the radar's *sweep-sweep* pattern appears on my moving map screen.

"So how do we get past this?" Jeremy asks. "How do we move forward as one pack?"

"Good question." I twist a knob on the center console to adjust the radar's tilt angle for our altitude so I can get an accurate representation of the storms. "I think it starts with our new pack leaders—the new United's management team—proving to our heads and to our hearts that the benefits of embracing our new United pack exceed the costs of resisting it." I look at Jeremy. "The head part is easier, I think, because most of it is transactional."

"Like the seniority lists for us and the other work groups?"

"And the contracts, routes, and bases. Things like that, although some of those will be tough because of the contentious, winner-take-all battle mentality they sort of foster. But—"

"This route was ours, and now it's theirs. This hub was ours, and now it's theirs. That kind of thing?"

"Exactly." I notice that the radar returns on our displays appear to be about 160 miles—or at least 20 minutes—ahead of us. "And so both sides have to see quantifiable benefits. That's step one. But then we need the heart piece, too," I say, tapping my hand on my chest, "because without it, I think it's easy for employees to focus on what their pack is losing instead of what we're all gaining."

"And how do you propose we do that?"

"Another good question." I pause to consider it for a moment. "I think I'd start with a compelling vision of where management intends to take us—one framed in a way that resonates with people on the line and reflects what they value, not simply the business mumbo-jumbo that appeals to investors."

"Like the 'merger synergies' we constantly hear about?"

"Precisely," I say. "It's not that synergies aren't important; it's that front-line folks need to understand why those synergies will help them as well as the stockholders."

"I can see that."

"And I also think we need a good story to bring our two sides together emotionally. We need to show that this isn't the death of our legacy companies but rather the evolution of them. And one common link I believe might be effective is Walter Varney."

"Didn't he start Continental?"

"He did, indirectly. He started Varney Speed Lines in the 1930s, which was sold to Robert Six, who renamed the company Continental Airlines."

"That's right," Jeremy says, nodding.

"Well, Varney also started a different airline several years before that. And as it happens, he sold that airline to a company that eventually changed its name to United Airlines."

"No kidding," Jeremy says, reaching up to his dashboard to turn on his weather radar, too. The tall, billowing clouds look more and more menacing the closer we get to them.

"And so as I see it, our two subsidiaries are like long-lost brothers—or maybe half-brothers—who lived separately for decades and never got that close. We went our own ways, each of us evolving and growing, struggling and thriving at various times. Until one day, after we both had matured, we realized nothing was stronger than a *united* family," I say, emphasizing the united part. "So we came back together. And right now, we're going through predictable growing pains as we learn to live together under one roof. There are jealousies. There are misunderstandings. But we are family. We are brothers and sisters. And we understand that if we focus on building each other up instead of tearing each other down, we can fly anywhere. The sky's the limit."

Jeremy smiles. "You know, I like that."

"It's a little cheesy, I get that."

"It is, but the analogy works."

"And maybe the Varney story isn't the right one," I say. "But—"

"We need the heart," Jeremy says, finishing my sentence.

"Yes. We need something to emotionally unify us, something to rally us around a common crusade of beating the other airlines, not ourselves."

Jeremy pauses, thinking about our discussion. "So, this is all well and good, but what if management doesn't do it? What can you and I do to make a difference?"

"Well, I say we should follow Arthur Ashe's advice that if you want to change the world, start where you are, use what you have, and do what you can."

"I've heard that before," Jeremy says. "Great quote."

"It is. And what else *can* we do but do our roles the best we can and hope everyone else does the same?"

"Not too much," Jeremy says.

"But you know what?" I ask rhetorically. "There's opportunity in that—if only on a small scale."

"Yeah. And if enough of us did that, it *could* really make a difference."

"I agree. It's grassroots change. It's harder, but—"

"It's possible."

The conversation lulls for a bit as the two of us turn our attention to the storm clouds we see out our front windows. With dusk setting in, the clouds are bathed in backlighting from the sun. The rounded white edges are clear and bright, while the shadowed portions appear a mesmerizing purplish tint. The hot summer air and the mountains near Mexico City create strong currents of rising air—the lifeblood of a thunderstorm—that drive the clouds higher. Even from over 100 miles away, we see the tops billowing upwards like a child's vinegar and baking soda volcano. The collection of storm clouds is beautiful to see, with some clouds rising taller than Mount Everest and as wide as a marathon's twenty six-mile course. But Jeremy and I know that clouds on such massive scale mean the storms are powerful beyond measure.

"What sort of factor do you think these storm cells are gonna play on our approach?" Jeremy asks.

"Well," I say, staring at my map display and the *sweep...sweep... sweep* of the radar. The heart of the beast paints in intense reds and magentas—areas that, if we were to penetrate them, would likely toss our jet around like a ragdoll. Beside the largest and most intense cell on the left are smaller clusters of bumpy-but-safe yellows and easily navigable greens. "The worst of it seems to be off our routing."

"For now," Jeremy says, changing the scale of his radar to see if he can zoom in to get a better look at the radar's returns.

"We'll have to work our way around the system's outer edges."

"And the mountains don't give us much room for that."

"Not at all," I say, "especially since there's only the one pass we fly through to get to the airport."

The two of us study the charts clipped to our windows, evaluating the heights of different terrain areas near our routing.

"This could get tight," Jeremy says.

I look toward him. "Yes, it could."

I check a few things on our flight plan as we switch ATC frequencies again. Then I peck around in the flight computer before asking, "What are your thoughts on our fuel?" I've already evaluated the situation myself but don't want to prejudice Jeremy's opinion by offering my thoughts before he's made his own assessment.

He grabs the flight plan from atop the center console and punches a few buttons on his side's flight computer. "Well," he says, "Acapulco is our alternate." He pauses again, crunching some numbers in his head about how much fuel it will take to fly from Mexico City to Acapulco if need be. "So, I'd say we have about..." He pauses, double-checking himself. "I'd say we have about fifteen minutes of fuel to play with before we need to head to Acapulco. Twenty at the most."

"I agree," I say, taking comfort that his mental math has matched my own. "Think there's any chance ATC will swing us around and bring us in from the south?"

"I don't know," Jeremy says. "I've never had them do that."

"Me, neither."

"Holding," which is where a plane flies an oval racetrack pattern above a specific location on the ground, "seems more likely. Maybe until the storm passes completely."

"Agreed." I take another sip from my water bottle. "Have you landed down here after it has rained?"

"Not that I can recall," Jeremy says. "But I did see the notes about possible hydroplaning in the ten-seven pages," which are the company-curated notes for every airport to which United flies.

"It can get a bit sporty," I say, implying that we should not take lightly the note's warnings. "Don't be surprised if some taxiways are completely flooded."

"Perfect," Jeremy says. "I should be surprised the drainage is so bad at one of the busiest airports in the world, but then—"

"It's Mexico City."

"Exactly."

Another lull in the conversation. "Well, shall we make it official and brief this up?" I ask.

"Sounds good," Jeremy says.

The two of us banter back and forth for several minutes, discussing the many critical aspects of our descent, landing, and taxi. Then we run through our required checklists, and Jeremy makes a pre-arrival announcement to the passengers.

Only a sliver of daylight remains along the western horizon as the Mexican controller instructs, "United One-Five-Six-Six, descend to one-five-thousand feet," which is the equivalent of 15,000 feet. Jeremy reads back the clearance, and I command the autopilot to begin our descent.

I snap my shoulder harnesses into my seatbelt and take another long swig from my water bottle. My heart beats faster as I think about the many parallels between the challenges for our flight and those of the Cali, Colombia, accident I had studied in the *Role of the Captain* course.

Relax, Korry, I tell myself. *And leave yourself an out.*

I focus on the radar sweeping back and forth on my map display like a windshield wiper on its slowest setting. With each subsequent pass, the radar "paints" an updated depiction of the storm's location and intensity. And with night all but upon us, those synthetic images are the only way for us to *see* the gigantic storm . . . that is, except for when lightening bolts flicker eerily within it, illuminating the billowy cloud like a photographer's soft box strobe light, which happens frequently.

Sweep...Sweep...Sweep.

"They're drifting," Jeremy says, referring to the storm cells.

"I see that," I say. The edge of the storm's heart—the red and magenta radar returns—now paints directly overtop of our course line. I had hoped to stay on charted airways all the way to the airport, since doing so makes it substantially easier to determine our clearance above and around the mountains. But that's not going to happen with the storm's location. "We're gonna have to deviate."

"I agree. How much do you want? Twenty right?" he asks, meaning degrees right of our present course.

"That will work for now."

Jeremy makes the request with air traffic control.

"Roger, United One-Five-Six-Six. Deviation right of course is approved. When able, proceed direct DATUL."

"Heading select," I announce, pressing the button on the dashboard that commands the autopilot to point the jet's nose toward a specific magnetic direction, or "heading," instead of following the published airway that we have programmed into the flight computers.

I rotate the heading control knob, and the plane starts a shallow bank to the right. And the thunderstorm grows closer still.

Flicker. Flash. Flash-flash. Flicker.

Jeremy checks his charts for the terrain heights in our area. "We've got several thousand feet to play with around here."

"Great."

"Much tighter in a few minutes, but good for now."

"Okay. We'll go back on course by then."

The radar shows a tightly packed cluster of bright reds on the course line, which is now to our left. Yellow returns extend for a few miles beside them, and green returns continue for a few miles after that.

"Given the terrain, do you see a way we avoid the greens?" I ask.

Jeremy checks his chart again. "Not really," he says. "We might even catch a bit of the yellow."

"And how do you feel about that?"

He shrugs. "I'm okay with it. We can basically see the worst of this thing, and those cells are way off to the left."

"Okay."

"So, it's just a short section of the tail that we've gotta punch through. And those returns aren't nearly as intense—heavy rain at the worst. It won't be bumpy for more than a minute or two."

"I agree completely," I say. "And if it gets worse than we expect, we'll go around and either try again or divert."

"Sounds good, Korry."

"Why don't you call back to the flight attendants and ask them to be seated."

"Sure thing," he says, picking up the interphone.

Flicker. Flash. Flash-flash. Flicker.

"United One-Five-Six-Six, can you proceed direct to DATUL at this time?" the controller asks, knowing as we do that we need to get back onto the planned airway soon to ensure we can slip through the mountain pass.

Jeremy looks to me for an answer.

I purse my lips, evaluating the radar returns and their proximity to our course. "DATUL is gonna put us right on the edge of the reds. How about LUCIA?" I ask, suggesting a fix farther down the airway.

"Let me check," Jeremy says before querying the controller.

The radio is silent for several seconds. The bursts of lightening within the clouds are bright enough to light up the dark cockpit.

Flicker. Flash. Flash-flash. Flicker.

"Roger, United One-Five-Six-Six, proceed direct to LUCIA and rejoin the arrival," the controller commands.

"Direct LUCIA and rejoin the arrival," Jeremy confirms.

I type the new clearance into the flight computer. "Like it?" I ask.

Jeremy studies the change on the computer and the map display. "Looks good."

"Great. Execute," I say, pressing the computer's key and the LNAV button on the center dashboard, which commands the autopilot to track the course line again. The airplane begins a gentle left turn.

Flicker. Flash. Flash-flash. Flicker.

A few minutes later, the landing lights begin illuminating a wall of solid gray clouds. I reach down to the center of my five-point safety harness and pull the belts a bit tighter.

"Here we go," I say, looking to Jeremy.

And then *SWOOSH!* We are inside the clouds, our windshields glowing from the refraction of our bright landing lights against the clouds' moisture. My shoulders press into the tight seatbelts as the light turbulence begins, jostling us left and right in our seats like a jet skier skimming across choppy waters. My left hand grips the control wheel, which jiggles as the autopilot works to keep the wings level.

Sweep...Sweep...Sweep.

"Just greens so far," I say, almost to myself. Light rain cascades like sand granules across the windshield. "Yellows are coming our way. Speak up if you get uncomfortable."

"Looking good, Korry."

"United One-Five-Six-Six," the controller interjects. "Descend to one-two-thousand feet. After San Mateo," which is the next fix after LUCIA, "cleared I-L-S D-M-E Runway Zero-Five-Right."

Jeremy reads back the clearance and spins the altitude knob to 12,000 feet. My heart races with adrenaline. Behind the cockpit wall, I hear ceramic plates and coffee mugs clinking inside the stowed first-class galley carts.

Just a few more miles and we'll be out of this, I think.

I twist the knob for the radar's range, zooming in to evaluate the conditions with even greater precision. As we crest through the edge of the yellow returns, the rain intensifies. It's now hard, driving rain, and it pelts the windshields as though someone is pouring a bag of tiny marbles against the glass. Its sound consumes the cockpit. But Jeremy and I stare ahead stoically; we've flown through heavy rains in the past, and we know how to block out the distraction.

"We're coming through the mountain pass now," Jeremy says, his map screen displaying the terrain instead of the radar returns. Moments pass as the rain continues to pound the glass in front of us. "Okay, we're all clear of the terrain."

"Roger that," I reply. "Turning onto final now." And the airplane banks hard to the left.

"United One-Five-Six-Six, contact tower on frequency one-one-eight-decimal-five-five."

"Over to tower, United One-Five-Six-Six," Jeremy responds.

"Gear down, flaps fifteen, landing checklist," I command.

Jeremy lowers the gear lever, adding even more noise to the cockpit.

"Speed brake, armed. Gear, down three green," he says, reading from the laminated checklist card and visually verifying each item is correctly positioned.

"Down, three green," I confirm. "Flaps thirty, set target."

Jeremy moves the flap lever several more notches, and he rotates the speed knob to reflect our final approach speed. "Flaps thirty, green light. Landing checklist complete," he states, sliding the card into its slot above the dash.

"United One-Five-Six-Six, you are cleared to land Runway Five-Right," the tower controller instructs.

"Cleared to land, Five-Right, United One-Five-Six-Six," Jeremy says.

Sweep...Sweep...Sweep.

At the same time my map display shows us leaving the green radar returns, the clouds vanish and the rains and bumps subside, just like clockwork. The sprawling urban mass of Mexico City surrounds us. Homes and businesses of the city's 19 million inhabitants—some 40% of whom live in abject poverty—drape over and around the rolling hills. Dense shantytowns spill out the eastern break in the mountainous bowl. A thick layer of smog covers the city like a permanent blanket, its particulate fibers glowing orange from the city lights.

But it's the smell we notice most of all—a bitter stench that wafts over the city from sewage and landfill systems overtaxed by Mexico City's explosive population growth. I scrunch my nose as the pungent odor makes its way into the flight deck. I know U.S. cities like Los Angeles and Houston have bad reputations for air quality, but they seem like pristine wonderlands compared to Mexico City.

I turn my attention to the two long parallel runways in front of us. At night, only the white runway edge lights are visible, and the dearth of ambient light around the runways themselves makes it look like we are descending into a black hole—a challenging visual illusion for landing, particularly with respect to judging depth perception.

"Autopilot and autothrottles coming off," I announce a few miles before the runway's threshold. Jeremy monitors my flying and calls out any necessary corrections to airspeed as we descend. When the airplane's automated voice calls twenty feet above the ground, I pitch the nose of the airplane up while retarding the throttles to idle. The main wheels touch down softly onto the wet and glistening runway, but the runway's pavement, which is badly in need of resurfacing, takes away any hint of a good landing. The plane shakes as its wheels and struts try to accommodate the uneven surface. And out of the corner of my eye, I see large puddles of water pooled along the runway's edge, reminding me to be ready for possible hydroplaning.

"Eighty knots," Jeremy calls.

I continue slowing the jet to taxi speed, and my heart rate slows as I turn off the runway. I take a deep breath, sarcastically thinking, *That was fun*.

After parking at our gate, Jeremy and I shut down the jet and gather up our things. When the last passengers are off the plane, the entire crew forms a small conga line and heads down a drab corridor to the customs and immigrations hall. There, long queues of passengers weave back and forth, waiting patiently for immigration officers to inspect their travel documents. Thankfully for us, the crew line at the end of the hall is much shorter.

As captain, I feel an added responsibility to ensure the crew enters Mexico without any issues, so I motion for Jeremy and the flight attendants to go ahead of me. One by one, the gruff-looking immigration officer inspects the crew's documents. And after everyone else is cleared, the officer motions for me to step up to his desk.

"*Buenas noches*," I say to the officer, handing him my passport.

He doesn't respond, except to raise his eyes toward me for a brief moment. Then he scans my passport and pecks away on his computer. Leaning back in his chair, he lets out a sigh as he holds up my passport to compare its picture with my face. Apparently satisfied, he grabs the large metal stamp on his desk and flips through my passport's pages until he finds one with room for yet another stamp.

Ka-thunk!!!

He closes the little blue book and extends it back to me. "Welcome to Mexico City, *Capitan.*"

With our entire crew through customs and immigration, I feel like my captain responsibilities are over until we return to the jet the next day. But I have it all wrong, and two weeks later I'll learn that the role of the captain doesn't stop at the jet's door or even the exit of the customs and immigration hall; the role of the captain continues wherever the crew goes. It will be, perhaps, the most important leadership lesson I will learn my entire first year in the left seat. And it takes an utter failure on my part to learn it.

The turbine engines of the high wing de Havilland Twin Otter whine mightily as its pilots apply takeoff power. The craft wobbles atop its half-submerged floats, struggling to accelerate as the thrust from its whirling propellers blasts a caustic mist of water droplets dozens of yards behind the plane. Slowly, however, the plane begins to move, and as it does, a trail of frothy wake lines forms behind it. After building up enough speed, the floats pop up on top of the water's gentle ripples.

"See that?" Todd asks, leaning forward in his chair while pointing to the Twin Otter. "They're up 'on the step.'"

"On the step?" I ask.

"That's what it's called when the plane skims across the water instead of barreling through it like a boat. They'll be airborne in no time." And a moment later, the plane climbs away from Vancouver Harbour into the cloudless Canadian sky.

I try to imagine what the pilots see out their windows: the glistening blue water, the sailboats passing off their wingtips, the undulating, tree-covered slopes of the North Shore Mountains, and the dozens of glass-faced, high-rise apartment buildings that surround the harbor.

"That view must be incredible," I say to Todd, my first officer for this trip. "Even better than ours a few hours ago."

"Oh, for sure. They're right in the middle of everything," he tells me, using the same central Pennsylvania dialect I know so well from home—one that makes miles sound more like *mawls*. "But that's seaplane flying for you—absolute freedom at its core."

"That's so awesome," I say, smiling as I watch the Twin Otter disappear behind one of the mountains.

The two of us sit under a large red umbrella, munching away on burgers and fries at a harbor-side restaurant on a perfect summer evening. Todd isn't fully finished with a bite of his burger when he asks, "Do you think you'll ever get your seaplane rating?"

I take a swig from my glass. "It's definitely on my bucket list."

"Korry, you've gotta do it. You'll love it."

I chuckle. "That's what I'm worried about."

"Why's that?"

"Because then I'll want to get one," I say as I chomp down on my burger.

Todd laughs. "And what's the problem with that?"

"No problem," I reply, dabbing my mouth with my napkin, "except I'm certain my wife would say a seaplane is outside my toy budget."

"See," Todd says, "there *are* some plusses about being single—like a bigger toy budget and no one with veto power."

I laugh. "Honestly, her veto probably serves me well most times," I suggest. Returning to the topic at hand, I ask, "So, how did you learn so much about seaplanes?"

"Oh, I've been flying them for years—long before I joined the airlines. Spent something like three thousand hours instructing in them to build flight time."

"Three thousand hours?" I ask incredulously, knowing such flight time amounts to more than three years of full-time work as a low-paid instructor.

"How do you think I got all this gray hair?"

I chuckle, even though his hair looks to be more salt-and-pepper than gray.

"Then again," he continues, "It probably came from one of my five furloughs."

"Five furloughs?" I ask in disbelief.

"I wish I was joking," Todd says, taking another bite, "but I'm not."

"How does that even happen?"

"Easy: bad timing and lousy seniority numbers."

"I guess," I say, shaking my head. "But that has to be some sort of record."

"I doubt it. My luck isn't even good enough to win at that."

I chuckle at his attempt to make light of his career's incredible volatility. But I'm at a loss for words and manage only, "That's wild," as my reply.

"A wild ride, for sure," he says. "Five furloughs, four corporate bankruptcies, and soon I'll add my ninth pilot uniform to my closet."

"You worked for nine airlines?"

"Well, seven, if you count United, Continental, and the new United as one company."

"Still. That's a lot."

He takes a drink. "It wasn't a goal I set for myself, I'll tell you that."

"So, who all did you fly for?"

"A regional to start," Todd says. "Like a lot of pilots, I hoped to work for a major airline one day and fly globally. But after quite a few years in the regionals, the only call I got was from a startup flying 737s in the U.S. It was a better gig than where I was, so I took the job.

Unfortunately, they went bankrupt within a year. That was furlough number one."

"Oh, man," I say.

"The good news was that I saw it coming. So by the time the furlough actually happened, I had a class date lined up with another startup airline." He looks out to the water momentarily. "Seemed like a lucky break. But that airline lasted only six months." He looks back at me and smiles. "And so began furlough number two."

"Good grief."

"Now, it's not like I didn't know the startups were risky," Todd says, "but they seemed to be my best options both times. And if either of them had panned out, I would have been sitting pretty with seniority, since it's always good to get hired at the beginning of a wave."

"Absolutely."

"So I sort of saw it as a risk-reward type of thing. It just turned out to be more risk than reward."

I chuckle again. "At least you've got a sense of humor about it."

"Yeah, well, what else can you do?" Todd asks rhetorically. "Anyway," he continues, "United called me just before I started my second furlough. That time, I thought for sure I'd caught a lucky break. But then September 11 happened. And before I knew it, I was filling out job applications prior to yet another furlough."

I shake my head, completely dumbfounded. "That's unreal, Todd. Seriously unreal."

Todd continues. "AirTran in Atlanta came next. That's the first time I started to gain some traction. The airline was growing, I'd bought a house in Georgia, and within a few years, I was on the cusp of holding captain."

"That sounds promising."

"It was. But then United called me back."

"Oh," I say, surprised by the way he is making his recall sound like a negative.

"You see, I truly didn't know what to do—stay with AirTran where things were good but where I'd never fly globally, or return to United where I'd be at the bottom of the seniority list again, first to be furloughed if that happened again." He pops a fry into his mouth. "But you never hear about pilots getting furloughed twice from the same airline, so in my mind, that didn't seem to be a likely scenario." He sips his drink. "Still, I hedged my bets and delayed my United class date as long as possible, hoping to see how things played out. But eventually United said my choice was either to come back or lose my spot. So I took the recall and moved back to Chicago, which seemed like the better long-term play."

"But then?" I ask, grimacing from the suspicion that I know the next part of Todd's career journey.

"But then United parked its aging 737 fleet. The Great Recession hit. And fourteen-hundred pilots got pink slips—including me."

I put my hand up to my face, letting my fingers rub my brow in disbelief. "Dear lord, Todd. That's incredible. I haven't even lived through it, and it's painful to think about."

"You're telling me," Todd laments. "It felt like every time I stood up, I'd get knocked down again—to the street, to the bottom of another seniority list, and to the starting wages of yet another airline."

I take another sip of my drink. "How did you keep going?"

He smiles. "Guess you can call me a glutton for punishment."

"Because I'm not sure I would have been willing to keep trying."

He shoots me a puzzled look. "You mean you'd give up on your dream, just because it got tough?"

"Well, no, I…" I pause, leaning back in my chair, suddenly embarrassed. When my high school teacher had suggested to me that my dream was, in essence, out of reach, I had told him that nothing was going to stop me from realizing it, that I would never give up, and that I would find a way to succeed — whatever the odds. And yet now I'm suggesting to Todd that his dream might not have been worth fighting for. And who am I to tell him that? I feel like a complete hypocrite.

"The truth is," Todd continues, "I did eventually question my dream. But that wasn't until Korean Air pushed me over the edge."

"Wait. You flew overseas?"

"Oh, yes. After my second United furlough. Airline number six if you're keeping track. I commuted back and forth to Seoul from Chicago."

"That's a hell of a commute," I commiserate.

"It wasn't as bad as it sounds. Korean Air let expats like me fly business class, positive space," which is airline speak for a confirmed seat assignment like a paying passenger would have. "But it still got old."

"I imagine so. That's halfway around the world!"

"It is. But I could deal with the commute. What I couldn't get past was the culture." He looks to the water as another seaplane starts its engines. "I mean, the Korean norms, protocols, and expectations for pilots were so radically different from what I was used to with U.S. airlines. I just couldn't fit in. Figured I probably never would. So while it was fun to spend my layovers climbing Cambodian temples and exploring Vietnamese markets, after a year and a half, I had reached my limit."

"Can't say I blame you."

"So I came home and decided to quit the whole damn industry. A big part of me didn't want to quit, because I still loved aviation, but my experiences were making me hate it. I needed a break. I needed to feel like I had control of something in my life." He holds up his glass, smiling. "And that's where the toys came in."

I scrunch my face. "The toys?"

"Well, one in particular — my BMW K1200S motorcycle."

"Ahhh," I say. "That's quite a toy!"

"No," Todd corrects me. "It's a hell of a toy!"

I chuckle while watching another seaplane touch down in the harbor.

"I pulled in my garage after my last trip for Korean Air, and I saw that bike sitting off to the side, begging me to take it on the road. And not just for a ride around the block. It was telling me to take a big trip. A long trip. One that would last several months."

"So did you go?" I ask, intrigued by this turn of events.

"Heck no," he says before taking a sip from his glass.

"Why not?"

"Because I did what most pilots do; I overanalyzed it. I told myself the idea was crazy and irresponsible. I told myself it didn't matter that I had enough money saved to do it. I came up with a whole litany of reasons for why not to go."

"Oh."

"But I always had this feeling that I *should* go. I pushed that feeling down as long as I could, until one day, several months later, I looked at that bike and couldn't resist anymore. That day, I packed a small bag, crawled on the bike, and started riding—far away, but with no particular destination in mind."

"Wait. You just left?" I ask, amazed by Todd's spontaneity.

"I just left," he replies. "I rode across Indiana, Ohio, and Pennsylvania. I headed south through Virginia and all across the Carolinas. Eventually, I made it to Key West. I think I've even got a picture of that," he says, reaching into his pocket for his iPhone. He skims his photos for a few moments and then says, "Here it is," as he hands the phone to me.

On the screen I see Todd, straddling his sporty gray bike with bright yellow wheels. Key West's southernmost buoy is behind him, and standing beside him are six young, attractive, scantily-clad girls who appear to be heading out on the town for the night. But what I notice most is Todd's humongous smile and his gleaming white teeth. He looks truly and completely alive—a man free from stress and unburdened by the unpleasant realities of a career that hadn't gone as planned. A man without a care in his life, except for the here and now.

"It was the best summer of my entire life," he tells me as I hand his phone back to him.

"Todd, that's so awesome."

He smiles. "Awesome doesn't even begin to describe it, Korry."

I look out to the water as another seaplane touches down. I think about Todd's great summer ride, where there was nothing for him to chase but the wind and the open road—a place of true freedom and inspiration. And I wonder if I've every truly found a place like that in my own life, where I wasn't chasing anything but the present.

"So to make a long story short," Todd continues, "that's why you need a few toys. Because you never know when one of them may save your life."

The waitress sets two black check holders on the table, saying, "Whenever you're ready." We reach into our pockets for our wallets and slide two credit cards into the holders.

"So, obviously, you gave aviation another shot or you wouldn't be here," I suggest.

"I did. Because another thing that ride taught me was that I wasn't meant for an office job. Like most of us, I'd caught the flying bug—hard. And as much as I wanted to, I just couldn't give up on my dream. I got hired with a small cargo airline flying 747s all over the place. Most of our business was repositioning military equipment, but we flew all sorts of bizarre things—cows to Kazakhstan. Stuff like that."

"Whoa."

"Totally different than the flying we do here, but a lot of fun." Todd hands the check holders back to the waitress as she passes by. "Of course, as my luck would have it, when the war in Iraq drew down, the company lost its contracts, and I was furloughed yet again. Thankfully, by that time, United had already begun offering furloughees the chance to come back and fly on the Continental side, so I had a class right away. And now I'm here," he says, turning to watch a seaplane take off.

Once it lifts from the water, I say, "Todd, that's the craziest career journey I've ever heard."

"Apparently, I'm a big fan of the scenic route."

I chuckle. "Apparently!"

"That said, I'm okay if the twists and turns are over for a while. I'm not exactly looking for furlough number six anytime soon."

"Well, I'm cautiously optimistic things will go well for all of us now."

He offers a small smile, but I can tell it's a bit forced. "I hope you're right, Korry. Because I'm ready to catch a break. I've just grown skeptical over time."

The waitress returns with the check holders, and we scribble our signatures on the thin white receipt slips.

"So do you regret any of it?" I ask.

"Regret it?" Todd sighs as he wobbles his head back and forth. "I don't know. I wish I'd gotten on at one airline, built up good seniority, and enjoyed some stability. But I think the only regret I truly have is stressing about it as much as I did, because the stress didn't change a thing. It rarely ever does."

I nod, thinking for a moment about how much I've stressed about my career over the years. About its timing. About whether I was making the right choices. About whether things would work out. About whether I'd get where I wanted fast enough, or if I'd even get there at all.

"You know, in some ways, I guess I should be thankful. Because believe it or not, I've never missed a paycheck."

"Seriously?" I ask.

"Seriously," he says. "Not one missed paycheck."

"That *is* incredible," I say.

"Somehow every time I needed a job, a job miraculously came along." The two of us watch another seaplane slide gracefully into the water. Then Todd slaps his hands on the tabletop. "Well? You ready to head back? Our 4:30 AM van time is going to come early tomorrow."

"Way too early," I agree.

Ten minutes later, we're riding the elevator up to our rooms.

"Sleep well," Todd says, exiting one floor below mine.

"Same to you," I say.

And then the elevator doors close.

The recessed lights in the Vancouver Hyatt Regency's portico shine down upon Todd and me.

"Think we should call?" Todd asks.

"I don't know," I say, staring at my watch and brooding over what to do. "These vans are all prearranged. Let's give it a few more minutes."

"But Korry, it's already 4:45 AM. The van's fifteen minutes late and counting. You know these pickup times don't include much fluff."

"I know," I reply. And yet for no good reason I feel paralyzed by indecision. "Let's just give them a few more minutes."

Todd shakes his head. "As you wish," he says, tightlipped and frustrated. "You're the captain."

I try and tell myself that I can't make the call even if I want, since my cellphone doesn't work in Canada. But it's a lame excuse to concoct, since the hotel staff would gladly place the call for me.

I hear the *swoosh* of the hotel's rotating entry door behind us. Turning around, I see two more United pilots pulling their rollaboard luggage behind them.

"Morning fellas," the captain says. "You taking the 4:50 AM van, too?"

"4:30," Todd replies.

"Ouch," the first officer replies, his face contorted into a painful expression. "They running a little late?"

I feel my anxiousness rising.

"Yep," Todd says, looking at me, clearly annoyed.

Moments later, one of the transportation company's large Sprinter vans rounds the corner.

Yes! I think, relieved that this van is plenty big enough to accommodate both crews. *Problem solved.*

Stopping in front of us, the driver hops out to open the rear cargo doors. The four of us hand him our luggage and then pile inside.

Bags stowed, the driver takes his seat and studies his clipboard for several moments. Then he turns around, saying, "I'm only supposed to have two pilots. Flight Sixteen-Twenty-Five."

"That's us," the other captain says, raising his hand.

"Sir, something happened with our van," I jump in. "It's very late. So we're just gonna ride with them if that's okay."

The driver fidgets with his pen, tapping it against the clipboard. "I don't know. I'm only supposed to have the one crew. I'll have to check about that."

Todd and I look at each other, raising our eyes in bewilderment as to why this is an issue at all.

The driver dials his cellphone as he starts the minibus and pulls away from the hotel. Todd and I try, unsuccessfully, to listen as the driver talks with his company, a conversation that lasts for several blocks. And as soon as he hangs up, he turns the bus around, saying, "You two are gonna have to wait for the right van."

Todd and I furrow our brows. "Seriously?" Todd asks.

The driver seems nervous as he taps his hand on the steering wheel. "Look, I'm just supposed to have one crew. I'm sorry, but you'll have to wait for the other van."

"But that doesn't make any sense," I plead.

"Your company is contracted to take both our crews to the airport," Todd says, his frustration palpable. "Why can't we go with you?"

"I don't know," the driver says. "I don't make the rules."

"You've got to be kidding me," Todd huffs. He looks to me. "Korry, if we go back, there's no way our flight leaves on time."

"It's going to be very tight," I say.

"No, Korry. There's not a chance."

Todd motions for me to say something to the driver, to insist he take us to the airport. My stomach churns with indecision. And eventually, I say…nothing. Zip. Nada. I just sit there and go with it. I just let it happen—a passenger along for the ride…back to the hotel.

In no time, Todd and I are again standing under the hotel's awning, our bags beside us, watching the driver pull away with the other crew.

And now it's quiet. I look at my watch again: 4:55 AM.

"Want me to hail a taxi?" Todd asks.

The suggestion is wise, and I know the company will reimburse the expense with no questions asked. But I've given up. "Let's give it a few more minutes," I say without looking Todd in the eyes.

"Korry, why not?" he pleads. "This is the transportation company's problem, not ours."

But I'm defeated as I look toward him. "Just a few more minutes."

Todd shakes his head, staring straight ahead in the morning's quiet darkness, rightfully troubled by my inaction.

I keep checking my watch as though I expect it to magically tell me, "Okay, Korry, you've waited long enough. It's time to call a taxi." But all it tells me is the time is 5:00 AM. Then 5:05, 5:10, and finally 5:15 AM—forty-five minutes after our scheduled pickup time. We should already be at the airport by now—probably through security and at the gate.

Finally, our van arrives. Todd doesn't say a word to me the whole way to the airport, but then, he doesn't have to. I know he is right to be upset. I've been a passenger, not a captain; I've simply gone along for a ride instead of taking control and finding a solution. Todd deserves better from his captain. So do our passengers, who I fear will be delayed because of my inaction. And so does United, which entrusts me with the responsibilities of being a leader who gets things done.

But I've done nothing. I haven't tried to fix the situation. I haven't led. I've frozen up and failed miserably. I've been a captain in name only. And for the life of me, I have no idea why I have failed to act.

We end up departing Vancouver several minutes late, but short taxis and favorable winds let us arrive in Chicago on time. That doesn't matter, though. The damage is done between Todd and me. I know as much because Todd says little to me beyond our required briefings, callouts, and checklists. He barely says anything to me on our flights the next few days to Pittsburgh, Chicago, and Sarasota, either. It's not that he's being disrespectful; it's that he's seen me as the emperor who wears no clothes. I've lost him. And I deserve his silence. Because if I've failed to lead on an issue of trivial importance, then he must be wondering if I'll ever step up and take command...or if he'll have to do it for me.

The one good thing about Todd's silent treatment is that it provides plenty of time for me to reflect on the situation and how I must move forward. Leadership, I know, is about character. It's about setting a positive example for others to emulate. It's about stepping up and doing the right thing, all day, every day, even when it gets uncomfortable. And that responsibility sure as hell doesn't stop at the cockpit door; it continues everywhere. I know I can do better. I know I *must* do better. And I'm committed to doing just that.

The point is really driven home at the end of my trip when I reach the L train turnstiles at O'Hare. While pulling my transit card from my wallet, I notice the folded magazine cutout that my grandfather had mailed to me years earlier. It's a Warren Buffet quote, one that resonated with my grandfather and with me. And in many ways, it's the ethos by which I try and live my life. The quote reads: "It takes twenty years to build a reputation and five minutes to ruin it."

Well, my five minutes are over. Now, it's time to let the rebuilding begin.

As my first month in the left seat draws to a close, I crisscross the North American continent several more times, adding entries in my maroon pocket logbook for flights to Los Angeles; Washington, D.C.; Portland, Oregon; and Chicago. Each flight comes with its own unique challenges, but I can tell my focus on being a better leader inside and outside the cockpit is yielding significant rewards.

Nowhere is this more evident than on my last flight before starting a week of vacation in early September 2013. A line of small storms has veered north and mushroomed into supercells, unexpectedly shutting down all O'Hare arrivals and departures. The dispatcher informs the first officer and me of these developments via text message while we are still over South Dakota. Right away, the three of us begin playing the "what if?" game. If the storms stall over the field, how long can we hold, waiting for the storms to pass? What airport is best if we need to divert? How long will it take for us to fly there? How much fuel will that require? And given all of those considerations, what is our minimum "bingo" fuel figure—our line in the sand—that will delineate whether we continue to O'Hare or divert? We settle on Milwaukee as our best Plan B airport, and we figure we have about thirty minutes of cushion before a diversion becomes necessary.

About 150 miles from Chicago, we spot the massive storms along the horizon. Judging from our radar sweeps, the storms look to be east of O'Hare. And as we start our descent, air traffic control gives us the good news: O'Hare is accepting arrivals again. In fact, we will be the first plane to land.

The first officer looks at me apprehensively as if to say, "Oh, great. The first ones." No pilot likes to be first to land after a major weather system moves through. It's better to let others serve as the "pathfinders" who report back on what they discover.

"We'll take a look," I say, "and the moment either of us gets uncomfortable, we're off to Milwaukee. No questions asked."

"Sounds good," the first officer says.

We study the radar returns as we near the airport and the city.

Sweep...Sweep...Sweep.

We fly eastbound past O'Hare, directly toward the greenish-black behemoth, which is now just east of the city's Lake Michigan coastline, to set up for a westerly landing into the wind.

"Look at that rain," I say to the first officer, transfixed by the wall of water dumping out the storm's bottom into Lake Michigan.

"At least it's clear from downtown all the way back to O'Hare. I think this is gonna come together."

"Me, too," I say.

The radios are eerily quiet, making us wonder if we are the only plane in the sky at the moment. We turn south over downtown, where freshly-soaked roadways, rooftops and skyscrapers glisten from the orange light of the setting sun, and slip underneath the ominous mammatus clouds that trail the monster storm. Their bubble-wrap bottoms are evidence of thick churning air and extreme turbulence inside. But in the clear air below them, we don't feel a single burst of choppy air. In fact, it's silky smooth all the way down the glidepath to the runway, which probably makes most passengers believe the whole approach and landing is completely normal—at least until they see the forty planes waiting for takeoff on the drenched taxiways. Best of all for us, since those jets are on the taxiways, most gates are open, including ours. And so while the crazy weather has delayed thousands of other people, our 161 passengers arrive at the gate a few minutes ahead of schedule, unaware they almost ended up in Milwaukee.

With the engines shut down and the *Parking Checklist* complete,

I pull the Tank from its cubby and stand in the flight deck doorway, saying goodbye to the last few passengers. Then the Tank and I make our way for the "L" train, taking our usual spot near the emergency exit of one of the cars. Forty minutes later, I hoist the Tank up by its extended handle and schlepp it up the stairs of the Jackson subway stop.

Arriving street level, I'm hit by the wonderful smell of a nearby Garrett Popcorn store and the thick wall of summer heat and humidity, which has been magnified by the recently-passed storm. Beads of sweat form instantly along my forehead as I start the short walk back to my apartment. I loosen my tie and unbutton the top button of my shirt. But it doesn't help; the humidity is oppressive. So I trudge on, feeling the sweat slide down my face and tasting the salt from droplets that slip into the corners of my mouth.

Waiting for a stoplight to change one block from my apartment, I wipe my damp brow with my uniform's sleeve and gaze up at the Willis Tower across the street.

I bet the 27th floor is a mess right now! I think.

I picture the crew schedulers trying to get pilots and flight attendants back into position to cover diverted flights. I visualize the dispatchers texting back and forth with the pilots of dozens of flights, working to craft their own Plan Bs. And I think about the teams of people solving the giant puzzle of how to get misconnected passengers rerouted to their destinations.

It's a good time to be getting home, I think.

As the light turns green, a giant bead of sweat creeps down the small of my back. I *hate* that feeling. But then I feel a vibration, which distracts me. It's a single, long buzz, which can mean only one thing: a text message.

I pull the phone from my pocket and read the simple two-word message:

KURT: *It's out.*

CHAPTER 9

The List

"Man must rise above the Earth—
to the top of the atmosphere and beyond—
for only thus will he fully understand
the world in which he lives."
- Socrates

Chicago, Illinois – September 3, 2013

The apartment's door slams shut as my keys splash onto the small entryway table along the wall.

Jen pokes her head out from the kitchen to look toward me. "Hi, Husband!"

"The list is out," I say, wriggling out of my shoes.

"The list?" she asks.

"The seniority list. The new one."

"Ahhhhh," she replies. "How'd you make out?"

"Don't know yet," I say, grabbing the Tank's handle and hustling down the hallway. "But I'm about to check!"

The Tank and I zoom past Jen on our way to the bedroom.

"Don't I even get a kiss???" she asks.

I stop, mid-stride. "Oh…yeah!" I turn around and head back to her, leaning in to offer a quick peck on the lips.

"Ewwww," she says, wrinkling her nose as it touches the moisture on my face. "You're so sweaty!"

"I know," I say, scurrying into the bedroom. "It's crazy humid outside."

I plop the Tank in its usual spot next to my closet, remove my laptop from its bag, and then head over to the kitchen table. From there, it takes only a few seconds for me to pull up the Air Line Pilot Association's (ALPA) website. I log in and click through to the page containing all the transcripts, exhibits, and other documents from the seniority list arbitration hearings. Only now there is a new document available for viewing, titled "CAL-UAL ISL Opinion and Award."

I hover my pointer over the document's icon, nervous to open it because its contents will, for the rest of my career, control almost every aspect of my life and those of my 12,000 pilot colleagues. I wonder if the three arbitrators have built the new integrated seniority list using the methodology proposed by the Continental pilot representatives, the one advanced by the United pilot representatives, or some other methodology of their own design. Of course, there's only one way to find out, and so with great anticipation, I double-click on the document and start to read.

The 57-page PDF is full of legalese, opening with long summaries of the thousands of pages of testimony, which covers the history, economic status, fleet makeup, and pilot counts for both carriers on the date of the merger. I flick past more summaries detailing each side's suggested "list build" methodology and the panel's opinion about how those methodologies either address or don't address the three major tenets of ALPA's merger policy: career expectations, longevity with a carrier, and the type of airplanes flown.

Come on! I moan to myself. *Where's the list?!?!?!*

I keep skimming and finally arrive at a section revealing the panel's decision: "After carefully considering a large number of different alternatives, we concluded the [United Pilot] Committee's five-step list build model, with appropriate modifications by the

Board, achieved our goal of a fair and equitable [integrated seniority list] in this case."

Jen notices me sit back rather suddenly in my brown wooden chair. "What is it?" she asks.

I lace my hands behind my head and let out a long sigh. "They chose the United list."

"Is that bad?" Jen asks.

"I don't know, Wife," I say. "But it can't be as good for me as if they had picked the Continental list."

Honestly, I'm not overly surprised by the panel's decision to reject the Continental team's methodology; I had read every page of the transcripts, and like the arbitrators, I had found the United team's methodology to be more statistically compelling with respect to how it accounted for the major tenets of ALPA's merger policy. I suspect, however, that the complicated mathematical structure of the United team's integration methodology will make the final list more difficult for many pilots to understand or accept, since it seems to lack any sort of easily understandable or predictable pattern[12]. Instead, it often appears like a random spattering of pilots, at times featuring large clusters of pilots from one airline sandwiched between two pilots

---

[12] Seniority lists are often integrated using ratios. For example, the pilot seniority lists of Airline A and Airline B might be integrated using a ratio of 1.6 pilots from Airline A to 1.0 pilots from Airline B. Or the lists of Airline A and Airline B might be integrated using a series of ratios, such as 1.4:1 for the top third of the lists, 1.3:1 for the middle third, and 1.8:1 for the final third. The reasons for segmenting the lists in this way vary greatly, but the net result is a final combined list that follows a predictable and understandable pattern. In this case, the United methodology sought to integrate the Continental and United pilot lists with greater specificity than that made possible by the use of simple ratios. This culminated in each individual pilot receiving a final weighted average score based on his or her position on two integrated sublists, which were themselves ranked and ordered by separate criteria (the specifics of which are outside the scope of our discussion here). Pilots from both airlines were then, in essence, ordered in the final list based on their total combined scores. And while the resulting integrated seniority list was mathematically correct given the underlying methodology, it did not appear to follow a predictable or consistent pattern at all.

from the other. Then again, whether any pilot understands the list's construction doesn't matter. Nor does it matter whether pilots agree with its outcome. It is binding arbitration. The list is final. And it is simply a new reality for all of us to come to terms with — whether any of us like it or not.

I keep reading from the arbitrator's conclusion. "As in all such seniority integration exercises, the fairness and equity assessment is focused necessarily on the respective groups, not on each or any individual pilot….Regrettably but inevitably, there will be perceived disparities and mismatches by individuals on both sides…and the end result, no matter how crafted, never commands universal acceptance." In other words, while the arbitrators believe their list represents the fairest method for integrating all pilots, they understand there are bound to be individual pilots who view themselves as seniority winners or seniority losers. And I can't help but wonder within which category my friends and I now fall.

Nervously, I click on the link for Appendix A — the actual list itself — and scroll through the 236 pages of color-coded names. The top five spots belong to Continental pilots, as identified by the blue boxes with "CAL" lettering beside their names. Then there is one United pilot, identifiable by a red box with "UAL" lettering beside his name. Then one blue CAL pilot and two red UAL pilots. Then one CAL and three UAL. It alternates back and forth: one CAL, two UAL, one CAL, five UAL. Clumps and splatters. Sometimes in a regular pattern, and other times not regular at all.

As I skim, I easily notice the sections of the list where huge clusters of pilots from one side are bookended by pilots from the other airline. The largest such cluster places 388 United pilots between two Continental pilots at positions 4,530 and 4,920. Based on the list build formula the arbitrators have selected, I understand why such clustering is mathematically correct, but I suspect it likely doesn't seem "fair" to the CAL pilot at the bottom. After all, prior to the new list's publication, the bottom pilot's seniority afforded him a bidding power—for everything from the types of aircraft and trips he flies to the days he works each month and the specific vacation weeks he holds each year—that was basically equivalent to that of the CAL pilot at the top of the cluster. Now, with 388 pilots between the two of them, their levels of bidding power are substantially different. It's as though a switch has flipped and the bottom pilot instantaneously lost a year or more of seniority compared to that of the top pilot, solely because of the way the new integrated list is structured.

I keep scrolling, eventually finding my name on page 182—seniority number 9,606—roughly three-quarters of the way down the list. The pilot who had been one number senior to me on the Continental seniority list is now two numbers senior to me, with one United pilot sandwiched between us. And the pilot who had been one number junior to me is now three numbers junior to me, with two United pilots between us. And for the rest of our careers, that's precisely where we'll stay.

"Soooo," Jen says, looking up from the kitchen island. "What's the verdict?"

I let out a sigh. "I think I took a hit, Wife."

"That's not good," she says.

I turn around to face her. "It's definitely not ideal."

Jen nods her head slowly. "And what about your friends?"

I turn back to the computer. "I'm looking for their names now. But I suspect we're all in the same boat."

"Oh," Jen says.

One by one, I find their names on the list. And soon thereafter, rapid-fire text messages flow between us as we try to determine whether we are, in fact, seniority winners or losers. The consensus seems to be we are seniority losers. But how much seniority have we lost? And what are the practical ramifications of that loss in the short, mid, and long term?

Four days later, my friends and I wrangle with these and other vexing questions when we convene along with my parents in downtown Chicago for the long-scheduled party Jen has organized as a celebration of my captain upgrade.

Clink clink clink clink clink!

Kurt taps his spoon against his water glass as he stands up from the long linen-covered table in the second floor "boardroom" of Chicago's Sullivan's Steakhouse. "I hate to interrupt all the seniority list shoptalk," he says, tugging at the lapels of his navy blue blazer to straighten his jacket, "but I think it's time we turn our attention to the real reason we're here—celebrating Korry's captain upgrade."

It's quintessential Kurt, never afraid to take charge as a formal— or informal—emcee. Almost immediately, conversation dies down, and all fourteen sets of eyes turn toward him while two servers move around the room's edges, replacing our dinner plates and their trimmings of delectable rib eye steaks with decadent desserts.

"As you may recall," Kurt continues, "Jen asked us to come prepared with a few words of advice for Korry as he sets out on his new adventure in the left seat. I thought this was a fantastic idea, because I'm always up for giving Korry a piece of my mind."

Laughter all around.

"And so," Kurt says, pulling a folded piece of paper from his jacket pocket, "I thought I'd start us off."

I can tell Kurt is enjoying this. For all his shenanigans and jocularity—to which I've been party many times—Kurt loves formality, and he always comes prepared.

He turns to me, a few seats to his right, and says, "Captain Franke." He smiles slyly as he draws out the words for dramatic effect. "You are the first of our group of friends to become a major airline captain. For that I say congratulations…and don't mess it up!"

Everyone laughs again.

"Now, I realize I'm still a lowly first officer, so you'll probably take my words of advice with a giant grain of salt. And that's okay. Sooner or later, you'll realize the wisdom in these words."

I chuckle.

"Probably later," Kurt says, "since Jen assures me it often takes her saying things many times before you realize the wisdom in *her* words."

"Truuuuuth!!" Jen pipes in as the party-goers laugh in unison at Kurt's well-played joke.

"So with all that said, I'd like to offer a few suggestions as you continue moving into your new role." Kurt clears his throat and looks my way. "First, when interfacing with your coworkers and passengers, be wise enough to know when to get involved and when to stand aside."

As the Vancouver van debacle had shown, this is a major growth area for me.

"Second, when you do get involved, I encourage you to think over your words twice before they leave your mouth, because once they're out, you can't get them back."

It's sound advice and something I'm getting much better at doing. But there's room for improvement, as I've never been one to refrain from speaking candidly.

"Third, with respect to your first officers, flight attendants, and dispatchers, I suggest you follow Ronald Reagan's advice to 'trust but verify.' Each person has a role to play, and you can't do everything. So, engage and empower your team, but don't blindly follow them, because ultimately, you're still the captain."

I can't agree more, despite knowing how hard it is to achieve that balance.

"Fourth, use commonsense. The adages your flight instructors taught you as a student pilot, such as to 'aviate, navigate, and then communicate,' and to 'never let an airplane take you somewhere your mind hasn't been five minutes beforehand,' are as applicable in a Boeing 737 as they are in a Cessna 172."

Kurt is absolutely right. It's easy to get caught up in the complexity of airline operations. But flying—and leadership—truly revolves around several simple concepts, and if I focus on them, the other parts will work themselves out.

"And lastly," Kurt says, growing more somber as he glances around the room before returning his gaze directly to me, "never... lose...perspective." He pauses again. "Never forget to appreciate the intoxicating smell of jet fuel in the morning, the amazing sunrises and sunsets, and perhaps most of all, that indescribable feeling during takeoff when the earth falls away beneath you." He folds up his notes and tucks them back inside his jacket's pocket. "Those are my words of wisdom for you, Captain Franke. Congratulations, Korry." He raises his wine glass up for a toast.

I say thank you to Kurt as I clink my tumbler of single malt whisky with his glass and those of other friends around me.

"Good lord," I hear Ted say to Joe, both of whom were new-hire classmates of mine when we joined Continental Airlines in 2006. "I'm glad I don't have to follow that!"

But Jen does, and uncharacteristically, given her tendency to avoid the spotlight, she stands and speaks up immediately. "Well, Husband," she begins, "I'm very proud of you. And while I know you'll be a great captain, I'll leave the flying advice to your pilot friends. But I do have one *very* important reminder." A silly grin creeps across her face, making me wonder where she is going. "While you may be a captain for United, I hope you never forget that at our house, I will *always* be the check airman!"

The attendees howl, exactly as she has intended. I shake my head and offer, "Yeeessssss deeeaaaar," as she sits down.

My dad, Steve, speaks next. He moves around the room, placing his hands on the shoulders of each person in attendance, describing how it is that he's gotten to know each one of them over the years, some better than others. Finally, he gets back around to me. His hands squeeze my shoulders firmly. And as he speaks, I can almost hear the man I so greatly admire begin to choke up. "Clearly, I'm very proud of my son and the man he's become," Dad says. "But for that, I think you folks deserve a lot of the credit. Cindy and I couldn't have asked for Korry to have a better group of friends." I notice my friends smiling at this compliment. "I love seeing how successful you all are in your own ways, and as a dad, it means so much to hear you speak so highly of my son. So, like Jen, I'll leave the captain advice to the professionals, but I want to say thank you for helping to shape Korry into the man he is today."

I look up at Dad and smile, reaching to squeeze his hand, and knowing I'll probably well up with tears if I try to say anything. I love knowing how proud my parents are of me. And I know so much of my success has stemmed from the way they have raised me to value everyone, no matter who they are or what role they have; to strive for greatness; and to work hard every day. Mom and Dad are among my biggest cheerleaders, and their love, support, and encouragement never waver. I feel truly blessed to have them as parents.

"And if you'll humor me," Dad continues, "I'd like to add one more thing before I sit down." He pauses for a moment, and I notice everyone listening intently; he's firmly in command of the room. "As I've listened to you talk tonight over dinner, I've heard a lot of discussion about company growing pains as United works through its merger and about what the repercussions of the new seniority list might be for your careers—in the short term and long term. At the risk of sounding like an old fart, I'd encourage you to consider the true size and scale of those issues, because I'm wondering if they will appear as significant at the end of your career as they do now. And maybe they will. But I suspect they will not. I think you'll find that what matters most are the relationships you have with people like the ones in this room."

I nod as I look around the room, wondering where I would be—or who I would be—without the people sitting around this table in my life.

"Now, I know being an airline pilot isn't always as rosy as it might seem to an outsider like me," Dad continues, "but I think you're a lucky bunch. You're flying incredible airplanes all over the globe, to more locations in a year than I'll visit in a lifetime. I'll never know how exciting it is to fly anything bigger than a Cessna, and I only know that because Korry taught me to fly." I think back to that summer in 2002 and how fun it was to share the Cessna's tiny cockpit with my dad, how exciting—and terrifying—it was to send him off on his first solo flight, and how proud I was to stand beside him the day he successfully passed his checkride to become a private pilot. "I suspect when you look back in twenty or thirty years," Dad continues, "you'll see this career as a gift—even its challenging parts. You'll long for one more flight, and you'll deeply miss the camaraderie with your fellow pilots."

Dad pauses again. "You know, in my life, I've worked in anesthesia and in financial planning. I've talked with thousands of patients and clients who have worked in all sorts of fields. And I can tell you without equivocation that decisions will be made that you disagree with, no matter where you work. Outside events such as a merger, a seniority list, or a furlough will come along, change the game, and set you back. I've been there. And the worst part is you have no control over those things. But you *can* control whether you focus on the goods or the bads, the opportunities or the setbacks." I notice my friends nodding contemplatively. "You've got long careers ahead of you, and from where I'm standing, they look like bright ones. So my advice, not just to Korry but to all of you, is to try your best to see it the same way."

Dad's points are well taken, and deep down, I suspect we all know that he's right. There's no denying we have good jobs and even better friends. And my head knows this seniority setback is just a molehill, not a mountain, particularly when compared to some of the trials my first officers have endured. My heart, however, isn't as logical, and it's not ready to just take things in stride when our career outlooks have changed so dramatically by no fault of our own. Nonetheless, it can't hurt to at least try heeding Dad's advice to focus more on the opportunities ahead of us than the setbacks behind us.

The advice continues around the room, some serious, some sarcastic, and some a mix between the two. Finally, after Seth, we come to Paul.

"There's not much I can say that hasn't already been said," Paul begins, "so instead, I'll offer what I've been thinking as we've gone around the table tonight, which is that this is some very fine company. Fine people. Fine pilots. And if that's any indication, then this airline has a very fine future ahead of it, because, in many ways, *we* are the future of the new United." He looks around the table. "Despite the integrated seniority list's short-term impact, at least four or five of us will finish our careers with seniority numbers in the single digits," which is purely a function of our getting hired at a young age. "Most of us will serve as United captains for several decades," although some may choose to enjoy the scheduling benefits that come from remaining a senior first officer instead of becoming a junior captain. "Many of us are, or will be, in management," Paul says, looking to my friend Abe, who left his captain slot on a regional jet to earn his MBA and become a corporate manager at United. "And all of us will be mentors to new pilots and new employees over the years. So if you think about it, we have the ability to shape this airline into whatever we want it to become. Our past doesn't define our future." He pauses briefly. "And so as I've listened to the conversation tonight, I think Kurt and Steve are right—we need to keep things in perspective and enjoy the ride. Because we have a lot to be thankful for. I know I'm particularly thankful for the friendship of each of you."

It's somewhat ironic to me that the tenor of the night has turned so serious and reflective given most of our propensities for joking and lightheartedness. Then again, nights like this often have a way of reframing our realities, making the night's unstated theme of perspective impossible to miss.

This is particularly true after the dinner bill is paid and we head to the Signature Lounge on the 95th floor of the black and steel Hancock Building on Chicago's north side. From the lounge's floor-to-ceiling windows, we peer down onto the tops of fifty-story buildings and the antlike pedestrians and cars that roam the city's checkerboard streets. Gone are the sidewalk cracks and city grime that are visible at street level. Instead, the city looks crisp and clean, peaceful and serene. And that's only from 1,000 feet above the ground. At work, our perspective is thirty to forty times higher. From that height, Chicago's gigantic buildings are reduced to the size of Lego blocks. Even the entire city appears no larger than the palm of my hand. From our perch above the world, we look down upon entire regions, not cities. We see mountain ranges, not individual hillsides. How great is our perspective from that altitude? How big is our picture? And yet why is it so difficult for us to stop focusing on the street-level blemishes in our airline lives? I know it's natural to do so, but I also know that Dad is right: focusing on those things is a choice.

I place my arm around Jen and pull her tight against me as we gaze out the window. She looks at me and smiles. "I love you, Wife," I say.

"I love you, too, Husband."

And staring out the window beside my beautiful wife and the best friends and family a guy could hope for, the seniority list and the issues facing our company suddenly seem minuscule. I am more than lucky; I am truly blessed. And as long as these people remain in my life, I know I can overcome any adversity that comes my way. I just have to keep things in perspective.

Of course, getting others to see past their own perspectives is an entirely different thing altogether. And several weeks later, I find that to be particularly challenging to overcome when the perspectives of a passenger and a crew of flight attendants collide.

The gate agent stands at a small podium next to our flight's jetway door at the far end of United's Washington Dulles D concourse.

"So how are we coming?" I ask as I approach her side in the deserted boarding area. We have reached the scheduled departure time for our evening flight to San Francisco, and our passengers and crew are eager to get the long "transcon," which is aviation-speak for a transcontinental flight, underway.

"Immigration is all backed up," the agent tells me as she pecks away on her computer keyboard. "We're still missing eleven connectors from London, so Operations wants to hold for five more minutes."

"Gotcha," I reply.

"One of them is a first-class passenger," the agent continues. "Supposedly he cleared customs a few minutes ago. Not sure about the others, though."

I shrug my shoulders. "Well, keep us posted."

"You know I will...especially since you're my last flight of the night."

I smile. "And then you're off to go trick or treating?" It is Halloween night after all.

"Ha! Probably not. I wore this same costume last year," she says, motioning to her uniform. "Wouldn't look good to repeat."

I chuckle, saying, "I know the feeling."

As it happens, this is my first trip wearing the full captain "costume." Over the summer months, the formal suit jacket and traditional pilot cap are optional when operating flights within North and Central America. Now, the additional gold stripe I see on each of my jacket's sleeves and the leaf-shaped embellishments, affectionately called "scrambled eggs," that are sewn into my cap's brim make me feel as though I stand out even more than I did before. Even if that's not true, they definitely make me look more official.

"I bet this is him," the agent says, peering down the concourse to where a tall man is running at full speed while pulling a black rollaboard bag. Behind him, another United representative tries to keep up, while running in high heels and clutching a black satchel bag, which I presume also belongs to the passenger.

The passenger arrives at the podium, huffing and puffing. "Customs was a freaking fiasco," he exclaims, slapping his boarding pass onto the little podium.

"That's what we hear," the agent says.

"I was worried you'd close the flight without me, and I'm only home for one night before I head off to Dubai."

"That soon?" I ask, thinking about how much traveling such an itinerary is. "Sounds like you spend more time on airplanes than I do!"

"Wouldn't be surprised if I do," the passenger tells me, still trying to catch his breath. "But there's no place like home, so it's worth it."

I can't agree more. "Well, there's no reason to stress now. We won't be leaving without you."

"Thank goodness," the man replies, using the sleeve of his shirt to wipe away beads of sweat that cling to his forehead. "You had to pick the farthest gate away, didn't you?"

I look to the gate to our right and say, "Second farthest." Judging from the way the passenger rolls his eyes, I can tell he's unimpressed by my attempt at levity.

The agent scans his boarding pass and then smiles as she looks up. "You're all set. Welcome aboard."

The passenger thanks the agent and heads down the jetway with his rollaboard luggage and leather satchel in tow.

As he rounds the jetway's corner and disappears from our sight, the podium's phone rings. "Gate D-twenty-seven," the agent answers. Then a pause. "Okay, sounds good." She hangs up the receiver and looks at me. "Ops says it's time for you to get to work!"

I smile. "And time for you to go get some candy!"

"We'll see about that," she says, laughing.

I turn to head down the jetway, but I'm not even halfway to the plane before I begin to hear the argument.

"What do you mean I have to check my bag?"

"I'm sorry, sir, but the bins are already full. There's nothing I can do." The female voice sounds like one of the flight attendants, and as I round the jetway's corner, I see my assumption is correct.

"But I'm in first class on a full-fare ticket!" The passenger holds his carry-on at waist level with his satchel draped over his shoulder. In front of him, just inside the aircraft's entry door, the flight attendant stands with her hands up and her fingers outstretched as if to signal stop. The passenger hears me approaching, so he turns around, saying, "This is ridiculous! She's refusing to let me bring my bag on the plane!"

Here we go again, I think. *Another argument I didn't see but that I'll now have to adjudicate.* I understand that as the final authority for my flights, it's part of my role as captain to weigh in on all sorts of issues, whether flight-related or not, if only to help prevent the operation from bogging down. Admittedly, however, I'm surprised by the number of times I've already been asked to call such balls and strikes during my brief tenure in the left seat.

"You've got to do something," the passenger pleads. "She won't even let me look around to see if I can make space!"

"Okay," I say. "Let me see what I can work out."

The passenger moves to the side of the jetway and sets his bag down, shaking his head with his brow furrowed and his lips pulled tight together.

Personally, I find it completely reasonable for a full-fare, first-class passenger to expect his bag be accommodated in the cabin's overhead bins. In my mind, he's definitely paid for that benefit. But the overhead space isn't infinite, and on full flights such as this one, despite the best efforts of flight attendants to maneuver bags so that the overhead bins are packed as efficiently as possible, unfortunately, there often comes a time when there's simply no more room. The flight attendants then have the unenviable job of informing late-boarding passengers that they'll have to check their bags. And now, as I step aboard the jet, I'm wondering how I can bridge the divide and mediate this dispute in such a way that both the passenger and the flight attendants feel supported. At the moment, however, I'm struggling to see how any choice offers much chance of a win-win.

I step forward to the lead flight attendant, who is standing by her colleague, at their stations in the forward galley, and ask what seems to be the issue.

"The issue," the lead flight attendant tells me in a low voice, "is that he isn't listening to us when we tell him there's no more room. He keeps insisting we let him on so he can look."

"He's so animated," pleads the second flight attendant. "His face is beet red."

I glance back at the passenger. "Well, in fairness, he just ran all the way from customs," I offer. "Maybe he's just flushed."

"Either way, he needs to calm down," the lead says. "Otherwise, how can we know he's going to listen to us during the flight?"

The lead's point is well taken, even given my empathy for the passenger's frustration about his bag. Without a doubt, the flight attendants deserve to know each passenger is going to listen to what they say—something that's absolutely imperative in the event of some sort of in-flight emergency.

"Korry, do you honestly think he's calm enough to fly?" the lead asks me.

I take a deep breath, buying time to gather my thoughts. It's a trickier question than it first seems, and I know I must answer it artfully in order to avoid triggering unintended escalation. "What I think is…" I pause again. "What I think is if we work this out, all he's going to do is sit down and fall asleep."

The lead purses her lips. "Well, I hope you're right."

Me, too, I think.

"Look," I say, taking another long breath, "I'll talk to him once we work this out, okay?"

The lead nods.

"But right now, I'd just like to get this resolved as expeditiously as possible. And for me, that means finding a way to get his bag onboard." My decision is made; now I brace myself for the duo's response.

The lead nods more slowly this time. "Well," she says, shrugging her shoulders, "you're the captain."

Immediately, I grow disheartened, fearing I've lost her. I'm nearly certain she believes I'm choosing to support the passenger over my own crew. And while I understand and appreciate why she may feel that way, I don't know what decision I could make that would be fair to both the crew and the passenger. There are so many interests at play, so many nuances and potential repercussions to consider, and it's absolutely my objective to positively address as many of those interests as possible. After all, fostering a cohesive inflight team is a huge priority for me, as is keeping our passengers happy, since happy passengers make for returning passengers. But once again, a decision had needed made, and it was up to me to make it. So I own my choice and its consequences, and I'll work to find a way to get the lead and her team of flight attendants back on my side once we're airborne and on our way to San Francisco. For now, it's time to move forward, so I ask her if the bins are completely full.

"Korry, we wouldn't close them if they weren't full," she retorts.

"Would you mind checking one more time?" I ask, wondering if we might be able to move a few pieces around, like a game of overhead-bin Tetris, to make just enough space for the passenger's bag.

"Actually, I sort of do," she says.

The lead's tone carries with it a hint of defiance, which I tell myself is somewhat justified. After all, my question has unintentionally implied that I think the crew hasn't done their job as well as they could have. I consider insisting that one of the flight attendants look through the bins, if only to make the point that my question isn't really a question. But I firmly believe leaders should never ask questions whose answers they aren't prepared to honor. So I'll honor her answer by not making any of the flight attendants search for space, but that doesn't mean I can't look through the bins myself.

I set about opening several bins in first class, and as I glance down the aisle toward the back of the plane, I see a number of passengers in economy watching me with great interest, as is always the case when any pilot comes into the cabin. I offer a few forced smiles and then return to the task at hand, turning a few bags sideways and gently sliding jackets and small personal items on top of them. Before long, a spot opens up that appears just large enough for the passenger's bag. I walk to the jet's door and motion for the passenger to come aboard. His bag requires a small amount of cajoling to slide into the newly created space, but it fits—barely.

Once he sits down, I crouch beside him to ask a favor, again noticing the stares of economy passengers, some of whom are just a few feet away. "Look, I don't know what happened or what was said earlier between you and the flight attendants," I tell him. "Frankly, it doesn't even matter at this point. You're onboard, and so is your bag. But before we can leave, I need to ask for your help with something, okay?"

"What's that?" he asks.

"I need you to give me your word that during the flight you'll listen to the flight attendants and do what they ask. I've assured them you will, but I need you to promise me that you'll follow their instructions. They deserve that assurance from you, and so do I."

He nods, saying, "I just want to sleep."

I sigh at his non-answer answer. "Okay." I start to stand up, but then add, "And one more thing. I totally understand if you're frustrated about customs or this event. I would be, too. And if that's the case, I'd really appreciate if you'd vent those frustrations directly to me and not take them out on the flight attendants. They were just trying to do their job."

The passenger nods. I stand up to walk back to the flight deck, and as I turn away, I hear him say, "Thank you, Captain. For your help."

I turn around again, smile, and say, "No problem," although, in truth, I'm not sure if I've helped or not, given the rift my decision has seemingly caused between the flight attendants and me.

As I pass the forward galley on my way to the flight deck, I thank the flight attendants for respecting my decision. I also suggest my hope that we can put this behind us for the rest of the flight.

"Of course," the lead flight attendant says. But the stoic look she gives me doesn't leave me overly optimistic.

I thank them again before stepping into the cockpit, sliding around the center console, and wedging myself back into the captain's chair, ready to complete my preflight checks and get our flight underway.

A few hours later, after the flight attendants have finished their primary meal and beverage service, I ask the lead to come to the flight deck to chat. Once inside the pit, she stands by the door with her arms crossed, wearing the same stoic look on her face, which announces that her frustration hasn't abated.

I turn to sit sideways in my chair, so as to better look her in the eyes. "Look, it doesn't take a rocket scientist to know I'm a relatively new captain," I say. "I assure you I'm trying to do my best, I really am. But I know I don't always get everything just right. And so to help me become a better captain for you and your colleagues in the future, I'm hoping you might be willing to give me some honest and candid feedback about what you think I could have done differently this time."

"What you could have done was support your flight attendants and trust us," she snaps.

It's the response I had expected. "And why do you feel I didn't trust you?"

"Because you took his side, right from the start. And then you rummaged through the bins, even though we told you they were full. If you trusted us, why would you feel the need to do that?"

I see her point and can't really argue with it. It's well within my right as captain of the ship to open any bin I want, but it's equally critical for me—or any leader—to recognize the symbolic significance of my actions. And in this case, my actions implied a lack of trust on my part of the flight attendants. "I guess it just seemed like everyone was digging in their heels instead of working to find a mutually acceptable solution," which is the exact opposite of Rule #1 in negotiations: Always focus on interests, not positions.

"And that's what you think you did? Find a mutually acceptable solution?"

"Yes," I say.

"Mutually acceptable for whom, Korry?"

"For you and the passenger."

"The *first-class* passenger, maybe," she says, putting heavy emphasis on the *first-class* part. "He got his bag on, and he even secured a direct line to the captain to voice any frustrations he might have. But what about all the *other* passengers?" Immediately I realize she's referring to the economy passengers who had been watching me so closely. She notices the light bulb come on for me. "Had you even considered that just moments earlier, as they were boarding, we had asked a number of them to check their bags because the bins were full?"

I pause, running my tongue inside my lower lip as I contemplate her point. "Well, no."

"And do you think that fact was lost on them? I mean, what do you think went through their heads as they watched the captain step in and save the day for one passenger, but not for them?"

I shrug my shoulders.

"Well, let me enlighten you, because we've already heard it from a number of them: They think it's our fault. They think if the captain could find space for the first-class passenger, that probably means we could have found space for their bags, too."

"But that's not a fair comparison. There's far more space per passenger in the bins above first class."

"You and I know that, Korry. But even if the economy passengers know that, too, do you think they much care? Is their business or their bag any less important?"

"Well, no, but—"

"Because that's how it feels to them." She pauses. "And, not for nothing, while you get to close the cockpit door and press on like everything is normal and the problem is solved, our crew gets to spend the next five hours answering questions and listening to complaints about how, if we had only done our job, their bags would be in the overhead bin, not in the cargo hold on their way to baggage claim." I nod slowly, knowing she's right. "Not so mutually beneficial, is it?"

"No," I say, pausing for a moment. Then I look up, meeting her stare. "I'm sorry. I hadn't even considered that. But I can tell you this: I will now."

Her face softens just a touch. "I hope so," she responds, uncrossing her arms and letting them fall to her sides. It's the first time I feel like we're starting to make headway. She's not back on my side yet, but it's a start.

"And thank you," I add, "for your candor."

I notice the corner of her mouth tilt upward in a little half-smile. "You asked."

And I'm glad I had, because I needed that feedback. It's always hard to see things through the eyes of others, but it's imperative for a leader to consider those perspectives. Decisions, after all, are never made in isolation, and there are almost always unintended consequences. Only by fully understanding the various elements and interests that are at play in a problem or situation can a leader anticipate what the unintended consequences of a particular action might be. Sometimes, there is no way to make a choice that appeases everyone. And sometimes, that's okay or even necessary. But sometimes, the costs of acting can exceed the benefits. The line between the two is a fine one. And it's clear to me that I haven't yet figured out precisely where that line is.

A few moments later, the flight attendant returns to the cabin. I'm hopeful my receptivity to her criticisms and concerns has improved our working relationship. But as I stare out the window onto the orange light from the streetlamps that speckle the countryside of the Great Plains beneath us, I know there's no way for me to know for sure. Wounds, after all, rarely heal with just one conversation. But it's a start. And for now, I'll take it.

The "L" train's wheels screech as they round a corner of track far below our apartment's balcony a few days later. Jen and I stand huddled together, mostly for warmth, as we lean against the balcony's metal railing, gazing out at the skyline. Every few seconds, more lights turn on in nearby buildings as the last bits of dusk turn to night.

"I'm really going to miss this view," I say to Jen, slowly moving my gaze around to let each massive building, each intriguing layer of urban scape, burn itself into my memory bank.

"Me, too," she replies, doing the same. "But that's what pictures are for."

"They never do it justice, though. You've gotta see this firsthand."

A cool breeze blows across our faces, and Jen tucks her windblown bangs back behind her ears.

"Besides, I think I'm gonna like our new one even more," Jen says. "This one's so static. Makes me sad how something so beautiful simply became background after a while."

And Jen is right. The first time we walked into the apartment, the immersive skyline literally took our breath away by how it consumed every inch of the floor-to-ceiling windows. But after a while, it was as though the windows turned into giant picture frames containing artwork that simply alternated between day and night. Only when someone new came into the apartment and experienced the same visceral reaction to the view that we had first had would we remember just how special and unique it truly is.

In some ways, I guess the same could be said for my view at work. For all its beauty, there are many times, particularly during cruise flight at high altitude or at night, when it simply becomes background to the goings-on inside the cockpit, almost like we are slowly gliding above a giant atlas. Of course, when new flight attendants visit the cockpit in flight, I see the same awe and wonder on their faces that came over mine the day I stepped aboard the 747 high above the Atlantic, instantly reminding me how unique and special the view truly is.

"The sixth floor will be much more dynamic," Jen continues. "We'll actually see the cars and people going by."

And as I think about it, I realize that my favorite views at work are likewise the dynamic ones, where the scenery is rich with detail and full of movement. Like the sunrises and sunsets where the tints and hues of the sky constantly change. Or the departures and arrivals flown at lower altitudes, such as how New York City's skyscrapers pop with depth and dimension while flying up the Hudson River toward LaGuardia only a few thousand feet above the bridges and boats below, or how the approach to Portland, Oregon, places the pointy peak of Mount Hood at eye level, revealing the mountain's intricate and undulating combination of snow-packed lakes, twisting crevasses, and slithering streams that otherwise get lost from high above.

"Don't forget about the trains," I say to Jen, noting how three Metra commuter rail tracks pass just to the north of our new building in Chicago's West Loop neighborhood.

Jen rolls her eyes. "You can barely hear them inside." Which is true. "And you'll still get your skyline. It'll just be a bit farther away."

"I know," I say, recalling how the city's north side skyscrapers could be seen beyond the rail tracks and in between a few other nearby high-rise residential towers.

"And that sun," Jen says longingly, closing her eyes and smiling as she runs her hand up and down my back, no doubt imagining its orange rays bathing our corner unit. "It'll be so much brighter."

"Especially in the afternoons."

"So much more homey and less hotel-like."

"I know, Wife," I say, wistfully. "Lots of plusses to this move. Basically no negatives. I just wish it hadn't been forced on us."

"You're telling me, dude; moving stinks."

"Yes, it does," I agree, letting out a long sigh. "Rent to own," I mutter as I begin to recall the "perk" the developer had included in our first Chicago lease. "More like rent to own or get out."

Jen chuckles as she looks toward me. "It just wasn't meant to be our forever home, Husband."

"I know," I say, meeting her gaze.

"It was meant to be our first *together* home."

"But wasn't that Country Lane?" I ask, referring to the small 1960s rancher we had lived in after getting engaged.

"Meh," she says, looking away again. "That was yours long before I moved in, just like Bethlehem was already your town with your friends." She looks back. "But Chicago is *our* town. To live in and explore together."

I smile. "And it's been really good for us."

"Yeah, dude," she says, nodding. "Like your mom expected, it forced us to actually become an *us*."

I smile and pull her tight. "You think we'll end up staying here long-term?"

"Who knows," Jen says, sighing. "On one hand, it's hard to imagine raising a family in the city. But on the other hand, I never imagined living here in the first place. And I definitely didn't imagine liking it as much as I do. So, who knows. I wouldn't rule out anything."

"Yeah. Gotta trust our path, I guess."

"It hasn't let us down yet," Jen agrees.

"Well, for the most part, at least."

Jen looks to me, quizzically. "For the most part?"

"Well, yeah. I mean, I thought for sure that part of our moving here was so I could put my MBA to work over at Willis in Flight Ops management," I say, motioning across the open expanse to the Willis Tower a block away, the home of United's corporate headquarters. "But that's a door I can't seem to crack open, no matter how hard I try."

"Well, Husband, maybe it's not supposed to open, for whatever reason."

"Or maybe I just haven't tried hard enough," I say.

Jen pulls her hand away from my back rather suddenly, resting it on the balcony's rounded metal railing as she looks away.

"What?" I ask. "What did I say?"

She shakes her head slowly. "It's nothing."

"Wife," I insist, "what did I say?"

"It's fine," she says, drawing out the word *fine* in a way that indicates it is most definitely not fine at all.

"Come on," I plead. "What is it? What did I say?"

Jen looks to me, then returns to staring blankly at the cityscape. "It will never be enough for you, will it?"

I furrow my eyebrows. "What do you mean?"

She looks back at me. "I mean this," she says, waving her hand toward the apartment behind us. "Our life. You and me. Us. When will *we* be enough?"

"Wife, what are you talking about? Of course this is enough."

"No, it's not, Korry. You're a major airline captain, the youngest at United even. And yet it's not enough. You still want more." She pauses. "You'll always want more." Turning away again, she says, "I just need to get my head wrapped around that."

A long moment of silence hits us as I gather my thoughts. "Wife, I got my MBA for a reason, and it wasn't just to hang a fancy diploma on the wall."

She looks back. "But when does it stop, Korry? The chase. Because there will always be something more to chase after."

I shake my head, confused. "Wife, I don't understand why being driven is such a bad thing."

"It's not bad. But it's not everything, either."

"I'm not saying it's everything. But don't you want me to be professionally fulfilled?"

Jen shakes her head. "You seriously don't get it."

"Get what?"

"That if you can't be satisfied as the youngest captain at United, when will you ever be?"

"Wife, I *am* satisfied."

"Then why do you have to go be in management? Why can't you just be okay with where you are—with where *we* are?"

"Because I think I can make a difference over there," I say, raising my voice slightly as I point toward Willis.

"A difference for whom?" But Jen doesn't pause long enough for me to answer, which is probably good anyway. "Husband, I'm sure you'd make a difference there. I'm sure you'd do great in whatever role you had. But after a while, you'll say you can make even more of an impact by getting a different role with a better title. And so you'll work more. You'll email more. You'll chase more. And you'll climb more. Heck, maybe you'll even climb your way up to the C-suite."

"Oh, come on, Jen."

"And I'll be here. On this balcony—well, one like it—watching you climb. And waiting."

"Waiting for what?" I ask, increasingly annoyed with the turn the night's conversation has taken.

"For the time when it's just us." I stare at her as she pauses. "The time when *we're* enough."

I shake my head and turn away, resting my hands on the cold metal railing. "You're being dramatic."

"Am I?" Jen asks, still looking at me. "Or are you?" She steps closer to me. "Because you know what happens after you become CEO? Or VP? Or whatever? One day you retire." I look back toward her. "And that same day someone else gets promoted to take your place." She grabs one of my hands from the railing, letting her fingers mesh with mine. "And then it'll be just us." She squeezes. "Except it won't." She drops my hand and turns away. "Because we'll be strangers living in the same house."

"Jen, seriously," I say, perplexed by the way she's casting my ambition as a negative. She's always been my biggest cheerleader, and I'm confused as to why she sees the potential effects of my moving into a management role as completely different than when I pursued professional opportunities on the flight deck like moving to captain. Perhaps she's worried about the additional work demands of an office job, which is somewhat understandable, since I'm the first to admit that one of the best parts of being a line pilot—whether a captain or first officer—is coming home, hanging the uniform in the closet, and having no other work obligation to think about. No emails to answer. No phone calls to return. No meetings to attend. No nothing. Just time off. Clearly, a job in management would be different. But does she seriously think I wouldn't set limits there, too? And has she forgotten that I wouldn't be traveling half the month like I am now? I just don't understand.

Jen continues, "And maybe that's okay for you, but it's not for me. I want my husband. That's it. That's all I need." She looks to me. "You're all I want to chase."

A long pause fills the air, and mercifully, an "L" train's screeching rumble fills the painful silence. As I see it round the track's corner below us, part of me wishes I could hop on and ride away from this conversation altogether. But I can't. And just as I won't run away from the woman I love, I also can't escape the conflicting reality of my blind ambition that is now laid bare in front of me.

I turn to Jen. I look in her deep green eyes and see a part of me I'm suddenly not proud of. And my frustration melts. "Wife, I want that, too."

She looks up to my eyes. "I hope so, Husband." She grabs one of my hands. "I really hope we're enough."

"You are," I say, turning to hold both her hands. "And you always will be."

Jen offers a half smile. "I really, really hope so." Then she pauses and looks away. "I'm probably just overly emotional with the move and all."

"It's stressful for all of us," I say, hoping it really is just the move across town that has triggered this. But part of me also knows Jen has a point, even if I don't want to admit it out loud. I think a lot about the furloughees with whom I've flown and how content many of them seem with their rough and tumble paths. I wonder why I don't have that same "roll with it" attitude, why I can't just turn off my desire for the chase and the climb. I know I must be missing something, but I can't put my finger on what that something is.

A few moments later, in what seems to be an effort to lighten the mood, Jen begins to reminisce about a few of the many memories we've shared in the apartment, like how I made the mistake of pulling our U-Haul trailer inside the parking garage while moving in, only to realize the trailer had cleared the ceiling's water pipes by an inch at most. "Do you remember the looks we got from the other residents as they drove by?" she asks with a small laugh.

"Ohhhh, yessss," I say, grinning. "But they were nothing compared to the scowls I got for hauling all that stuff up on the regular elevator instead of the freight."

Jen laughs.

"Not exactly a great first impression," I sigh.

"Nor was Lollapalooza while you were on your trip that first weekend."

I chuckle, remembering well how Jen and our dog, Molly, had been less than thrilled by the throngs of edgy, raucous festivalgoers who were then roaming the city's streets, causing her to seriously question where in the world I had moved them to. "Thankfully, it got better," I say.

"A *lot* better," Jen adds.

The reminiscing continues as we recall the many nights we watched Navy Pier's weekly summer fireworks from the comfort of our balcony while drinking wine and talking late into the night. Or how we often woke up to the staccato tones of a street performer's terrible rendition of "Tequila"—that he played exactly the same way at least ten thousand times on his saxophone. Or how we sat in silence on our couch, holding hands in the darkness and wiping back tears as the two of us mourned the end of Molly's courageous two-year battle with canine kidney disease.

"So many memories," Jen says.

"And so many more to make," I add. "Come on. Let's go inside. We could stand here and do this all night."

I hold up my iPhone to capture one last panoramic shot, but as expected, it doesn't do the view justice, and it looks identical to all the other ones I've taken in the past. Jen is right; it's time for a change.

We make one final walk through the apartment, checking closets and cabinets for any items we may have missed. Then we place our keys and our parking garage clicker on the kitchen island's granite countertop.

"You ready to go?" I ask, my voice echoing against the apartment's barren white walls.

Jen looks up at me, smiling. "So long as you're going there, too."

I smile and place my hand on the small of her back to guide her down the long hallway toward the door. Once there, we turn around and take one final look at the *together* home that helped make us an *us*.

Another chapter of life is complete, I think. *Here's hoping the next one is just as good.*

I look to Jen and can tell that, like me, she has tears welling up in her eyes.

"Onward and upward, Wife," I say. "It's time."

Jen smiles.

We open the door, turn off the lights, and walk out.

CHAPTER 10

The Wanderer

"Many go fishing all their lives without knowing that it is not fish they are after."
- Henry David Thoreau

Dulles, Virginia – Early November 2013

My captain's hat blocks the steady, cold rain from drenching my hair as I heave the Tank and my laptop bag into the trunk of my Ford Focus rental car. After closing its lid, I scoot around to open the rear driver's-side door. I toss my cap onto the far-side seat and drape my uniform jacket neatly across the other two, which is when I first notice the cigarette burn in the fabric.

Looks like I've got myself a gem, I think.

My opinion solidifies when I slide into the driver's seat, close the door, and find myself quickly overwhelmed by the stale smell of cigarettes.

You've got to be kidding me, I think.

Normally, I'd ask for a different car, but I'm already behind schedule. The drive to my grandfather's hospital in Lancaster, Pennsylvania, will consume at least two-and-a-half hours of my fortuitously assigned 24-hour layover in D.C. And if I don't hit the road immediately, Papaw may be in emergency surgery by the time I arrive.

Whatever, I say to myself. *It's one day. Deal with it.*

I start the car and crack the windows a fraction of an inch, hoping the fresh air will circulate enough to cover up the cigarette smell without letting the rain drench the inside of the car.

After loosening my tie, I pull the seatbelt across my chest, sliding its end into the buckle. The belt falls awkwardly against the maroon pocket logbook on my chest, so I pull the tiny ledger from my shirt and set it in one of the center cupholders.

My logbook's pages have been filling up with great rapidity of late. Intermingled among new entries for flights to United's core "hub" cities like Washington Dulles, Denver, and San Francisco are entries for flights from those hubs to the various "spoke" cities to which they link, such as Buffalo and Sacramento, Las Vegas and Harrisburg, Omaha and Kansas City, and more.

As always, I write the names of the pilots with whom I fly at the top of each page. There are names of single pilots and married pilots, male pilots and female pilots, pilots with small children and pilots with children long since grown—each of them a new single-serving flying partner with new stories, experiences, and perspectives for me to consider…at least during the fleeting time we spend together trekking around the continent over the course of our trip. Then it's another handshake, another "hope we get to fly together again soon"-type of goodbye, and another L ride home spent romanticizing the more robust relationships fostered by Jen and her coworkers.

I get along well with almost all of my fellow pilots. But not with Scott, a 40-something first officer with short brown hair and a build that suggests fitness has always been a priority for him…at least it was until the recent stresses of his life took center stage. And as soon as I get on the highway, I call Kurt to vent about my frustrations.

"Korrrrrry!!!" Kurt answers in his big, boisterous voice. "What's happening?"

"I'm driving," I say. "And boy do I have a story for you."

Kurt lets loose one of his signature rapid-fire laughs as I glance over my left shoulder, signal, and change lanes to pass a slower car. "This oughta be good," he says. "What happened?"

"I just had a nonsensical argument with my F-O over the damn seniority list."

"Little early to pick a fight, isn't it?" Kurt asks.

"Way too early!" I exclaim. "It was barely 6:00 AM on leg one of a four-day, and I couldn't get him off the subject."

Kurt rips into another laugh. "Nice way to start your trip!"

"Tell me about it," I grumble, knowing an argument was the last thing I needed after the 2:30 AM wakeup call from crew scheduling assigning me the trip. "I mean, I hadn't even finished my first cup of coffee!"

"Now, *that's* unacceptable," Kurt says, his sarcasm dripping from the phone as I hear the pop, hum, and gurgle of a Keurig starting its brew cycle in the background. "So what was the deal?" he asks.

"Well, we're up at cruise altitude," with Scott and me both staring forward, our feet propped up, sunglasses on, and Starbucks coffees in hand, "going through the usual questions—where do you live? Are you married? Kids? Interests? Normal twenty-questions stuff. Only it's clear from his one-word answers that Scott doesn't want to chitchat, which is fine by me. So I'm—"

Use the right two lanes to join I-495 north toward Baltimore, my iPhone's GPS curtly interrupts.

"So I'm sitting there quietly," I continue, glancing over my right shoulder before signaling and changing lanes, "just watching the sunrise and making radio calls with A-T-C, when out of nowhere, he launches into his disdain for the new list. And I mean he was furious about the way it turned out. Just fuming."

"What was he so mad about?" Kurt asks.

I hear a clink in the background as Kurt sets his coffee cup on his kitchen island's granite countertop. "Mostly that he couldn't believe he didn't get more credit for his longevity with United."

"Gotcha," Kurt responds. "Furloughed guy?"

"Yeah," I say. "Double furloughee."

"Well, at least the arbitrators gave him *some* credit for his longevity when they built the formula for the list."

"Kurt, that was just the start," I say, easing off the accelerator so as to better time my merge with the slow-moving traffic I see ahead on the packed D.C. beltway. "And the more he spoke, the more I felt my anxiety level shooting up." I glance, signal, and change lanes.

"See, I don't get why guys wanna discuss the list on the flight deck. It's not like it's gonna change, so why even talk about it?"

"Exactly," I say. "It is what it is."

"Mmhmm," Kurt hums, as a water droplet falls from my cracked window onto my forearm.

I brush my arm against my pant leg to dry it. "So, in an attempt to deflect the conversation and avoid the topic altogether, I made some vague comment about how the formula used by the arbitrators was definitely complicated. But that didn't help. He kept going on and on about how it didn't make any sense for him to be integrated amongst Continental people who were hired in the mid-2000s when he was hired at United in the late '90s." I notice red brake lights ahead, so I glance left, signal, and change lanes. "He kept asking how that was fair."

"But it's not about fairness," Kurt says. "It's about whatever the arbitrators decided. That's the deal with binding arbitration."

"Right?!?! I really wanted to ask if he understood that the final list was basically the one advocated by his own union, but I didn't."

"Good move," Kurt adds.

"Instead, I said, 'I don't know.' And then threw in something like 'How about those Bears?' to make it blatantly obvious I wanted to change the subject."

Another round of Kurt's rapid-fire belly laugh. "You mean that didn't work?"

I merge back to the right. "You know, I think you're enjoying this a little too much."

"I sure am!" Kurt says. "Because I can see it happening. And I can imagine how awkward it would be. But please…go on."

The rain intensifies, and my wipers quicken. "So when he still wouldn't drop it, I said it sounds like we both are disappointed in the list, and perhaps the flight deck isn't the best venue for us to discuss it, if we should even discuss it at all."

"Good."

Another drip on my arm. "And then I asked about his kids or something, trying to change the subject again."

"But let me guess: He kept going," Kurt says.

"He doubled down!" I wipe my arm on my leg again. "He said the only fair method for integrating the lists would have been to use date of hire and only date of hire."

Another laugh. "Which, conveniently, would have made him senior to you."

"Bingo," I reply.

"So what did you say?"

"I said something like, 'Well, date of hire wasn't advocated by either side, which suggests both unions believed fairer methods existed for integrating the lists.' And then I again suggested we move on."

"But he kept going," Kurt says prophetically, clearly mid-sip.

"He wouldn't stop!" I exclaim. "He just kept saying there was no way it was fair for him to be integrated with pilots, some of whom hadn't even started flying at the time he was hired by United and some of whom now hold captain slots." Another round of Kurt's rapid-fire belly laugh. "It was like he was pointing his finger directly at me!"

"That's because he was," Kurt adds.

"I kept thinking, 'Is this really happening?' And I'm sure he isn't the first pilot who's flown with me to think it, but he's definitely the first one who's said it to my face." Red lights in between the rapid swipes of the wipers. "And he said it on leg one of a four-day trip!"

Another laugh. "Sounds like it's going to be a fun trip for you."

"This isn't funny!" I exclaim, rapping the palm of my hand onto the top of the steering wheel.

"Oh, yes, it is."

"I mean, can you imagine saying that to a captain?"

"Nope. Not even a little bit."

"Me, neither," I say. "Especially to question a captain's legitimacy so bluntly. It seemed surreal."

"I bet it did," Kurt says. "So what'd you do, Captain?"

I feel another plop of water onto my arm. I look down at it, annoyed. "Well at that point, I decided I had to say something, because clearly the topic wasn't going to change otherwise." Another wipe of my arm on my leg. "And I worried that letting Scott's passive aggressiveness toward me go unchecked could impact my ability to lead on the flight deck." I press the button to close the window. "Not to mention that I didn't want to listen to him complain about all this stuff for four days." Instantly, the smell of stale cigarette smoke returns. "So I drew a line in the sand."

"Oh, boy," Kurt says. "Here it comes!"

I crack the window again, accepting my wet fate. "I said something like, 'Scott, I've tried to politely change the topic many times now. I've suggested this isn't the right venue for us to discuss this issue. But since you're not gonna let me change the topic, then at least answer a few simple questions for me." Brake lights ahead as traffic slows. "Were you furloughed at any point while Continental was hiring between 2005 and 2008?'"

"Dude, you—"

"He replied yes." I slide left to pass. "So I asked if he had ever applied to Continental during that time, and he said no. And when I asked why not, he sort of hemmed and hawed, talking about United recall rights and Continental domiciles being too far from his home." And now back again to the right as traffic speeds up. "It was logical reasoning, but it identified that he'd made a choice not to apply. So I interrupted his stammering, suggesting that if he *had* applied, he might very well be senior to me today, which would likely mean he'd also be a captain today, too."

"Oh, my," Kurt bellows. "I bet that went over really well!"

"Honestly, I think he was surprised I was pushing back."

"Probably so."

"Then I asked him if he had been furloughed on the date of the merger, and he said yes. And I asked if he was aware of any other merger where pilots on furlough at the date of a merger were integrated with actively flying pilots of the other carrier. Unsurprisingly, he was not, and neither was I. So I said that all things considered, it seems he got a pretty good deal."

"Korrrrrrrry, Korrrry, Korry," Kurt says. "You actually said that?"

"I did," I say, scrunching up my face.

"But why would you say that?"

"Because it's true!" I exclaim.

"But who cares if it's true or not? That's like stoking the fire. Actually, that's like pouring gasoline on a fire that's already raging."

"Look, something had to get his attention." Another drop on my arm.

"And I'm sure that did," Kurt says, letting out a long sigh. "So what did he say then?"

"He didn't say a word."

"Well, there's a surprise," Kurt says sarcastically. "But I'm guessing you did."

"Correct." Another wipe of my arm. "After a second or two, I said something about how all of us try to make the best possible choices for our careers and for our families given the information we have at the time." I see slower traffic ahead. "Sometimes, those decisions work out really well. Other times, they don't." Glance. Signal. Lane change. "And when they don't, we often wish we could get a do-over. We tell ourselves we would make a different choice. But the truth is, if we had it to do over again, knowing only what we'd known then and nothing more, chances are we would make the exact same choice." And back to the right. "Because sometimes shit just happens. And when it does, it's understandable to be frustrated. I told Scott I'm sure I would've been frustrated if I'd been in his shoes. But then I said that for him to think, as a furloughed guy, that he should be integrated above someone like me who has been actively and continuously flying for several years before the merger, well, I told him, quite frankly, I find that to be ridiculous. And then I said, 'Next topic.'"

Kurt lets out another rapid-fire laugh, stammering, "Dude, you are…I just…I bet that went over reaaaaaally well!"

"Look, I know it was a bit overly harsh, but it had the desired effect."

"Which was what?" Kurt asks. "To build a giant freaking brick wall between the two of you?"

"To get him to stop talking about the damn list!" I shout, rapping my steering wheel once again.

"Well, I hate to tell you this, but you probably did both."

I rub the side of my face. "I'm a little afraid of that," I say. "But what was I supposed to do? Say nothing?"

"I don't know, man. I just don't know," he says. "But probably not that." Kurt tells me to hold on a second. I hear a sliding glass door open as he yells, "Daisy! Come here, girl." A few seconds pass before I hear the clicking of paws on Kurt's wooden floors and the *swoosh* of the door once more. Then he's back. "Oh, buddy," he says, pausing briefly. "You have to admit it must be tough for these guys to sit down next to you right now. You're such a young captain, and the list is such a fresh wound."

"Oh, I get that, Kurt, but how —"

"And you're what?" Kurt interjects. "Ten, fifteen years younger than most of these F-Os?"

"That's about right. Sometimes the spread is even greater," I respond. "And let me tell you—it can feel really awkward at times."

"I bet," Kurt says as yet another drip hits my arm. "You know, I'm just wondering. Do you think it's possible that pilots like Scott aren't really frustrated with you?"

"What do you mean?" I ask.

"Maybe they're just frustrated with what you represent."

"What I represent?"

"Yes," he says. "The career they wish they'd had."

I take a moment to consider Kurt's point. "I guess I can see that."

"Especially since it generally takes you much longer than one flight to get under someone's skin."

I wish Kurt could see me rolling my eyes, but I know he can hear me chuckling.

"Seriously, though," he continues, "can you imagine going through what they have?"

I shake my head. "Not really."

"I mean, imagine what it would feel like to look your wife in the eyes as you wonder if you'll actually be able to make your mortgage payment next month once your income drops back at the regionals?"

I let the imaginary scene play out in my mind. It's shortly after Jen and I have paid the final bill for our wedding in 2010, perhaps the most precarious financial position of our lives to date. I'm sitting on the couch in the living room of our old Pennsylvania home, holding the pink slip that tells me I'm about to be furloughed, staring at my open laptop and the Excel doc that is bleeding red from projected overages to our budget. And in that moment, Jen walks in. She looks at me and sees the concern on my face and my fear that I'm failing at my duties as the provider for our family. I know it's a completely fictitious scenario as I drive on the D.C. beltway, and yet I feel an incredible sense of overwhelm creeping over me. And that's without any kids to consider either. I let out a long sigh.

"I mean, that stress must have been awful," Kurt says.

"No, Kurt," I say as the rain eases. "It must have been hell."

He pauses. "So you gotta figure that each furlough, each setback had to feel like a punch to the gut for these guys. And there was nothing they could do about it, so they kept taking the punches, hoping to catch a break eventually." I change lanes again as Kurt continues. "Maybe Scott saw the seniority list as his last chance to catch that break. And when that didn't happen, and when he sat down next to a 31-year-old who was significantly senior to him, his frustration simply bubbled over."

I nod, saying, "I could see that." I merge back to the right.

"Just as it could have for anybody," he says.

"But what was I supposed to do, Kurt? Pass on the upgrade? Say, no, there are other people who should upgrade before me? No one would say that."

"You're right, Korry. And deep down, I bet guys like Scott know that, too. But that doesn't mean it doesn't suck for them in the moment."

"Yeah, I know," I say.

"And don't forget that if one or two little things in our career had gone differently, we could have been in their shoes. We could have been born one year earlier or one year later. We could have interned with United or American or Delta instead of Continental."

"Oh, you're right, Kurt."

"And who knows what type of effect those things might have had on our careers."

"Which again makes me wonder if our careers are controlled more by the choices we make or by dumb luck and timing," I say.

"I'd like to think our choices control a lot," Kurt says. "But it's probably a combination of the two. And maybe more the latter than we'd like to admit."

I rub my forehead as I let out a long sigh. "I'm definitely starting to wonder if that's the case."

"The bottom line is we've got a lot to be thankful for. Left seat or not."

"Amen to that," I agree.

I hear another clink of Kurt's coffee mug. "So how do you honestly think the rest of your trip will go?"

"Boy, that's the question of the hour." I take a moment to think. "I guess I'm cautiously optimistic, because about fifteen minutes after that conversation, Scott started chatting with me again. So maybe, like you said, it was just his frustration bubbling over. Guess I'll find out tomorrow."

"Well, good luck, Korry. I'll be curious to hear how it goes."

"You and me both!"

"And keep me posted on your grandpa. I got your text about him last night. Sorry to hear he's having trouble. Nice this trip worked out so you can see him today."

"Yeah, I couldn't have planned it better."

"You think he'll be okay?"

My GPS interrupts again, saying, *In two miles, use the right two lanes to take exit 27 for I-95 north toward Baltimore.*

"I'm not sure, Kurt. I'm not even sure what I'm walking into. All Mom has said is that something happened with his gallbladder. But it's all come up so suddenly."

"Well, keep me posted. I'll be thinking of you and your family."

"Thanks, man. And thanks for letting me vent."

"No problem, buddy. I'll talk to you later," he replies.

"Later," I say, hanging up the phone.

Two hours later, I pull into the hospital's parking garage, thankful my rainy drive is over. The hospital is busy, but I'm able to find a spot rather quickly. And after shutting off the car, I text Mom that I just parked. Her response comes almost immediately.

MOM: *Hurray!*

As I step out of the car and close the door, a second text arrives.

MOM: *Papaw's still awake. He'll be thrilled to see you.*

Using my reflection in the car's window, I snug up my tie and center it along my collar. Then I take a few deep breaths, nervous about what I'll find inside, and walk toward the hospital's entry doors. The Wanderer himself awaits.

*H*e *doesn't even look like Papaw*, I think as I peer through the open doorway into his hospital room. It's as though someone has replaced the fighting patriarch of our family with a tiny, frail, old man. I wonder if he's cold, given that his hospital gown barely covers his shoulders and his bedsheets only come partway up his chest.

Come on, Korry. This is Papaw, I remind myself. *Even if he's cold, there's no chance he'll admit it.*

Still, I can't imagine he's comfortable, especially with the needles stuck into his wrists, the tubes taped to his arms, and the incessant *beep...beep...beep* of his EKG, which chimes softly in the background. Then again, there's a strange comfort in those beeps; they indicate Papaw hasn't yet lost the biggest fight of his life.

I rap three times on the wooden door before walking in.

Papaw's eyes turn toward me, and a big smile spreads across his face. "There's the pilot," he says in a soft, fragile voice to the nurse kneeling beside him.

"I see that," she says with a tiny laugh, tapping Papaw's hand as she stands up. She grabs her clipboard and begins jotting down a few figures, glancing up at me at one point to ask who I fly for.

"United," I say.

"This kid's been everywhere," Papaw tells the nurse.

I chuckle, correcting, "Maybe not *everywhere*. But a lot of places, for sure."

Papaw scrunches his nose and repeats to her, "Everywhere."

"Well," the nurse says, "one of these days I wanna build up enough courage to get on a plane and go *somewhere*. But I'm not quite ready yet." She looks sheepishly to me. "I bet you probably think that's silly."

"Not at all," I say, smiling as I shake my head. "It's all what you're used to."

"I guess so."

"And it helps that I'm usually at the controls," I say, hinting at what I believe is the primary driver for most people who share the fear of flying—the complete lack of control.

"Yes, I'd say that helps a lot," she says, chuckling. Then looking to Mom, who is standing on the other side of Papaw's bed, she says, "Anyway, they're looking at his records now to make sure the anesthesia will be okay with his current medications. Once we get that approval, I'll be back to take him up for surgery."

"We'll be here," Mom replies.

As the nurse leaves, I walk over and give Mom a hug.

"I'm so glad you're here, Korry Mike," she tells me, smiling.

"Me, too," I respond. "How are you holding up?"

"Pretty well," she says. And for the most part, I believe her. But the concern on her face is easy to spot, and there's no doubt her unexpected all-day vigil has taken its toll. Papaw is, after all, her dad.

Over the years, the two of them have shared a unique and complex relationship. Mom has always adored her dad, and few things have seemed to bring her more satisfaction than his approbation. But Papaw has never been one to show emotion, and his praise has not always flown freely. Instead, the evidence of his approval more often surfaces in the form of a subtle nod or simple gesture, a smile or a wink, not through an easily discernable written or spoken word. At times, that has left Mom wondering if she actually measures up to her dad's incredibly high expectations. But that uncertainty has never stopped her from trying her best to please him, especially when she was a kid.

Times were tight inside the modest two-story house in the Pennsylvania countryside where Mom grew up. To make ends meet, Papaw ran his own plumbing and heating business in addition to his full-time job as a pipefitter at a local factory. And for her part, Grandma Janet worked from home, somehow balancing the tasks of managing the office for Papaw's business while raising Mom and her older brother and ensuring the family's precious resources—like the food grown in the family's large garden or the pieces of coal that were fed into the basement's furnace—weren't squandered. So when splurges were made for Mom to take private piano lessons, she practiced diligently, learning Papaw's favorite old-time songs to prove such sacrifices had been worth it. And when Mom saw her dad taking his finicky, old, but paid-off car to the shop again and again instead of buying a newer, more reliable one, she understood he did so because his top priority was saving money to put toward sending Mom and her brother to college. So Mom studied extra hard, striving to become valedictorian of her high school class in hopes that such a distinction might earn her a full scholarship to college. And that's why she made such a production out of the letter she received from Thiel College's scholarship committee in the spring of her senior year in high school.

From the home's wide front porch, Mom eagerly awaited Papaw's return for dinner between his two jobs. Eventually, she watched his car turn onto the long, tree-lined driveway. As usual, Papaw looked tired and haggard as he walked from the car toward the house. And as soon as he stepped inside the kitchen, Mom began criticizing his rickety old car.

"Dad, I think it's time you get a new car," she told him.

"A new car??" he asked incredulously. "That car is just fine."

"No, Dad. It's old. It's constantly breaking down. And it's time you trade up."

Flabbergasted by Mom's suggestion, Papaw asked, "Now, Cindy Lou, how on earth do you propose I pay for a new car? Take on a third job?" His anger was almost palpable; Mom had him right where she wanted, and it was all she could do to conceal her enjoyment of the moment.

"I don't know, Dad. I just think it's time."

"It's time?" Papaw asked, shaking his head. "Well, I'll tell you what I'll do then. I'll take all that money I've been saving for your education, and I'll spend it on a new car. How about that?"

Mom beamed. "I think that's a fantastic idea," she said.

"You what?" Papaw asked, astonished by her brazen response.

"I said I think that's a fantastic idea," she repeated, "because I don't need that money anyway. I got the full scholarship!"

Instantly, Papaw melted with pride, and Mom burst out in laughter. It wasn't easy to pull one over on Dale Hartman, but she had done it. And doing so for such an important issue made it all the more satisfying.

Of course, Papaw had always been proud of Mom and her accomplishments, even if he didn't say as much. And as we sit by his bedside, I call tell he is proud of her now—his daughter, the lawyer— by the way he smiles and nods and sometimes raises his hand up to make the sign for "okay" as the three of us talk.

It's several hours before the nurse comes back with the news. "There's a bit of an issue," she begins. "The doctors are concerned about how your father's diabetes medications will react with the anesthesia. And so to lessen the risk, he's going to need a much longer prep period than we anticipated. Unfortunately, that means we're going to have to move his surgery to tomorrow morning."

Mom thinks contemplatively for a moment before asking, "Is it safe for him to wait that long?"

"The doctors say he's stable and the risk of moving forward with the surgery now outweighs the risk of waiting."

I can tell Mom is torn about what to do. "Well, if that's what's better and safer for him, I guess that's what we'll do."

The nurse offers a comforting smile. "If they had any doubts, I promise you they'd operate now."

"Okay," Mom says. "It's not worth rushing things if doing so could further complicate his condition."

"Absolutely," the nurse says. "We'll keep a close eye on him tonight. And first thing tomorrow, we'll get him all fixed up."

Mom gives a forced smile that fails to hide her concern for her dad before saying, "Thank you."

Once the nurse leaves, Mom sits down next to Papaw and holds his hand as she explains the latest update. "Does that make sense, Dad?"

He nods and holds up another "okay" sign with his hand.

"And are you okay with me going home to get some rest?"

Another nod and another "okay."

"Alright, Dad. I love you. I'll be the first person you see in the morning." Mom gives him a kiss on the cheek and then begins to gather up her things. "Stay as long as you like," she tells me as she puts on her long trench coat. "We'll see you at the house when you get there."

"Sounds good, Mom."

She gives me another hug before heading for the door.

And then it's just Papaw and me...and the constant beeping of his EKG. Given the weakness of his voice, I know he can't talk much, despite how much I desperately wish he could. I want to hear him retell the stories about his Costa Rican fishing trips or his grand adventure in Alaska. I fear it might be the last time I'll get to hear the stories from him, and so I want him to tell them to me again and again so I never forget even the tiniest details.

But I know that's too much to ask. So I talk instead, sitting beside his bed, holding his wrinkly ninety-year-old hands, admiring his long thin fingers and their callused skin, hardened by many years of strenuous work. I describe trips I've recently taken, and I recount many of my favorite memories of the two of us, like when he'd take me fishing in the Juniata River or on his small boat at Raystown Lake. Again and again, he'd coach me along from cast to catch, squeezing my shoulder as my arched rod lifted my pugnacious prize above the water's ripples, and grinning satisfactorily a few moments later as I lowered it back down to the surface and released it into the realms below. "We shared so many good times, Papaw."

He smiles and nods.

"You were always there for me, pushing me to grow. And I hope you know how important you are to me—how much you've influenced my life."

He smiles again.

"You know, I still have the magazine cutout of the Warren Buffet quote you mailed to me years ago," I say. "The one about how a reputation takes twenty years to build and five minutes to ruin. I think about that quote a lot, and I'm trying my best to avoid those five minutes."

Papaw gives me another "okay" with his hand.

"Did Mom tell you I've finally started reading your manuscript?"

He turns his head to me, smiling, before shaking his head no.

"It's really good, Grandpa. Seriously. I'm about halfway through and can't put it down. I'm actually embarrassed it took me this long to start reading it."

Papaw scrunches his nose and tosses his fingers in a wave that suggests, "Don't worry about it."

"It's so vivid and beautifully written. I feel like I'm walking along the rimrocks with Jeb," I say, referring to the book's main character. "I'm really surprised it never got published, but I'm hoping to change that if you're okay with it." Papaw looks at me, intrigued. "Jen scanned it into the computer, so now we have an electronic copy of your manuscript, which will make it much easier to work on. I'm thinking that if we clean up some typos, segment it into chapters, and put a good book proposal together, *Wonders of Wanderers* will find a great audience. I've already started thinking of ways we can market it to hikers and hunters and conservationists. Outdoorsmen of all types. It will be right up their alley."

Papaw smiles with approval. I squeeze his hand, and I feel him squeezing back. Tears begin to well up in my eyes as I pray, *Lord, please don't let this be the last time I see Papaw.*

"Anyway," I say, fighting the tears back, "I'm just really enjoying it. And I wish I would have read it years ago."

Papaw coughs a bit, clearing his throat. "You're reading it now," he says, offering another "okay" with his hand.

For close to an hour, I sit beside him and ramble on about all the memories I have of the two of us, about Chicago, about Jen and our hopes to start a family soon, about all sorts of things. But eventually, I know it's time for me to go.

"You've got a big day tomorrow, so I should probably let you sleep," I say, although I hate the thought of leaving him alone in the hospital. "I'm so sorry you're not well, Papaw."

He shrugs his shoulders. "I'm old."

"You're also a fighter," I say, hoping his fighting days aren't over. I lay my hand on top of his. "They're going to fix you up, okay? You'll get through this. I know it."

He gives me another "okay" with his hand, but there's no smile this time. And that lack of a smile makes me wonder all sorts of things, like if it's possible that Papaw doesn't really believe he'll get through this. And if not, I wonder if he's okay with whatever lies ahead. I wonder if he's scared or if he's just as strong as ever. I wonder if he'll talk to God when he's alone in the room later that night. And if he does, I wonder what he'll ask the Great Architect of the Universe. It makes me wonder so many things—if he's happy with the twists and turns his life has taken, if I've been a good enough grandson for him, if there's anything else he wishes he could do. And the more I wonder, the more I feel tears welling up inside of me again. The more I want him to get fixed and be back to his old self, so the two of us can sit along the riverbank again, casting our lines into the water and talking about anything and everything. So he can teach me more about plumbing or gardening. So he can tell me about the inspiration for his book. So he can tell me why he ventured off to Alaska as a young man in the first place. There's just so much I want to talk with him about, so much I want him to show me. And now it seems our time is so short.

I squeeze his hand and lean in to give him a peck on his stubbly cheek. "I love you, Grandpa."

He looks me square in the eyes and squeezes my hand. "I love you, too, Korry Mike."

I choke up instantly, knowing how rare it is for him to actually use those words. "You'll get through this, okay?"

Another "okay" with his hand.

"And I'll see you soon?"

Papaw nods.

"I'm gonna hold you to that," I say, earning a small smile from him as I give him one last hug. Then while standing near the door, I turn around and say, "Goodbye, Papaw."

And Papaw smiles.

I leave the dimly lit room and close the door. I meander through the maze of hospital hallways, numb with emotion. Eventually I arrive at my cigarette-smelling rental car. I spend the hour-and-a-half drive to my parents' house listening to music from my iPhone on shuffle. At times I turn the music up loud, hoping to block out the melancholy feelings that consume my soul. But it's a worthless pursuit, especially when I hear the unmistakable organ lead-in to one of my favorite songs—a song I understand was written about the death of a family member.

I think about skipping to the next track, but instead choose to embrace it, turning up the stereo even louder, listening to the anthem's powerful lyrics, and finding solace in its stanzas. And then the driving guitar riff begins, signaling the start of the song's final buildup. I grip the steering wheel tighter, staring straight ahead down the lonely nighttime highway. The drums kick in, and the riff pulses forward. Eventually, the lead singer cries out about tears streaming down his face, and I notice tears streaming down *my* face as my emotions overflow. But I don't bother wiping them; I just let them slide down my cheeks, their wet streaks chilled by the car's air conditioning. And I sing, belting out the lyrics I know so well, until the powerful chorus suddenly quiets, leaving only the simple piano chords and the artist's haunting voice to bring the soulful song to conclusion. And as it ends, I find myself wishing there were something I could do for Papaw, some way I could help make him well again. But I know there is likely nothing I can do, and possibly nothing the doctors can do either. This time, it just feels different.

The call comes two weeks later as I sit in the captain's seat beside Vince, a former U.S. Navy fighter pilot, waiting for the last few passengers to board our flight from New York's LaGuardia Airport to Houston. It's Dad. Part of me doesn't want to answer, because I have a sinking feeling I know what he's calling to say. I stare at my iPhone's screen, but after a few rings, I answer the call and say hello.

"I know you're working, Korry, so I hate to tell you this, but—"

"Papaw died," I interrupt.

"Yes," he says solemnly.

I let out a long sigh. "I had a feeling that's why you were calling. Is Mom okay?"

"Actually, I think she is," he says. "She seems at peace."

"That's good," I say.

"It's kind of crazy, really. Mom had been camped out in Papaw's room at the nursing home all morning. Grandma had gone to lunch, and as soon as she returned, Papaw's breathing changed significantly. Mom said he took three short breaths and was gone."

I feel tears starting to well up in my eyes. "He wanted his family with him," I say.

"Yes, he did."

I let out another sigh. "Okay, Dad, I've got to go. We're about to push for Houston. Let me know what the plan is, and I'll call United to work out my schedule. I suspect Jen and I can get home tomorrow."

"Sounds good, Korry. I love you."

"I love you, too, Dad."

After ending the call, I tell Vince what has happened.

"Are you okay to fly, Korry?"

"I really am, Vince. I'm actually strangely okay. Almost relieved. Because he's at peace now."

"Well, there's no shame in it if you're not."

"I know," I reply. "And if I thought I wasn't okay, I wouldn't fly. But truthfully, the distraction of work is probably good for me. This isn't going to feel real until I'm home in Pennsylvania."

Vince nods. "I know exactly what you mean."

Vince turns to look at his navigation chart. "Are *you* okay with me continuing?" I ask.

He looks back. "I am, Korry," he says, nodding. "It's two legs. We'll be back in Chicago tonight."

"If that changes, just let me know and I'll remove myself, no questions asked."

We fly to Houston without event. And after landing, I call the

Chief Pilot who oversees all Chicago-based United pilots to ask that he remove me from duty for the next few days.

"Consider it done, Korry," he tells me. "I'm also authorizing two positive space passes for you and your wife to fly home."

"Oh, that's fantastic," I say, knowing how much peace of mind will come by having confirmed seats home instead of needing to rely on my hit-or-miss space-available travel privileges. "Thank you so much."

"You bet," the chief pilot says. "Go be with your family. That's what's important right now."

I smile, thankful more than ever to work for a company that doesn't view its employees as numbers but vital parts of its 80,000-member family.

The next morning, Jen and I pack up and fly home. I bring Papaw's book with me to read on the flight. And as I'm reading about Jeb's adventures in "the western parts," one passage jumps off the page the moment my eyes scan its text. It reads:

> *The only riches Jeb considered genuine and which he coveted were those of a spiritual nature. His wandering eyes had beheld the indescribable beauty of countless sunsets and many mysterious rainbows that arched across the moisture-laden sky, adding their wondrous beauty to the wilderness of which he was a part and which he shared with no one. His nose had often scented the musty odor of fresh fallen leaves during the sultry Indian summer evenings, when the air hung heavy beneath the golden autumn moons, while he rejoiced in the whispering silence. Many times he had stood in immense wooded ravines beneath gigantic chestnut trees and had been bombarded with the ripened nuts as they fell from the burr-laden branches that tossed about in the gusty winds high above his unprotected*

head. The tasty nuts lay so deep beneath them they formed a mahogany carpet where walking without falling was seldom possible. Many times he had been lulled to sleep by a murmuring mountain stream as it cascaded downward over moss-bound rocks. He had watched in wonder as the churning flow sent tiny white fairy wings of foam dancing downstream to a never-ending jig.

These memories were Jeb's riches. These were the legacies stored in the depositories of his resourceful mind. The most clever thief could not unlock the vault where his riches were stored, and if one were so fortunate as to gain entrance to the vast accumulated cache, he might never understand its great value.

When Jeb's rambling days were over and his strength was failing, his mind would feast on these nourishing recollections and be at peace. Jeb might be faulted by some for lacking ambition. His accomplishments left no lasting benefits and bore no social significance. It is oft-times difficult to make a good case for ambition. Ambition nullifies contentment and cultivates overindulgence. The satisfaction of contentment contributes more to a peaceful world than does naked ambition.

I close the manuscript and lean back into my chair. *He's talking about himself,* I think.

I picture Papaw, pecking away at his typewriter as his mind returns to the beauty and solitude he had experienced during his grand adventure in Alaska. Back when things were simple for him—when he was young and free and felt like he could do anything, even with the lingering effects of his polio. Back before he shouldered the stress of working two blue-collar jobs to put food on the table for his family. Back before his son's incredible potential was stolen by schizophrenia. Back before he noticed the first subtle signs of Alzheimer's in his beloved wife. These were the moments he looked back on to find peace as he tried to make sense of his meandering journey through life and all of its unexpected twists and turns, many of which were completely outside of his control. And I can't help but feel like he's trying to tell me something about how I should approach my own journey through life, too.

Oh, Papaw, I think. *What I wouldn't give to have you here so I can ask exactly what you mean.*

I think back to all the times when I spoke with him about my desire to move up to the next rung on the career ladder, or how I hoped to one day get into management or run for political office. Had he been inspired by my drive and determination? Or had he listened to me talk, hoping one day I'd realize an even greater goal exists than that of blind ambition—the goal of contentment and fulfillment in life?

If only I'd read his book sooner, I think, *maybe I would have had time to discuss it with him.*

But now, I'll never know exactly what he meant. Now, I'll have to ponder this riddle on my own. And maybe that's to his liking anyway—to leave me one last great mystery to solve. And maybe his final lesson doesn't have an answer he could simply give to me, even if he had wanted to do so. Maybe this lesson requires that I discover its meaning for myself. On my own time. In my own way. And it dawns on me that maybe Papaw's book is just another clue.

CHAPTER 11

Winter

"What I am looking for is not out there, it is in me."
- Helen Keller"

Chicago, Illinois – January 2014

Piping-hot orange fluid streams across the 737's cockpit windows as though we are in a car wash on the O'Hare tarmac. Instead of cleaning off dirt and grime, however, this wash removes snow and ice from our jet. And instead of adding a protective and beautifying wax, this wash bathes us in a viscous liquid that forms a resistant shield against Chicago's rapidly falling snowflakes. Of course, the viscid armor won't last forever, and we can only take off safely if our wings are completely free from snow and ice. So the clock is ticking for my first officer Rob and me to get airborne before reaching the fluid's tested "holdover time." Otherwise, the shield's protective qualities can no longer be guaranteed, and we'll have to return to the gate and start the entire de-icing process again. Unfortunately, nothing happens quickly on snowy days.

"You know what stinks?" I ask Rob as the de-ice shower temporarily stops while the tanker truck and its long articulating sprayer arm repositions farther down the side of the jet.

"I'm afraid to know," he chuckles.

"This stuff is gonna drip all over our new uniforms," I say, referring to the notorious tendency of the 737 to squeeze out any liquid that finds its way around the side windows' seals prior to the pressurization system kicking in during takeoff.

"Probably so," Rob laughs. "Hope you have a good drycleaner."

I smile, watching a particularly thick gob of de-ice fluid slowly ooze down the outside of the heated windows in front of me.

"So what *do* you think of the new unis?" Rob asks.

I run my fingers over my new midnight blue tie and across the tiny gold ALPA wings I've pinned halfway down. "I don't know." I lift up the bottom of the tie to inspect more closely its polyester design. "Not sure I like the stripes."

"Me, neither," he says, glancing down at his own tie's thin golden stripes. "Probably just need to get used to them."

"Yeah," I agree. "They'll likely grow on us . . . after a while."

There's no doubt, however, that the new, common uniform is a good thing; it's time for all of us to move on and let our past identities as Continental or United pilots be just that—parts of our pasts.

Rob looks to me. "So weird to see everyone dressed the same in the crewroom this morning, wasn't it?"

"For sure."

"Although I had to laugh at the couple guys I saw wearing their old pilot wings."

I chuckle. "You mean the one-man warriors?"

Rob nods.

"I noticed a few of them today, too," I say, glancing to my left breast, where my new, art deco-ish wings are pinned. "Sooner or later, I hope they realize their efforts are better served trying to shape the change of our company rather than resisting it."

Rob rolls his eyes. "Don't bet on it."

With nothing for Rob and me to do until the de-icing crew finishes its work, we wait patiently, watching the snowplows scurrying around the ramp, shoving churning piles of snow into any unused corner they can find. But the snow is falling at such a frantic pace that the plows barely clear a path before it's covered again.

"This place is a mess," Rob says. "Glad we're heading to Cancun."

"You can say that again," I say while pulling my tiny maroon logbook from my shirt pocket. I flip past entries for Newark, Fort Lauderdale, Cleveland, and Baltimore before finding a blank page to record the flights for this trip. I've barely finished writing Rob's name into the ledger before a voice comes over the radio.

"Iceman to flight deck. Your de-icing is complete. One hundred percent type one and four applied. Application of type four began at thirteen-twenty zulu," or 7:20 AM in Chicago—the start time we will use for determining the end of the de-ice fluid's effectiveness.

"Roger that," I reply over the radio, scribbling furiously to record the info, especially the de-ice start time, on the paper I clipped to my control wheel. "Thanks for your help."

"No problem," he says.

And now the snail's-paced race to the runway begins, with each second bringing us closer to the de-ice fluid's holdover time. We push back from the gate, start our engines, and complete the *After Start* checklist. When the ground crew is safely away from the aircraft, I flash my taxi light and return the marshaller's salute.

"Call for taxi," I instruct. I take a deep breath, knowing the most stressful time of our entire flight—and perhaps of my entire captaincy thus far—will come next. This is the first time I've taxied with more than a trace amount of snow, and of course, it's now a full-blown blizzard.

Rob keys his mic to request taxi instructions from ground control.

"United Eleven-Ninety-Eight, O'Hare Ground," the controller responds. "Taxi to Runway Nine Right via Bravo, Alpha Seven, Juliet."

Rob reads back the clearance and then says to me, "Clear right."

I twist to look out my windows. "Clear left."

I reach up and twist the control knob for my windshield wiper.

The wiper swipes across the glass, flinging de-ice fluid from the surface. *Here we go,* I think, taking a deep breath as I push the throttles forward, quickly realizing I need far more thrust than normal to get the jet moving with the snow. I tweak the throttles forward a bit more. The resulting thrust of our engines causes a rooster tail of powder to rise up behind us. The jet's tires begin to roll, and as they compress the snow, I hear a crunching sound that's similar to the one my boots make when I walk on Chicago's snow-covered sidewalks.

Soon, we exit the ramp area, and I'm amazed by how different O'Hare looks. All I see is white. It obscures nearly all the visual references I usually rely upon for taxiing around the complex airport. It restricts my forward visibility no differently than a thick fog. It covers the taxiways and hides their yellow centerline stripes, which I now realize have been extremely helpful for guiding me and ensuring I keep the big jet's tires on the pavement. White even shrouds the yellow and black taxiway name signs, making it much more difficult to determine precisely which taxiway is which. And without those visual cues, I have to rely solely upon the sea of tiny blue taxiway edge lights to determine where the taxiways actually are. But with O'Hare's maze of curved and intersecting taxiways, and with the snow falling so rapidly that the tracks from preceding jets are quickly covered up, I find it extremely difficult to decipher which blue lights are the ones I'm supposed to taxi between. And if I make the wrong decision, I'll likely taxi straight into the now-frozen grass.

For a split second, a cascade of make-believe images flash through my mind. First, it's a CNN Breaking News banner with the headline "United Jet Slides Off Chicago Taxiway" plastered across the bottom of the TV screen. Then Wolf Blitzer narrates over the snowy video of our jet, its nose wheel sunken into the frozen earth and its perimeter surrounded by several fire trucks with flashing lights. In the corner of the screen, there's a bus gathering up passengers who are evacuating via mobile stairs. Then come screenshots of tweets and Instagram photos posted by several passengers. I envision Jen and my parents watching the coverage as I step off the plane on national TV, and I picture the surreal way my name stands out to my friends as they read the front page of tomorrow's *USA Today*. Finally, I picture a drab conference room in the Willis Tower where Rob and I sit patiently, sipping from cups of stale coffee while we wait for a slew of United management pilots and safety experts, our ALPA representatives, and the government's FAA investigators to file in so our post-incident investigation can begin.

My stomach churns. Thankfully, the distressing images drift away as quickly as they had appeared. But they have done their job to reinforce that it's incredibly important for me to get this right.

"Rob," I say, interrupting his study of the O'Hare airport diagram beside him, "Please keep me honest on this taxi, okay?"

He looks over and nods. "You bet, Korry." Then he turns back to his chart. "Bravo looks to be the second left turn."

"Agreed," I say, creeping forward. We pass over the compacted tracks of preceding jets on intersecting taxiways, causing the 737's struts to creek and moan as they accommodate the bumps. "Starting the turn now."

"Yep," Rob confirms. "This is Bravo."

With my left hand, I pull the tiller backwards to start the left turn. Almost immediately, I feel the nose wheel start to skid. Adrenaline floods my veins. I straighten the tiller and tap the brakes to correct the understeer, quickly regaining traction. But the tiny slip startles me. I exhale and remind myself that in these conditions, a slow taxi isn't slow enough—especially during a turn.

Take a deep breath, Korry, and stay controlled, I tell myself. *Just a few more turns and you'll be at the runway's end.*

Two sharp turns, to be exact. And I'm relieved when, after completing them, our takeoff runway comes into view beyond the three airplanes ahead of us. I reference the time I wrote on the piece of paper clipped to my control wheel before comparing it with the time on our dashboard's clock. "Looking good on the holdover time," I say to Rob, referring to the de-ice fluid's time limit.

He leans forward to peer out the front windows. "Still nothing sticking on the nose."

"Excellent," I say. "It's all coming together."

A few moments later, I call for the *Before Takeoff* checklist. Rob picks up the microphone to tell the flight attendants to be seated. As the plane ahead of us takes off, we watch its thrust launch dusty plumes of snow dozens of yards behind it. And as the plane rotates toward the end of the runway, the blowing snow turns into opposing swirls, evidence of the invisible wake created by the air sliding over the jet's wings.

"United Eleven-Ninety-Eight, Runway Nine-Right, line up and wait."

Rob reads back the tower controller's clearance, and we both reach up to the overhead panel to turn on a variety of external lights. I creep forward onto the runway, making one final 90-degree right turn to swing the nose around to align with the runway's centerline. I'm comforted to see the runway almost entirely cleared of snow, but I can't shake the thought of how dicey a rejected takeoff could become. Then again, that's why we have adjusted our performance figures to account for any possible reduced traction, and that's why our preferred method for handling most issues today is to take off, address the issue in the air, and return for landing. That way the full length of the runway is at our disposal, instead of an ever-shortening part of it, as would be the case for getting stopped during a high-speed rejected takeoff.

"United Eleven-Ninety-Eight, Runway Nine-Right, cleared for takeoff. Fly runway heading."

Rob reads back the clearance.

I look to my right. "Well?"

Rob looks to me. "Let's get the hell out of here."

I flip on the landing lights, start the clock for our elapsed flight time, and push the throttles up to full thrust. The engines whine mightily, and the jet pushes against our backs as it begins to accelerate. My heart pounds as I grip the control wheel and the throttles. Faster and faster we go, the falling snow starting to look as if it's moving horizontal with the ground, zipping past us in a constant blur of white specs.

"One-hundred knots," Rob announces. And as if right on cue, small amounts of the orange de-ice fluid starts dripping onto my left forearm as the aircraft's pressurization squeezes it from the window's seams. "Vee-one," Rob calls, triggering me to move my right hand away from the thrust levers. "Rotate."

I pull back on the control wheel, and the nose hops off the ground. Moments later, the runway falls away beneath us—just as Kurt had described at my captain's party.

Click!

"Positive rate, gear up," I say.

I steal a quick glance out my window as Rob raises the gear lever. Snow covers everything around us—highways, houses, and everything in between. Seconds later, we slip into the thick clouds, bopping around as the wind pushes against the jet. It takes only a few minutes for us to climb above the blizzard into clear blue skies where brilliant sunshine reigns supreme.

Three hours later, we are gliding above warm turquoise waters surrounding the Yucatan peninsula's coastline. Cancun's famous lagoon is visible in the distance, as are the many hotels peppering its eastern and northern shores. Our approach, however, keeps us far away from the trendy resorts, instead putting us above thick forests, a handful of dirt roads, and evidence of the real Cancun—pockets of dense shantytowns. I wonder how many tourists enjoying the luxurious accommodations on the coast will venture inland to see the real Cancun. My hunch is not many.

Rob and I are among those who do not, although our regular travels throughout United's international network provide plenty of opportunities for us to witness firsthand the abject poverty and broken-down infrastructure that so often plague the developing cities frequented by business, not leisure, travelers. Today, however, we will enjoy luxurious accommodations after landing, clearing customs and immigration, and taking our prearranged transportation to the opulent Marriott Casa Magna hotel on the beach.

Once inside my spacious room, I hang my uniform and long black winter coat in the closet before changing into shorts and a t-shirt. I pull back the translucent draperies covering the sliding glass door that opens onto a large fifth-floor balcony. I step out and admire the view overlooking the hotel's deep blue pool and the ocean waves cascading on the beach. I turn around and snap a selfie with the view of the tropical paradise in the background. Then, in an admittedly risky move, I text it to Jen with the caption:

ME: *Cancun would be great if only it weren't so hot. Wish you were here.*

Moments later, Jen's reply pops up on my phone.

JEN: *Gotta run. Locksmith is here. Lol.*

I deserve her lighthearted rejoinder. But she needn't worry; I soon get my karmic payback.

Two days after my relaxing Cancun layover with Rob, one of United's crew schedulers calls to inform me that he's tagged an extra "turn" to and from Jacksonville, Florida, onto the end of my trip. It is part of the crew schedulers' efforts to solve the massive logistical puzzle created by the preceding blizzard that had left many pilots out of position for their flights.

As an on-call "reserve" pilot, I'm not surprised by the reassignment. I am, however, disappointed that the dinner reservation Jen has made for us at a trendy restaurant in our neighborhood needs to be rescheduled. But such is life on reserve; plans are always subject to change. And as my seniority improves, so will my schedule's predictability. In the meantime, we must go with the flow. And thankfully, Jen is up for the ride.

Now, five hours after receiving that call, I'm descending through dark skies toward Chicago when the small printer at the back of the 737's center console begins humming and pulsing rhythmically as it scrolls off the latest O'Hare weather report, breaking my gaze at the orange city lights far ahead in the distance.

"Excuse my reach," says Mike, the 37-year-old first officer who has also been added onto the turn. He reaches back to grab the shiny printer paper, grazing the knee of Sam, our flight deck jumpseater, in the process. Of course, Sam takes no offense; the 737 isn't known for having a spacious cockpit, and with Sam—or anyone, for that matter—occupying the fold-down flight deck jumpseat, what extra space there is becomes non-existent.

Mike tears off the weather report. Then he maneuvers the eyeball light above his seat to cast a wide beam onto his control wheel. "Let's see," he says, folding the printout in half. "O'Hare information Sierra." He makes several more meticulous folds, slowly transforming the large printout into a tight piece of flight deck origami, where only the most crucial weather information is still visible. "Winds one-eight-zero at twenty-nine, gusting to thirty-nine. Clear skies—"

"Wait," I interrupt, turning sharply toward Mike. "Did you say thirty-nine knots?"

Mike smiles mischievously. "Sure did. That ought to be fun for you."

My eyes grow wide. "Seriously."

He smiles slyly again. "Especially since they're landing on the Two-Sevens."

"Even better," I moan.

Landing on 27L or 27R with the reported winds out of the south amounts to one of the most difficult landing configurations pilots can face: a stiff, direct, and gusty crosswind, just a few knots away from the demonstrated crosswind limits of the 737.

"Arriving from this direction, I'd guess Two-Seven-Left," Mike suggests.

"I agree. Let's set up for that, and when you're ready, I'll give you a quick brief."

The two of us flip switches and tune navigation instruments in preparation for the approach. With every button I press and every knob I turn, I feel my adrenaline ratcheting up as I contemplate the O'Hare winds. There will be little room for error on this approach.

Time to bring your A-game, Korry, I think.

Once Mike and I are set up, I talk him through my plan for the approach, landing, and taxi in. In addition to our usual items, we review the 737's maximum crosswind limits that, if exceeded, will require us to abandon the approach and go around. I also ask Mike to calculate our landing distance based on slippery runway conditions, even though such conditions aren't presently reported at O'Hare. I just suspect we may find snow from the preceding blizzard drifting across the runway, which might reduce our traction upon landing.

"Given the conditions, Mike, I want us to be ready for anything."

"Totally agree," he says.

"And that includes a go-around if you don't like how something looks, including my flying. Just say the words, and we'll go around. No questions asked."

"Thanks, Korry."

Briefing complete, we run through another checklist. Then the three of us sit quietly, staring out the front windows toward the big black hole of Lake Michigan ahead of us.

I glance over my right shoulder toward Sam. The overhead panel's backlighting casts a dim light over his button-down shirt and khakis, and I notice him fidgeting aimlessly with his shoulder straps. "You good, Sam?"

He stares straight ahead, deep in thought, missing my question.

"Sam?" I ask again.

He still doesn't hear me. Perhaps the discussion Mike and I just had about the approach's challenges is weighing heavily on his mind. After all, most jumpseaters are fellow pilots who are well-accustomed to seeing tough approaches in person. But Sam is not a pilot; he's a flight dispatcher for United on one of his required annual observation flights. Normally, he plans flights *around* the weather from the comfort of his high-tech workstation at United's Network Operations Center on the 27th floor. Now, strapped into the jumpseat, he'll get to see what it's like to actually fly *through* it.

"Sam?" I ask once more.

"Yes?" he asks, as though I've jolted him away from his thoughts.

"You good?"

He shifts again in his seat. "Yeah. All good."

I nod slowly, not fully believing him. "Great." Then I turn around to review the arrival chart again. *I'm guessing this isn't what he had expected when he picked up what he had called our "little Jax turn."* It is, however, an excellent eye-opener into our world.

The bumps begin as soon as we're below 15,000 feet. They start as gentle pulses, like the jet is skimming across small ripples on a lake. I look up at the seatbelt sign and see it's already on. But as the pulses of choppy air grow more pronounced, I decide it's wise for the flight attendants to take their seats, too. I tell Mike my plan as I pick up the interphone's handset from beside the printer.

"Great idea," Mike agrees. "It's only gonna get worse."

I press the flight attendant call button. Jess answers from the aft galley. I pass along to her the reports of moderate turbulence we have received from air traffic control and suggest that her team members take their seats.

"Thanks for the heads up," she says. "Can you tell the passengers?"

"Sure thing," I reply.

I replace the handset in its cradle and then pick up the handheld PA microphone. "Folks, from the flight deck, this is Captain Franke." My words interrupt the plane's entertainment system, commanding the attention of most passengers. "I suspect you've noticed we're now flying through a little bumpy air." It's perhaps the understatement of the evening. "Unfortunately, I expect the bumps to stay with us all the way to landing. In fact, there's a good chance they may even intensify." This is probably the last thing a nervous traveler wants to hear. "Because of this, I've asked the flight attendants to be seated for landing at this time." It's the prudent thing to do, but I can almost feel the anxiety of nervous travelers skyrocketing as the words leave my mouth. After all, I know passengers often gauge the seriousness of a situation by the actions and mannerisms of the flight attendants. My asking the crew to be seated earlier than usual undoubtedly causes some concern in the minds of these nervous travelers. I have to say something to reassure them so they can understand that this represents only an abundance of caution, not an indication of impending danger. "Now, I know a lot of you are experienced flyers who understand turbulence is just a nuisance, not something to fear. But I also suspect at least a few of you aren't quite as at ease with the bumps." Statistically, it's almost a quarter of all travelers. "If that's you, I encourage you to think of the bumps as something that adds a few white caps to your coffee or makes completing your Sudoku puzzle a bit more challenging. They're the potholes on a country road, while our flexing wings are the shock absorbers trying to smooth out the ride." I wonder if my analogies are helping at all. "More than anything, I hope you will take comfort knowing that this airplane is designed to handle bumps of far greater intensity than any one of us—myself included—would ever want to experience." I glance toward Sam and notice he's listening intently to my announcement. "So please bear with us, and in about fifteen minutes, we'll be safely on the ground. Thank you."

I hang up the hand mic and tell Mike I'm back.

"No changes," he says. "We're in L-NAV and V-NAV, out of twelve thousand, descending to eleven. You have the aircraft."

"L-NAV, V-NAV, twelve for eleven. I have the aircraft," I confirm.

With that, we crest over Lake Michigan's southern coastline, the lights of Gary and Chicago ringing the big black hole. And the lower we get, the more the bumps intensify.

"United Twelve-Hundred, descend to seven-thousand feet," the air traffic controller instructs. "Expect Runway Two-Seven-Left."

Mike reads back the clearance.

Descending through 10,000 feet, the bumps reach full force. It feels like the wind is slamming into the side of the jet. It shoves against our big tail, jolting us from side to side, jerking the control wheel left and right as the autopilot fights to keep the wings level.

"Good lord," I say to Mike, my hands hovering atop the controls, ready to take over from the automation at a moment's notice. "I'd definitely call that constant moderate chop."

An even stronger jolt slams into us. "Maybe more," Mike jokes.

I smile, but notice Sam isn't amused.

Mike reaches up to the cabin temperature control knobs on the overhead panel and tweaks them lower, knowing the bumps can make some passengers feel nauseous, especially toward the back of the plane where the ride is always worst.

A few moments later, Mike says, "I've got two good IDs," referring to the identifiers for the navigation aids that will guide us to runway 27L.

"Excellent. *Approach* checklist, please."

Mike grabs the laminated card and runs through the checklist's items. Meanwhile, the bumps continue unabated. The turbulence bops us around, at times thrusting us hard against our snug seatbelts and shoulder harnesses. Mike watches me as I monkey with the vertical positioning of my seat. "Just can't seem to get comfortable tonight," I say to him. And in my head, I know the truth is it isn't because of my seat.

Mike grins. "Look at you, already making excuses for your landing."

I chuckle, appreciating Mike's levity. But once again, Sam does not. He's gripping his legs, tense from the bumps, trying to convey that he's at ease when he's clearly not.

"United Twelve-Hundred, turn left to three-zero-zero," the controller instructs. "Maintain four thousand until established. Cleared for the I-L-S Runway Two-Seven-Left."

"Three-zero-zero, four-thousand until established, cleared for the I-L-S Two-Seven-Left, United Twelve-Hundred," Mike replies.

I spin the autopilot's heading knob and press the button to link the plane up with the electronic glideslope. "Approach is armed."

The plane banks hard to the left to line up with the runway, which extends in front of me in the distance, beyond the shoreline and downtown's skyscrapers. Steam trails move horizontally from the tops of many buildings, evidence of just how strong the winds are near the surface.

My heart races as we descend, mostly from excitement. Like most pilots, I love these types of challenges. I feel like a star quarterback, lining up for the big play at the end of an important game. Yes, the stakes are high. Yes, everyone is counting on me to get this right. Yes, it's the end of a long day. And yes, I definitely know the approach and landing won't be easy. But then, the most satisfying things rarely are. I know my limits and those of the airplane, and I'll respect those limits and abandon the approach if need be. But for now, there's only one thought in my head: *I want the ball.*

I take a few deep breaths as my fingers lightly grip the controls. *It's time to hike the ball and make the play.* I look to Mike and announce, "Autopilot and autothrottle are coming off." Three short sirens sound as I press the disconnect switches for both systems. The plane is now completely in my hands, and I feel every gust, every blast of wind trying to shove our craft around the dark sky.

When a particularly strong gust hits us, I hear the muffled *Woos!* coming from behind the cockpit door of what has to be a sizable number of passengers. I know many of them are gripping their armrests, eyes closed, nervous, and eager to be on the ground. It's humbling to think of the level of trust they are placing in Mike and me to get this right. But despite the pressure and the adrenaline racing through my veins, I am strangely calm. I'm in the zone, focused on the runway and the constant adjustments that are necessary to keep the plane on glidepath and on speed.

"Flaps ten," I call to Mike as the controller switches us to O'Hare tower frequency.

Mike moves the flap lever down another notch as he checks in with the Tower and receives our landing clearance. The drooping flaps cause the nose to rise, and I push forward on the control wheel to counteract the aerodynamic shift.

Gust after gust hits the plane, forcing me to make constant corrections. I grimace as I fight the elements, first to the left, then back to the right. Again and again. The same goes for the throttles in my right hand. I push and pull on them aggressively, commanding crescendos and decrescendos in the motors' symphonic whine as I chase after the jittery airspeed. All the while, I focus on keeping the jet moving directly for the runway. Like a rowboat trying to move across a swiftly flowing river, I angle the jet into the stiff southern wind. In fact, my "crab angle" is so substantial that I almost find myself looking out the first officer's front window to see the runway. It's a completely bizarre feeling, one I've rarely experienced outside the simulator. Thankfully, from several thousand feet above the ground, altitude provides options. But with each foot we descend, the margin for error slips away. And as it does, I feel my heart rate increasing.

"Gear down, flaps fifteen, landing checklist," I command.

Mike pulls the landing gear lever out and down before sliding the flap lever back another notch. Three green lights appear on the forward panel as the wheels thump down into place. Unfortunately, the extended wheels act like keels, catching the wind and causing the jolts of turbulence to grow even more pronounced.

Mike reads from the checklist. "Speed brake, armed. Gear, down and three green."

"Down, three green," I confirm. And after our speed decreases, I add, "Flaps thirty, set target."

Mike moves the flap lever to its final position for our flight. He watches the flap gauge's needle rotate. "Flaps thirty, green light," he says. "Landing checklist is complete."

"Thanks, Mike."

The flaps hang like barn doors below the wings, and the wind grabs hold, shoving us with unrelenting energy. I hear more *Woos!* from the cabin.

"One-thousand," Mike calls, indicating we are closer to the ground than the tops of the downtown skyscrapers.

"Set missed approach altitude," I reply. Then to myself, I think, *You're almost there, Korry. Stay focused. You've got this.*

Mike sets 4,000 feet in the autopilot's altitude window. "Missed approach altitude is set."

My eyes dart between the altimeter—900 feet now—and the runway, which seems to shuffle near the right edge of my front window. Now the airspeed. *Three knots fast.* I tweak the throttles back a touch. Another gust sends the airspeed racing. I pull back on the throttles. The engine noise quiets. Back to the altimeter—800 now. I feel the gust suddenly die away, so I push the throttles forward to catch the speed from bleeding off too much. Tweaking. Adjusting. Fighting.

A momentary calm settles on us for a moment as we pass through 700 feet above the ground. I peek out of the corner of my right eye and find Mike staring stoically ahead. "You okay with this?" I ask.

He looks to me and nods. "Looking good, Korry."

600 feet.

"The moment you're not, just say the word, okay? No questions asked."

"You bet," Mike says.

I look to Sam; his face is white.

500 feet.

We skitter down the glidepath, bouncing and shifting in the gusty winds. Like the quarterback in the pocket, I'm focused and intense as we descend through 400 feet, resisting the pressure from the wind and keeping my vision downfield toward my endzone—the runway that looms larger and larger with each passing second.

300.

I twist the controls and push the throttles, listening to the moan of the engines and the *Woos!* of the passengers.

200 feet.

My chest thumps. *123 people are counting on you, Korry! You've gotta get this right!*

Crossing the airport's fence, the raging river of wind becomes apparent as I notice dry snow drifting eerily across the runway's dark pavement, churning like a rapid's frothy top.

"One hundred," Mike announces, our landing lights now brightly illuminating the runway's threshold.

Left and right. Left and right. Power in and power out. Adjusting. Shifting. Battling the winds all the way to the ground. The room for error is gone.

Almost there, Korry!! Stick with it!!

"Fifty," the airplane's computerized voice proclaims. We are over the runway and still heavily crabbed into the wind.

"Forty…thirty…twenty…"

I pull back on the control wheel to begin my flare. Simultaneously, I push hard onto the right rudder pedal, twisting the airplane's nose into alignment with the runway. To keep us from drifting off the runway with the wind, I turn the control wheel sharply left.

Don't worry about a greaser, Korry. Just get this bird on the ground!!

"Ten…"

I'm fully into the flare, still jostling the controls, still fighting the gusty winds to keep the jet heading straight ahead. The plane floats down the runway, a few feet off the pavement.

Come on!! I plead. *Get on the ground!!*

The controls are nearly to their stops, indicating our craft can't handle much more crosswind. I need the plane to touch down right now or else I'll have to go around. *THIS* is the limit.

Get on there!! I exclaim to myself, grimacing as I battle the elements.

Then I feel a *THUD!!* as the left wheel touches down! Then another *THUD!!* as the right wheel meets the pavement.

YES!!! I think.

I push the control wheel forward, lowering the nose wheel onto the runway with another firm *THUD!!* It shimmies a bit before aligning perfectly with the dashed white centerline. We are down!

The autobrakes grab, jerking our heads forward. I hear the speed brake lever whirl backwards automatically, commanding the metal panels to pop up on top of the wings to help kill our lift and slow us down. My right hand's second and third fingers pull up on the reverse thrust levers, roaring the engines back to life. The whole time, my feet dance upon the rudder pedals while I push the control wheel full forward to ensure the nose stays firmly planted on the ground.

"Eighty knots," Mike calls.

The runway seems to have plenty of grip, but there's no telling how slick the taxiways might be. So I slow the plane to ten knots—barely faster than a slow jog—before I start to leave the runway's centerline.

"United Twelve-Hundred, turn left at Alpha One," the tower controller radios. "Give way to the regional jet moving right-to-left on Alpha, then continue with me to the north port."

Mike reads back the clearance, and I press the brakes to bring the plane to a complete stop while we wait for the regional jet to pass. My legs quiver from the adrenaline pumping through my muscles.

What a rush! I think.

Behind the cockpit door, I hear clapping from relieved passengers who are thankful to be on the ground. A huge smile creeps across my face. Part of me wants to pump my arm like Tiger Woods after sinking a putt to win the Masters.

Now THAT'S what flying is all about! I think. It had been challenging, but not overwhelming. Near the limits, but never beyond them. We had walked right up to the line in order to get the job done. But that's what professionals are paid to do, and on this day, we have definitely earned our wages.

"Great job!" Mike says. "Craziest approach I've seen in quite a while." And as I notice the color slowly returning to Sam's face, I'm certain he wholeheartedly agrees…at least with the last part.

After parking at the gate and running our final checklists, I stand in the flight deck doorway, saying goodbye to exiting passengers. As a man in a suit exits, he offers, "Great job." Another asks, "Wasn't that fun?" before adding, "Thanks for getting us here safely."

It's a steady stream of compliments from the exiting passengers. The compliments are admittedly nice to hear, particularly since I feel like the quarterback who has made the big play when the game was on the line. But as I see the relieved looks on so many of their faces, including a woman guiding her two young children who says nothing but who holds my gaze for longer than is comfortable, almost like she is trying to size me up, I start to wonder if I have perhaps misinterpreted the reason for the compliments. Are the passengers complimenting me for making the key play in the big game? Or is it possible they are complimenting me for not throwing an interception?

I mull these questions on the "L" train heading home. Yes, professionals are always expected to make big plays when the pressure is on, whether in the NFL, the airlines, or any other field. They're expected to walk the fine line between pushing enough and pushing too hard. But who's really the better quarterback? The one who launches the Hail Mary pass and gets lucky when a receiver in the end zone hauls it in for the win, or the one who sees the pressure coming, realizes the play isn't coming together, and is disciplined enough to throw the ball out of bounds so the team can play another down?

With the stakes so high for me as an airline captain, lucky isn't good enough; lucky is dangerous. Success depends on discipline, on maintaining focus under pressure, and on never losing sight of the risks involved. Of course, nothing is completely safe, and trying to eliminate all risks or to operate without any risks isn't just impractical; it's impossible. The best quarterbacks understand the key is preserving the right balance between pushing forward and pulling back. And as I ride the train home, thinking about the difficult approach and landing at O'Hare, I start to wonder if maybe one of the most important—and yet underrated—leadership skills is the ability to effectively manage the downside risk.

Thankfully, several off days and a week of vacation provide me at least a short reprieve from any potential encounters with that fine line again. Kurt, however, isn't so fortunate. And as he ping-pongs around the country on a four-day trip, he lands in Chicago as the second of back-to-back blizzards slams O'Hare. With his outbound flight canceled, he calls to tell me he's unexpectedly stranded in Chicago.

"So what are the schedulers telling you?" I ask.

"To hunker down," Kurt says. "Sounds like it's going to be at least one day—maybe longer—until they figure out how to get me back to Houston. O'Hare is in full-on meltdown mode right now."

"So does that mean you're free for dinner tonight?"

"Dinner…breakfast…lunch. I'll be around," Kurt jokes.

"Great. Jen and I will come pick you up in, say, an hour from now? We can show you our new digs and then walk somewhere close by for dinner."

"It better be really close," Kurt says. "I didn't bring much for a winter coat."

"No worries," I assure him. "I know just the spot."

Chicago feels abandoned as Kurt, Jen, and I trudge single-file through the blizzard's raging winds, biting cold, and fourteen inches (and counting) of freshly fallen snow. When a particularly strong gust hits me, I look skyward, thankful I'm battling this storm with my feet planted firmly on the ground instead of dancing atop the rudder pedals like they were during last week's tough approach to O'Hare.

The howling wind also makes it difficult to understand what Kurt is shouting at the top of his lungs from behind me. "What did you say??" I shout back over my shoulder.

"I said, 'I thought you said this place was close!!'"

"It is!!" I holler back. "Just two more blocks!!"

"Well, it feels like we're crossing Antarctica!!"

"Welcome to Chicago, Kurt," Jen mumbles through the scarf covering her face.

Just then, a gust rips across our frozen faces, carrying flecks of snow that cut like razor blades across our cheeks. In my head, I start reciting the mantra that has helped me get through previous Chicago winters: *I love Chicago in the summertime. I love Chicago in the summertime. I love Chicago in the summertime.* But with the actual temperature -20º F and the wind chill approaching -45º F, even my mantra can't change the reality, which is that the weather simply sucks.

Mercifully, we reach the Haymarket Pub and Brewery a few minutes later, stomping our feet to remove the snow from our shoes as we push through the restaurant's revolving door.

Kurt lets out a sigh as he pulls his much-too-small beanie off his head. "Explain to me again why you both want to live here?"

Normally I'd expound about Chicago's restaurants, arts, lakefront, and sports. But given the conditions outside, all I can muster is, "Sometimes, Kurt, I really don't know."

A hostess guides us to the dining room, where we have our pick of any table we want. We settle in and order a round of beers, burgers, and pretzel bites. And once our pint glasses arrive, I raise mine, offering, "It's good to see you, Kurt. Cheers!" The three of us clink our glasses together.

"It's good to see you both, too," he says before looking to Jen. "Although I have to ask: How the hell did you train for your marathon in this weather?"

Jen laughs. "Well, it wasn't ideal."

"Tell him how you got hit by the wave," I suggest.

"You what?" Kurt asks.

Jen nods sheepishly. "It's true."

"Kurt, I couldn't stop laughing when she walked back into the apartment looking like a giant icicle from her eyebrows to her shoelaces."

Jen rolls her eyes. "He's exaggerating a bit."

"But not too much," I add as our waitress drops off the basket of pretzel bites.

"Well, better you than me," Kurt says before sipping his beer. "Hopefully all that effort was worth it."

"It definitely was," Jen says. "They're such great events. So energizing."

I reach for a pretzel bite. "Kurt, I almost liked watching more than running. It was surprisingly emotional for me."

"How so?" he asks as I dip the warm pretzel in its accompanying cheese sauce and pop it in my mouth.

"Well for starters," I say, still chewing, "I knew how hard Jen had worked to prepare for the race. So it was awesome to be there to cheer her on as she climbed her own personal mountain." I sip my beer to wash down the pretzel. "But then you watch this endless river of runners go by. Thirty-thousand or so. And you realize each one of them is climbing their own mountain, too. Maybe it's to prove they can finish the twenty-six-miles without keeling over."

"Which is a hell of an accomplishment in its own right," Kurt adds.

"For sure," I agree. Then continuing where I left off, I say, "Others run in support of beating diabetes or M.S."

"Or to prove those ailments can't keep them down," Jen interjects.

"But all of them," I continue, "including Jen, were running for something." I notice Jen nodding. "Out there putting one foot in front of the next, racing toward a finish line that will undoubtedly drive them to pursue even bigger goals in their lives. And it's just inspiring to see."

Kurt nods contemplatively.

"Tell him about the shirts," Jen says, popping another pretzel bite. "Like the sixty-something man whose said, 'Beat cancer. Double knee replacement. Still running.'"

Kurt smiles.

"The one that really got me," I say," was this young guy, maybe thirty, wearing a Marine Corps shirt and carrying this huge U.S. flag… while he's running on a prosthetic blade for one of his legs."

"Oh, wow," Kurt says.

But the truth is, running isn't really even the right word. Gliding is more like it. Effortless and confident. Proof for everyone to see that nothing, not war or a lost limb, can keep him down. An unstoppable force. "Really puts things in perspective, you know?"

"For sure," he says.

I sip my beer again and recount watching Jen cross the finish line. "You should have heard that crowd." I look toward Jen. "Or the joy in Jen's voice after she got her medal." Jen smiles. "It was an incredible moment to be a part of." She reaches over and squeezes my hand.

"That's very cool," Kurt says. He takes another sip of his beer. "You visit Daytona while you were there?"

"Actually, we did. First time back since we met at the conference in 2006."

"Guessing it's changed a lot since then."

"Oh, my, Kurt," I say. "It's totally different. So much construction." The waitress drops off our thick burgers, French fries, and sweet potato tots. "Speaking of Embry-Riddle, did you hear Vishal just got hired by United?"

"Oh, really?" Kurt asks. "That's great news."

I pick up my burger. "Yes, it is. Long overdue, if you ask me."

"Agreed," Kurt says.

"Talk about someone whose path would have been a lot different if September 11 hadn't happened."

"How's that?" Jen asks, picking up her burger.

"Well," I say, "Vish had been on the exact same track as Kurt, Dianna, Paul, and me. We were RAs together. We flight-trained together. And Paul, Dianna, and I had even interned together with Vishal at Atlantic Coast Airlines." I take a bite, relishing how the creaminess of the avocado perfectly contrasts with the crisp bacon and savory beef. I cover my mouth as I start to talk. "But Vish was a Kenyan citizen—at least he was until recently when he gained his U.S. citizenship." I finish chewing and swallow. "And some sort of regulation issued after September 11 restricted non-U.S. citizens from training in advanced simulators for large airplanes. So even though

Vish is a fantastic pilot and an all-around great guy, the stroke of a pen upended his career plan and left him questioning whether his dream of becoming a U.S. airline pilot was actually viable anymore."

"That's crazy," Jen says.

"I think he even thought about leaving Riddle to become a doctor at one point."

"Isn't that why he ended up doing charter?" Kurt asks. "Because those planes were beneath the restriction's weight limit?"

"Believe so," I say, popping a sweet potato tot into my mouth.

"Piaggio P-180s, right?" Kurt asks.

"Yep," I say, turning to Jen as I finish my bite. "It's like the Italian sports car of turboprops. Super fast with killer looks. Like a sleek catfish with pusher props on the back."

"Interesting," she says, unimpressed.

"He's flown all over in that thing," I continue. "Met a ton of interesting people, too. Business leaders and celebrities."

"That's cool," Jen says.

"Really made a name for himself there when one of his planes experienced a major mechanical problem in flight. His leadership as the flight's captain helped save the plane."

"That's right," Kurt says. "I remember that now. Isn't that how he ended up instructing in the Piaggio simulator?"

"Something like that," I reply.

"A little ironic, isn't it?" Kurt asks.

"Just a bit," I say with a chuckle. "Anyway, I'm glad he stuck with aviation, because the rule changed and now he's here doing what he's always wanted to do. Just can't believe it took him so long to jump through all the hoops."

"Crazy," Kurt says.

"I mean, we've got almost eight years of seniority on him, and all of us started from basically the same place."

"That's the airlines for you," Kurt says. "Dianna's husband is gonna be in the same spot."

"Yeah, but Mark knew about the ten-year service commitment for Air Force pilots before he willingly chose to walk through that door. Vish didn't have that choice."

"That's true," Kurt says.

"And if my vision had been better, I would have made the same tradeoff to fly a fighter. I mean, can you even imagine how fun that must be?"

"Not even a little."

We both laugh. "So here's the thing, Kurt. You, me, Dianna, Mark, and Paul—we're all doing what we wanted to do, when we wanted to do it. To get here, we needed certain doors to open, and they actually opened for us. But that wasn't the case for Vish. And it wasn't the case for the furloughees I'm now flying with all the time. And I'm just trying to reconcile why our doors opened while theirs did not."

Jen jumps in. "Are you sure their doors didn't open? Or were they perhaps just different doors?"

"Well, I'm sure Vish would have chosen to be here years ago. And I doubt many of the furloughees actually chose to be furloughed."

"I'm not saying they chose it," Jen says. "I'm suggesting maybe those were the doors they needed to walk through for some reason."

"I'm not sure I'm following you," I say, scrunching my face.

Jen leans forward, shifting in her seat. "Think about all the things you just said Vish got to experience at his company. If he had gone straight to the airlines, he wouldn't have met those people or flown to those places or had those opportunities."

"Okay," I say.

"And you just said you would have made the same choice as Mark if you could have, because you wanted to be a fighter pilot. That's why you were applying to the Naval Academy. But your eyesight didn't meet the Navy's standards at the time, so that door never opened."

"I'm still not tracking with you," I say.

"What I'm saying is, maybe the Navy wasn't the right door for you to begin with. Maybe it was just a door that needed to stay open long enough so you could meet the academy guy—the one who recommended Embry-Riddle to you. And then the Navy door needed to close so you would walk down the hallway and find the Embry-Riddle door—the airline door—the door that led you here."

I nod my head, contemplating Jen's suggestion.

"She may have a point," Kurt says. "I've never thought about it like that."

"And let's be honest," Jen says, smiling from ear to ear. "The best part about that door was that it led you to me!"

I roll my eyes as I take a drink.

"Whatever, dude," Jen says. "You know you can't even begin to imagine your life without me in it!"

Kurt and I laugh. "Yeeessss," I say. "Life without Jen. That would be…" I pause, making a smug grin as I decide what to say next.

"You better choose your next word carefully, bucko," Jen says.

"Terrible. It would have been absolutely terrible."

Jen nods in agreement. "I know," she says. "So be thankful about that, okay?"

"Mmhmm," I mumble, as my mind wanders off for a moment, imagining what my life would have looked like if I had gone into the Navy. Perhaps I would have still met Jen, just under different circumstances. Then again, perhaps my life would have looked completely different. I wonder which people would have been major players in that life. Where would that path have led me? It's like the movie *Sliding Doors*, where one seemingly insignificant moment changes the complete trajectory of a life. For a disciplined planner like me, the randomness is slightly terrifying to consider.

"Well, that's great about Vish," Kurt says, breaking me out of my thoughts. "Glad he finally made it here. And I'm glad we've had the chance to walk through the doors we have. They've led us to some awesome places so far."

"No doubt about it," I agree.

Kurt lifts his glass. "Here's to hoping they continue guiding us well."

"I'll toast to that," I say, raising my glass.

"And to the end of this G-D winter!" Jen exclaims.

Kurt laughs. "Now *that's* something we can all drink to!"

And the three of us clink our glasses together.

A few weeks later, my eyes open groggily as the early morning light streams around the sides of our bedroom's window shades. I roll over, noticing Jen heading into the bathroom. Given how late my trip through Boston; Washington, D.C.; and Aruba had finished the night before, I figure it's much too early to get up. So I roll back over and let the white noise of the fan at the foot of our bed ease me back to sleep.

It's close to a half-hour before the bathroom door opens again. And when it does, Jen scampers back to bed. She crawls under the sheets and nestles up close to me.

"Huuuusssssbbbaaannnnddd," she whispers in my ear.

"It's early, Wife," I moan as I roll toward her. "What are you doing up?"

"Can't I cuddle with my husband if I want to?"

"Of course you can," I say. "Just don't be mad if I sleep while you do it."

"But don't you want to talk with me?" Her voice is full of energy.

Later, I think. *After two cups of coffee.* But I know that's not the right answer. I rub my eyes before taking in a deep breath and stretching my arms way above my head. "What are you so excited about?" I ask, still not awake.

"Oh, you know. Nothing really." She gives me a little peck on the lips.

I smile. "Sure doesn't seem like nothing."

Jen turns to rest on her elbows. "Well, there is this one thing I'm excited about."

"And what is it?"

"It's silly, really. But…well…I'm excited I won't be changing the cat litter for the next nine months because…" She pauses for effect. My eyes open wide. I'm suddenly wide-awake. "Because I'm pregnant!!!"

"Really???" I ask.

"I am!!"

Jen giggles as I wrap my arms around her and give her a big kiss. "Wife, that's awesome!!"

"We're going to have a baby!!"

"Yeah, we are!!" I exclaim. "You're going to be a mom!!"

"And you're going to be a dad!!"

I give her another big hug and a kiss. Then the gravity of her words hits me, and I reiterate, "Holy crap!! I'm going to be a dad!!"

Jen bursts out laughing.

A million thoughts run through my head as we lie on our backs, staring at the ceiling, talking about what awaits us. I have no idea what being a dad will actually involve. I have no idea how drastically our lives will change. But I know there's no turning back. It's exciting and terrifying all at once. And I know it will change everything for us—as individuals and as a couple.

"It sort of feels like the end of a season, doesn't it?" Jen asks. "The season of just us."

"It does," I say, taking another deep breath.

I see her look my way. "It's gonna be a hard season to beat."

I smile. "Yes, it will," I say, thinking how this Chicago season has been the most exciting season of my life. "But we've got this."

"Yeah, we do."

The thought strikes me that life is just a collection of seasons. Some are happy, some are challenging, and some are in between the two. But each season has a beginning and an end. And while it's often difficult to spot the demarcation between two seasons, today it's easy to see.

I wonder what our next season will bring with it. I hope and pray it will be a happy one. But the only thing I know for certain is it will be impactful, one way or the other. And as I'll soon discover, the most impactful moments of all are the ones I can't see coming.

CHAPTER 12

The Red Sea

*"Success depends almost entirely on how
effectively you learn to manage the game's two
ultimate adversaries: the course and yourself."*
- Jack Nicklaus

Southeast of Boise, Idaho – March 2014

I know they're out there," my first officer Jeffrey says, referring to the Boise Mountains lining the valley into which we are descending. "But I can't see them."

"Me neither," I say.

The range's barren peaks have disappeared under the moonless sky. They do, however, show up on our terrain displays as various shades of green, yellow, and red. And with every foot we descend, the greens turn to yellows, and the yellows turn to reds.

Adding significantly to our flight's complexity, a thin, dense fog layer clings like a plush carpet to the valley floor. The fog had not been forecasted to arrive until much later in the evening, so it catches us somewhat by surprise. But it's here now, so as with any of Mother Nature's curveballs, we adapt.

The major problem with fog is that it restricts forward visibility at the surface to less than one-quarter mile, not even one loop around a high school's running track. That means we'll be lucky to see more than a handful of the evenly spaced white runway lights after we break out of the fog. And since we'll be covering nearly the length of a football field every second upon landing, such conditions will make it impossible for us to visually identify the airport in time to safely land the plane. Thankfully, in situations like this, *we* won't be landing the plane at all.

"Unless you have any questions, comments, or additions, Jeffrey, that completes the approach briefing for our autoland tonight."

"No questions, Korry. That all sounds good."

"Great. *Approach* checklist."

I'm actually quite excited for this approach. Autolands are always impressive to experience, but they're particularly impressive at night. Like most airline pilots, I've practiced countless autolands in the Box during training. Throughout my entire career, however, I've performed, at most, a handful of night autolands in the real world. And I've yet to do one from the left seat.

As the name suggests, autolands are where the autopilot lands the plane. Not surprisingly, a slew of restrictions and conditions must be met before such a landing can be performed, including special certifications for the pilots, the airplane, and even the runway itself. But once those i's are dotted and t's are crossed, an autoland is actually a very routine procedure, despite its requisite high level of precision and miniscule margin for error. In fact, the only real difference between an autoland and a normal approach is that the pilots search for reasons to abandon the approach instead of reasons to continue it.

Our absolute limit tonight is that we must see the runway by at least fifty feet off the ground. That's one-quarter the normal limit of a hand-flown approach and ten feet less than the distance between a pitcher's mound and home plate. Given the thickness of the fog, it's entirely possible we will dip below the treetops surrounding the airport before we actually see the runway. Of course, the airplane can land without any forward visibility at all, but such "zero-zero" landings make taxiing to the gate nearly impossible for the pilots. Thus the fifty-foot limit.

The air is calm as the air traffic controller vectors us around the night sky. In the quiet moments between instructions, I double- and triple-check that the flight instruments are set correctly. And as we fly past the city, which glows a muted orange through the fog, I catch myself wondering about Jen and the baby growing inside of her. But just as quickly as the thought arrives, I force myself to push it away and compartmentalize. On this night, my sole focus must be this approach.

The controller issues instructions for us to make several sharp right turns to join up with the electronic beam known as the Instrument Landing System, or ILS, which will guide us to the runway about ten miles away. As a diamond-shaped dot starts moving left to right along the bottom of our primary flight display, the airplane makes a final right turn to lock onto the horizontal portion of the ILS beam, the localizer.

"Loc capture," Jeffrey announces.

Soon, another diamond-shaped dot starts moving down the right side of our primary flight display, identifying the vertical portion of the ILS beam.

"Glide slope capture," Jeffrey calls as the autopilot locks onto the beam and starts a gradual descent to follow the dot all the way to the runway.

"Roger that. Gear down, landing checklist," I command as the approach controller switches us to Boise Tower.

Jeffrey switches radio frequencies and moves the gear handle down. As we slow to our final approach speed of 140 knots, or roughly 162 miles per hour, he extends the remaining flaps on schedule and completes the checklist.

"United Twelve-Eighty-Three," says the Boise air traffic controller, "you're cleared to land Runway One-Zero-Right."

"Cleared to land, One-Zero-Right, United Twelve-Eighty-Three," Jeffrey acknowledges.

My hands hover atop the controls, monitoring the autopilot as it jiggles the yoke and tweaks the throttles to track the ILS beam and remain on our final approach speed. The tip of my right hand's middle finger rests upon a small, scalloped button attached to the throttles that, if pressed, will command the airplane to go around. For now, all is going well, so I monitor the instruments and allow the autopilot to keep flying the approach. But I'm ready to press the go around button at a moment's notice. I take several deep breaths, watching the altimeter tick lower.

"One thousand," Jeffrey announces.

"Set missed approach altitude," I reply.

Jeffrey reaches up to the autopilot control panel and dials in 6,000 feet. We are still well above the clouds, which feels strange for this low height above the ground. Given how thin the fog layer is, however, we will likely be in the clouds for at most one minute—one extremely important minute.

Down the glidepath we slip, growing closer to our landing spot obscured beneath the clouds.

"Five hundred," Jeffrey states.

I look at my displays and announce, "Flare armed," after confirming the autopilot's landing mode has appropriately armed.

No go around yet, I think. *Everything is looking good. Continue.*

"Four hundred."

The air is still. We are focused. And our bright landing lights begin illuminating the top layer of the fog.

"Three hundred."

We slip in and out of the fog's wispy rounded edges. They zip past us in a blur, turning our windshields bright white and then black again like a slowly flickering strobe light. In and out. In and out. Black to white. Then less black and more white.

"Two hundred."

If this were a normal approach, this would be our limit. I'd likely see a long stretch of steady approach lights leading to the runway's threshold. I'd see buildings and cars and airplanes moving around on the approaching taxiways.

But not tonight. Now all I see is the solid white of the clouds that are moist and damp, evidenced by the minute water droplets forming along the rear edge of the windshield wiper at the bottom of my front window. The air is so smooth it feels like we are gliding on ice skates toward the runway I cannot yet see. I wiggle a touch in my seat as we head lower, wrapping my fingers tightly around the control wheel and throttles, the tip of my middle finger tracing the rounded portion of the tiny go-around button.

Come on, I plead. *Show me that runway!!* But all I see are thick white clouds.

"Approaching minimums," Jeffrey calls.

This is it! One hundred feet to go till we reach our fifty-foot minimums. We are now over the airport grounds, flying lower than the peak of a golfer's wedge shot. I tense up, looking for signs of the runway that I know must be directly ahead of us. But all I see is white. My middle finger slides fully into the scalloped go-around button, but I won't hit it early—or late for that matter. On this night, every foot counts.

Stay in the pocket. Be ready. And wait for it.

My eyes fixate on the altimeter showing our height above the ground and the flight instrument needles that show us perfectly on course and on glide path.

One hundred.

Ninety.

Eighty.

Come on!!! Show me something!!!

But all I see is white.

Seventy feet above the ground.

And through the white haze, I notice a few faint orbs of light. With each foot we descend, the orbs grow brighter and new sets appear farther in the distance. The dewy fog disguises them, but they are unmistakable.

YES!!! I think. *The runway lights!!!*

Sixty.

And now I see them clear as day. "Landing!" I announce, realizing we are already overtop of the runway, beyond the large identifying numbers painted on its threshold. Only the runway lights and the thick centerline stripes are visible. But that's enough to identify the runway, so I pull my fingertip away from the tiny black go-around button and let the autopilot finish its work.

The computerized voice makes its final altitude callouts: "Fifty... forty...thirty..."

The autopilot's flare mode activates, and I feel the control wheel move backwards rather mechanically as the plane begins to pitch up.

The runway lights zoom past us, and as they do, new ones emerge through the fog. The extreme brightness of the lights nearly blinds us, but such intensity has been necessary for us to spot the lights through the thick fog in time to land.

"Twenty...ten..."

The throttles inch backwards automatically, and we wait for the main wheels to settle onto the runway.

Ba-bump! We are down! While I wouldn't call it the best landing I've ever seen, it's far from the worst.

The wheels straddle the runway's centerline and its embedded lights. The speed brake handle whirls backwards, and I pull up on the reverse thrust levers. The nose wheels settle onto the tarmac, offering a small *chirp* as they kiss the pavement. And with the autopilot's job complete, I press the disconnect button on the control wheel and take over the task of steering the jet on the ground.

"Eighty knots," Jeffrey calls as the plane continues to slow.

I move my feet up to the tops of the pedals and press firmly on the brakes. My eyes search the runway's edge for a taxiway, but the dense fog makes it difficult to see anything. So I slow to a crawl and creep forward until I find an exit.

Jeffrey spots one first. "There's Delta," he says, pointing to the taxiway labeled with the letter D ahead and to our left.

I barely see it through the haze, but then I notice its yellow lead-in line painted on the runway and curving off to the side. "I've got it now," I say, grabbing the tiller to begin my turn.

Jeffrey checks his airport diagram. "Looks like this crosses the inboard runway and leads directly to the main terminal," he says. "Super easy."

"No complaints there." Easy is good on a night like this.

"United Twelve-Eighty-Three, when able, cross Runway Ten-Left and taxi to the ramp. Report clear of Ten-Right. You're completely obscured from the tower," the controller instructs.

"We're clearing Ten-Right now at Delta. Cross Ten-Left and taxi to the ramp with you, United Twelve-Eighty-Three," Jeffrey says.

It takes several minutes for us to arrive at the gate area given our slow crawl through the fog. And when we do, we struggle to spot the correct gate, since the large illuminated gate numbers affixed to the terminal are nearly invisible from our location. Jeffrey notices a ramper's lit wand off to our side, however, and we turn to follow the ramper's lead. Another ramper guides us the last hundred feet to the gate. I'm relieved when he crosses his wands above his head—the stop signal—so I can set the parking brake and shut down the engines.

While such low visibility flights are stressful, they're also extremely satisfying. The thought strikes me that I'm much more at ease commanding stressful flights than I was at the beginning of my time in the left seat. Clearly I'm growing into my new role, which makes sense, given that it's early spring—roughly seven months after

I first took command. Which is also a good thing, because a few weeks later, a cascading series of events raises the stakes yet again.

M iami Center, United Sixteen-Ten requests flight level three-eight-zero," I say over the radio.

"United Sixteen-Ten, unable due to traffic. We're going to need you at thirty-six for a while. In fact, you can expect that as a final."

I look to my first officer Katherine, shaking my head, before depressing the control wheel's push-to-talk switch and plainly and unemotionally replying "Roger" to the air traffic controller.

Katherine sighs. "Well, that's just perfect."

"Yep."

"I'll grab some new winds for the box and see what that does to our F.O.D."—the calculated amount of fuel remaining over our destination.

"Sounds good," I say, watching her thin fingers peck away at the flight computer.

We're a little more than two hours into our five-hour flight home from St. Thomas in the Caribbean. It seems that each mile we fly brings various events that slowly chip away at our adequate-but-not-excessive fuel reserves. And should the trend continue, Katherine and I are wondering if a fuel stop short of O'Hare may become necessary.

It all started when the prevailing winds in St. Thomas necessitated that we take off from the airport's relatively short runway pointed toward the lush, undulating ridgelines of the nearby mountains instead of away from the hills, over the water. Doing so placed significant requirements on our flight's takeoff and initial climb performance, which limited our maximum takeoff weight, since a heavier plane takes longer to accelerate for takeoff and climbs more slowly once airborne. Given the flight's full passenger load, however, the only way for the dispatcher to meet those weight requirements without removing passengers was to plan our flight with a relatively lean fuel load. Of course, lean didn't mean unsafe; I would never accept a plan—nor could the dispatcher legally create a plan—that didn't include adequate margins to account for unexpected events during the flight. Lean simply meant those margins were not excessive. But I also knew the line between the two was a fine one.

So as soon as I saw the flight's paperwork, I dug into its nitty-gritty details, questioning and evaluating every assumption it contained, all to determine if the dispatcher's plan seemed reasonable and achievable. I dissected the routing, the weather forecast, the planned altitude, and cruise speed, knowing every extra mile flown would burn more fuel, as would every non-optimal altitude and airspeed assignment by air traffic control. Having flown the St. Thomas to Chicago route several times, my personal experience led me to conclude that the dispatcher's plan was tight but realistic and built with sufficient slop to afford some wiggle room if things didn't go 100% according to plan. But as Katherine and I discovered soon after takeoff, little about our flight would go as planned.

Our first clue had come when the Caribbean air traffic controllers slowly stepped us up to our cruise altitude instead of allowing us to climb directly to 36,000 feet. Each step, each momentary pause, had burned away tiny amounts of our fuel cushion. A bit later, the controllers had required us to fly slightly faster than planned to accommodate other, faster traffic behind us on the same routing. And once again, a bit more of our extra gas had slipped away. Now, we have learned that we will fly the duration of the flight two thousand feet lower than planned, which both of us know will siphon away still more of our reserve fuel. And while any of these events on its own does not impact our flight, taken together, they complicate our fuel planning significantly.

"Winds are here," Katherine says, responding to the "CRZ WIND UPLINK" prompt on our flight computers. She loads the updated wind forecast into the computer and then switches to another page to see the uplink's effect. "The box shows five-point-one for F.O.D. now," she says, meaning 5,100 pounds of fuel.

"Starting to get tight," I say. "Katherine, just for planning, what would you say is the minimum number you're comfortable landing with in Chicago or at an alternate?" I ask, not wanting to prompt her with my own personal minimum, since I prefer to base our divert decision off the most conservative figure.

"Probably four point five or so," she says. "That's enough to go around and still be on the deck with at least forty-five minutes of gas."

"Perfect. That's the number I had in mind, too," I say. "So, we'll use that to determine if we need a fuel stop or not."

"Sounds good," she says.

"Now we just need things to hold together."

"Agreed," she says.

DING!! the interphone chimes.

I pick up the handset on the center panel and say hello to the flight attendant in the forward galley.

"Do you two want your crew meals?" the flight attendant asks.

"Come on, now. We're pilots," I joke. "When have you ever known us to turn down food?"

"Good point," the flight attendant chuckles, knowing that pilots are always interested in food, whether on the plane or on a layover. "I'll put them in the ovens and will call you back when they're done."

Twenty minutes later, the flight attendant calls to pass our meal trays up to the cockpit. After closing the flight deck door, I hand one to Katherine before maneuvering carefully around the center console to sit down with mine.

"Mmmmmm," I joke to Katherine as I pull back the aluminum foil covering my entrée and prepare to dig in. "Just like home cooking."

Katherine rolls her eyes, but truthfully, the meals are pretty good—braised short ribs, asparagus, a small salad, and an individually wrapped brownie for dessert. In between bites, the two of us make idle chitchat while we check to ensure the fuel over destination number on the flight computer stays constant—which it does.

"That sunset is gorgeous," Katherine says.

I glance to my left and smile. The sun is fast approaching the western horizon line. Its rich golden rays flow outward in all directions except for where a few wispy clouds create shadowy streaks through the sky. The bodies of the tall, billowy clouds rising up from the water appear purplish from the sun's backlighting, their edges trimmed a brilliant white.

"They always are in the Caribbean," I say. "Just spectacular."

Katherine pauses to take a bite of her salad. "My husband and I have talked about bringing the fam down here for a little spring fling. Feel like we need a reset after the Midwest's awful winter."

"Great idea," I say, recalling how the city's salt and snow have added wear marks to the toes of my black work shoes and a slight squeak to one wheel on the Tank. "Doubt the polar vortexes reach all the way down to the Caribbean."

Katherine chuckles. "Let's hope not."

I pull off a bite of the tender ribs with my fork. "How many kids did you say you have?"

"Two," she replies. "A boy and a girl. Seven and nine." She reaches into her bag and pulls out a family photo, handing it to me.

I smile. "That's awesome," I say, wondering whether I'll have a son or a daughter of my own in a few months.

"They're great kids. Miss them to pieces when I'm on a trip."

I hand the photo back to her. "But they do okay with you on the road?"

"It's all they know," she says, looking at me. "But it's always tough to leave, especially when they were younger. They'd see my uniform and know Mommy only wears it when she's going away."

Katherine takes another bite of her meal. "We've had more than a few meltdowns as I'm trying to walk out the door."

"That has to be tough."

She looks at me. "Tears your heart apart," she says, her face clearly pained. Then returning to her meal, she asks, "What about you? Any kids?"

"No kids yet, except for the furry kind," I say. "But we did find out several weeks ago that my wife's expecting."

"Really??" Katherine asks, a big smile spreading across her face. "Congratulations!"

"Thanks!" I say. "Honestly, it's a bit surreal." I pick at my salad with my fork. "We planned and planned and planned for this, and now that it's actually happening it's like, 'Oh, man. This is for real.'"

Katherine laughs. "Been there. Our first one was planned, too. But the second, well, he was a bit of a surprise. But that thought hits you either way."

"There's just so much to consider." I glance at the flight computer and see our fuel over destination is still holding steady. Then back to Katherine. "I mean, we were at the store the other day, looking at diapers and strollers and car seats and all that stuff. It's a whole new world."

"Yes, it is," she says, opening up her brownie. "But it's a great one."

I smile. "We can't wait. Not so much for the diaper part, but the starting new traditions and being a family part."

"Don't forget the get-no-sleep part," Katherine says.

"That, too," I chuckle.

"It's all worth it, though. You'll hear your kids laugh or see them smile and your heart will just melt." She pauses for a moment. "That's so exciting!"

"Thanks!" I set my silverware down on the plate and lay the cloth napkin over the tray. "Our first ultrasound is in a few weeks." I twist around to set the tray down on the cockpit's floor. "Should really be interesting."

"No, it's incredible," Katherine says, glowing. "Seeing your baby and hearing its heartbeat for the first time is just magical." She circles around and sets her tray on the floor next to mine. "You'll have to let me know how everything is going the next time I see you."

In six months...or three years...as we pass each other in the terminal, I think, remembering the single-serving nature of most of my flying partners. But it's a nice thought nonetheless.

"Definitely," I reply.

The miles tick by, and so do the states. Katherine and I banter back and forth about the usual topics, and I spend a good half hour or so staring out the window in between radio calls and minor flight duties, wondering what it's really going to be like as a dad. How will I handle being away from my child? How will Jen manage being a solo parent when I'm gone? Will she be envious of my quiet time in hotels or the dinners out with my colleagues? Or will I be the one who is envious of her time with our baby? How will the dynamic between the two of us change? There's so much uncertainty, so many things that are impossible to know. Most of all, I just hope I'm ready for whatever may come.

Soon, we're over southern Indiana with our F.O.D. calculation holding steady at 5,100 pounds when air traffic control requests we descend to 28,000 feet—much earlier than we had expected.

"Indianapolis Center, United Sixteen-Ten. Any chance of delaying that descent?" I ask.

"Unfortunately not," the controller replies. "Lots of crossing traffic. We need to get you down."

I spin the new altitude into the control window on the dashboard's center panel, and Katherine commands the autopilot to begin the descent. With each foot we descend, the air grows thicker, and the engines slurp down more fuel in the process.

Katherine points to the flight computer's updated fuel calculation based on our new altitude. "Four-point-nine now."

I rub my chin, contemplating what to do. "I'm a little concerned they're going to keep stepping us down."

"Me, too," Katherine says. "I wonder if the dispatcher can work something out with ATC to keep us higher."

"Worth a shot."

"I'll also grab a new ATIS to make sure the weather is holding up in Chicago."

"Great," I say. "Would you also ask if he has a preference on where we stop for fuel if necessary? Cincinnati? Indianapolis? Somewhere else?"

"Can do," Katherine says. She pecks away on the flight computer's tiny keyboard for a minute before announcing, "Sent."

The dispatcher's reply comes a short time later. I read the message on the flight computer's screen to Katherine. "Dispatcher says, 'Checking with ATC desk here on 27. Not too optimistic. Suggest Indy for fuel stop if needed.'"

In the distance, Indy's lights are easy to spot against the sparse Indiana farmland, even though dusk hasn't completely given way to night. A beltway rings the city. And from its downtown's hub, other highways articulate outward in every direction like spokes of a wagon wheel.

A few minutes later ATC instructs us to descend to 15,000 feet.

"You've got to be kidding me," I grumble before keying the mic and replying over the radios, "Down to one-five-thousand, United Sixteen-Ten."

I set the new altitude, and Katherine commands the plane to descend lower.

"Four-point-seven now," she says after checking the recalculated fuel figure on the flight computer.

I sigh as Indianapolis passes off our left side. The lights of Chicago shine along the horizon. "Katherine, we're gonna have to make a decision soon," I say, both of us knowing we are approaching the point where returning to Indy will burn more gas than continuing to Chicago.

"I agree," she says.

I plug away in the flight computer, loading a new fix onto our routing. I point to the map display screen and say, "That fix is halfway between Indy and O'Hare. That's our decision spot, okay?"

"Deal."

We descend in silence, trying to anticipate ATC's next commands and calculating in our head the effects such instructions may have on our fuel. Approaching the halfway fix, I notice a snow line crossing our path on the ground—the edge of a recent storm's snowfall—demarcating our decision spot.

"Talk to me, Katherine," I say as we approach the line. "What are you thinking? I want to make sure we're on the same page."

She presses a few keys on the flight computer to make one final evaluation of our situation. "Well," she says, picking up the O'Hare ATIS printout, "according to this, O'Hare's weather looks good. Clear skies. Winds out of the south. Landing to the west on the Two-Sevens and Two-Eights, which is what we have loaded. So I think the box's calculation should be pretty close." She sets the ATIS printout down and looks to me. "We had said four-point-five was our minimum to account for our reserve fuel plus some extra cushion, and we're not quite there yet. Given all of that, I'd suggest we press on to Chicago. I think we'll be fine."

"My thoughts exactly," I agree, nodding my head. "Chicago it is." And we pass over the snow line; our decision is made.

A few minutes later, I check in with Chicago approach control.

"United Sixteen-Ten, good evening. Expect Runway One-Zero-Center," the controller responds.

My head jolts toward Katherine. "Did he say Ten-Center?"

"Tell me they're turning the airport around," she replies, leaning forward and typing vigorously in the flight computer to pull up a new weather report for O'Hare. As the weather printout confirms, that's precisely the case. And now, instead of landing straight in to the west, we'll have to fly well beyond the airport, turn around, and land to the east.

"That's gonna add dozens of air miles," I gripe.

"We can't catch a break today." Katherine reprograms the flight computer with the new landing runway. "Down to four-point-three now."

"Damn," I say, shaking my head. I let out another sigh and look to Katherine. "You thinking what I'm thinking?"

"Min fuel?" she asks.

"Yep."

"We gotta do it."

With our fudge factor above our forty-five minutes of reserve fuel all but gone, and with our divert door firmly closed, we're committed to Chicago. Now, with O'Hare in an east flow configuration, we have to tell ATC that we cannot accept any more delays. Otherwise, we'll have to play our final card—a fuel emergency declaration—which will allow us to disregard ATC instructions and fly directly to the airport, forcing the controller to part Chicago's air traffic like Moses did the Red Sea. But declaring a fuel emergency is only to be done in the direst circumstances, and despite the precariousness of our situation, we aren't quite there yet.

"Chicago Approach, United Sixteen-Ten, we need to declare min fuel at this point," I say. "How long is the final tonight?"

A brief pause fills the air. "Roger, United Sixteen-Ten. Copy min fuel." Another pause. "Everything's jammed up right now as we swap runways. Expect about a thirty-mile final."

Thirty miles??? THIRTY MILES?!?!?! Thirty miles is two or three times as long as a normal final approach at O'Hare from this direction. Thirty miles is well beyond the western edge of Chicago's suburbs.

"Approach, United Sixteen-Ten is unable to take any lower altitudes until joining the glideslope."

Another pause fills the frequency's air. I picture the controller conferring with his colleagues about our situation. "United Sixteen-Ten, are you declaring a fuel emergency?"

"Only if you can't keep us up here," I reply.

Yet another pause. "I'll work something out," the controller says before resuming his intense cadence of instructions to other airplanes.

Katherine and I keep our eyes glued to the fuel gauges. They tick down ever so slowly as we turn due west. O'Hare moves behind us off our right side as we keep flying farther away from the airport.

"Come on," Katherine moans as the distance readout from O'Hare clicks over to 30.0. "Turn us in."

And just then, the controller commands our turn back.

"I think he heard you," I joke.

Katherine chuckles as she spins the autopilot's heading knob. The airplane banks hard to the right to begin its turn to the north. "Four-point-one now," she says.

"At least we're heading the right direction. I think this is gonna work out. Might even have a bit to spare," since 3,700 pounds of fuel equates to the forty-five minutes of flying time we want as an absolute minimum.

The controller turns us one final time before switching us to O'Hare Tower. After receiving our landing clearance, Katherine disconnects the autopilot and autothrottles to hand fly the plane the rest of the way. She aims our craft at the southernmost rows of white runway lights on the south side of the massive airport complex, keeping our altitude constant until the small horizontal row of four red lights to the left of the runway switches to three red and one white and then two red and two white—the sign our plane has joined the ideal vertical glidepath to the runway. "Starting down," she announces, letting the plane's nose drop to follow the path. Shortly thereafter she says, "Gear down, landing checklist."

I lower the gear lever, extend the final flaps, and complete the checklist as requested.

Katherine notices the white position lights of the plane ahead of us. "Feels like we're closing in on this guy."

I look to my map display and the diamond-shaped traffic symbols that are overlaid on it. "He's a little more than two-and-a-half miles right now." I notice the diamond drifting backwards on the screen. "But definitely closing."

Just then, a voice from the Tower says, "United Sixteen-Ten, reduce to your slowest practical airspeed. You're ten knots faster than the regional jet you're following."

"He's in sight," I reply. Then to Katherine I say, "This is gonna be really freaking tight. Be ready for a go around."

"He better make one of the first runway turnoffs," she says.

"Let's hope." I shift in my seat, anxiously watching the regional jet's lights and its corresponding white diamond on our traffic displays as our spacing tightens up. I play out the potential go-around in my mind, rehearsing its steps and callouts, including the fuel emergency we'll have to declare and the routing we'll need for an immediate return for landing. "One thousand," I announce as the altimeter hits 1,000 feet above the ground.

"Man, this is tight," Katherine grumbles as she jiggles the controls to stay on path and on speed, drifting lower and closer to the runway with every passing second.

My gaze darts from the regional jet to the diamond on our displays and to our altitude reading. "Five-hundred."

"He's on the runway," Katherine says.

"Regional Forty-Two-Fifty-One," the Tower calls to the regional jet. "No delay exiting the runway. Traffic behind you on a one-mile final."

But with the regional jet slowing down now that it's on the ground, the gap between our two planes closes rapidly.

Our altimeter ticks down below four-hundred feet.

Come on! Get off the runway! We can't touch down unless the runway is clear.

Three-hundred.

But the regional jet isn't veering from the runway's centerline.

"He missed the first turnoff!" Katherine says, jiggling the controls to stay on speed and on the glide path.

"Don't worry. Stick with it." I'm locked onto the regional jet's white position lights, waiting to see it move toward one of the taxiways on the left.

Two-hundred.

"There he goes!" I exclaim. "This might work out!"

"Come on, man, keep it rolling," Katherine pleads. She's focused. Composed. In the zone.

One-hundred.

Halfway down the runway, the jet's lights creep across the runway's edge. "He's almost clear!" I bellow as we crest the airport's boundary.

"Fifty," the 737's automated voice interrupts. We're over the runway now.

"…forty…"

The jet's tail completely clears the runway's edge. "It's all yours!" I exclaim.

"…thirty…"

"Landing," Katherine says.

"…twenty…"

She pulls back on the controls to start her landing flare.

"…ten…"

Ba-bump! Touchdown.

The speed brakes deploy and the reverse thrust roars to life as the brakes kick in. We shake in our seats as the jet slows.

Just before 80 knots, I slide my feet up onto the pedals and move my hands to the throttles. "I have the aircraft."

"You've got the aircraft," Katherine acknowledges.

My left hand falls to the tiller on the sidewall and I steer the jet toward the same highspeed taxiway turnoff used by the regional jet.

"Wow, that was close!" Katherine exclaims after clearing the runway.

"One more second and we were going around."

She blows out a deep breath. "A game of inches," she jokes.

And in so many ways, she's absolutely right.

We meander around O'Hare's taxiways for ten minutes before pulling into our parking spot. Once there, I shut down the engines, and just as I do, the fuel gauges turn yellow, like the warning light in a car telling the driver it's time to fill up. It's the first time in my career I've seen the gauges turn yellow. And while I know there is plenty of fuel in the tanks to have safely accommodated a go-around and second landing attempt—if not a third—I hope it's the last time I see those gauges that color.

Riding home with the Tank propped between my legs on the "L" train, I can't stop thinking about how tricky it can be to manage the unknowns in the airline business. Our flight plans are incredibly accurate, and we do our best in flight to execute those plans with precision. But so many variables are out of our control. And when reality takes over, sometimes the only choice is to react.

I hear my private pilot flight instructor's voice in my head, reminding me, *That's why you plan ahead and always leave yourself an out*—a lesson as applicable in a 737 as it had been in the two-seat Cessna.

The hard part, of course, is that there's never time to consider *all* possible options, and few choices are ever cut-and-dried, since each one comes with its own pros and cons. Yet someone has to weigh those choices. Someone has to make the final call. And for my flights, that someone is me. Sure, that responsibility comes with a fair amount of stress. But I'm learning that by managing the decision-making process in an open way that engages my first officers and utilizes the resources at our disposal, the quality of our decisions is usually excellent. And it's hard to beat the fulfillment that comes from that.

Forty-five minutes after leaving O'Hare, I step off the train at the Grand Blue Line stop and schlepp the Tank up the station's dingy red tile steps to street level. The walk sign is lit, so I begin to cross the street, only to see a car come veering around the corner unexpectedly. I jump back, close enough to touch the car, thinking, *Sometimes you just gotta react.*

Two weeks later, I'll have to react again—this time with a passenger's life on the line.

H ave you seen *Good Will Hunting*?" Lee asks, looking cool and re-laxed in the right seat of the 737—especially for a fifty-six-year-old—with his sporty, wraparound Oakley sunglasses pulled tight against his face and his short white hair spiked up in an edgy, albeit professional, way.

"I love it, actually."

"Well," he continues, his right foot propped up on the dashboard's footrest, "I had to go see about a girl."

I shoot him a confused look. "You had to go see about a girl??"

Lee nods. "I had to go see about a girl."

I'm nearly at a loss for words with his reasoning. "Come on, now," I say as we speed toward San Francisco across the rugged, snowcapped peaks of the High Sierra Mountains. "You're gonna have to give me more than that. Because that's a great line for a movie and all, but it's not something you say to explain why you took a voluntary furlough when you were senior enough to avoid it."

Lee shrugs off my demands. "Sure it is."

"But those were your prime flying years. And you risked them... for a girl???"

He nods again, this time with a smile. "I sure did." His foot falls to the floor, and he shifts in his seat. "Look, I know it wasn't the smartest career move, but I never expected that furlough to last as long as it did. No one did."

"But, Lee—"

"What other option did I have, Korry? I was head over heels for her. She was getting furloughed no matter what. And I knew if she took that job flying overseas, the chance we'd stay together would be next to zero. So I asked if she'd stay if I took the furlough, too."

"She must have thought you were crazy."

Lee chuckles. "Oh, she did. And maybe it was crazy, but—"

"It definitely was crazy," I interrupt.

"—but I was in love, man," he says, leaning toward me, his voice animated. "And you know what?" He pulls his sunglasses off to look me straight in the eyes. "She was worth it."

I lean my head back against the left seat's headrest and kick my feet up onto the footrests, smiling as I tap my fingertips together. "Lee, I've gotta give you credit, man. That's a leap of faith if I've ever heard one."

"Not really, Korry. Because what was my alternative? Stay at United and be one of the most junior pilots at the company, working weekends and holidays and flying the least desirable trips? Or travel with the woman I love, taking my fifth wheel wherever the mood struck us? Wineries. National parks. Homes of friends we hadn't seen for a while. It was the trip of a lifetime!"

It was also preposterous, and any right-thinking pilot would have been thankful his or her number hadn't been up for the furlough. But

Lee is cut from a different cloth. And even though I've only known him a few hours, somehow it makes sense for the laidback, happy-go-lucky guy. In many ways, his toss-everything-to-the-wind-and-do-something-crazy attitude reminds me of Todd, the pilot with whom I had flown to Vancouver near the beginning of my captaincy, and the motorcycle journey he had taken after returning home from Korean Air—the trip he had said was the best few months of his life.

"So do you have any regrets?" I ask, glancing his way.

"Not a—"

"United One-Six-One-Seven, contact Oakland Center on frequency one-three-two-decimal-niner-five," the air traffic controller interjects.

I reach for the push-to-talk switch on the control wheel. "One-three-two-decimal-niner-five, United Sixteen-Seventeen," I respond, dialing the frequency into the center console radio.

"Not a one!" Lee exclaims, picking up where he'd left off. After I check in with the new controller, Lee continues, "We took that trailer all over the place. We'd drive into the mountains of Utah, find some gorgeous vista, and set up camp for a week. And this wasn't regular camping, Korry. We did it right. Steaks. Seafood. Fine wine."

"That's awesome."

"And no TV or cellphones, either. Just us, the stars, and a campfire—a million miles from anywhere. Peaceful rejuvenation at its finest."

I smile. "Sounds incredible."

"It was beyond incredible." Lee pauses for a moment. "Korry, I know this sounds like an old man talking, but you're gonna find that this job, as great as it can be, it's still just a job."

I sigh softly, staring straight ahead out the window. "Yeah, I know."

"Some guys cling to it like it's everything. Like it's their identity. But then they retire, and three months later they kick the bucket because their identity is gone." His tone grows serious. "You've gotta remember that this job doesn't define us, Korry. It's what we do, not who we are." I nod and look his way, knowing he's right. "And sure, maybe I'd have some more money in the bank if I hadn't taken that furlough. But in the end, who cares? I would have missed out on that trip. I would have missed out on my awesome girl." He pauses. "So was it worth it? Would I do it over again?" He looks me straight in the eyes. "Abso-freakin-lutely. And I hope you get to do something equally crazy someday."

I smile. "Lee, that's a hell of a story," I say.

In a way, the Chicago move sort of feels a little like that type of trip for Jen and me, although it had, admittedly, been much less risky than a voluntary furlough with no guarantee of a call back. But I know the two of us will look back on it as an adventure we will never regret. And maybe that's what Lee is talking about. His spontaneity is inspiring, especially to someone like me who is such a planner and so driven to reach ever-higher career goals. Stepping away from that chase seems difficult to imagine. But seeing how passionate Lee is about that season of his life, I almost find myself envious of him.

I ask myself, when have I truly put everything on the line like that? My savings and my career? Granted, Lee's military pension guaranteed that at least some money would keep flowing in during his trip, but that doesn't negate that he and his girlfriend still took a massive pay cut by forgoing two full-time airline pilot salaries. All for an adventure without a set end date. An adventure that, as it happened, extended on for several years. I wonder under what circumstances I would truly be willing to take such risks? What reward would seem worthy of trading stability for uncertainty, to give up the pursuit, to just go and be and live?

DING!! My thoughts are interrupted by the chime of the cockpit interphone.

I look to Lee asking, "You want anything? Bathroom break? Another Coke?"

"Nah, I'm good."

I pick up the handset saying, "Flight deck, this is Korry."

"Captain," says the lead flight attendant, Ashley, somewhat frantically, "we've got a passenger in row ten who is having a seizure." I sit up and grab my pen from my shirt pocket to start scribbling notes on the slip of paper attached to my control wheel. "He's on the floor in the aisle now," Ashley continues. "We asked if there was a doctor on board, and thankfully, there was. He's evaluating the passenger as we speak. I'll get back to you with info about his vitals for when you talk to MedLink," the medical group that helps crewmembers respond to medical issues. "How far is San Fran?"

"Well, we were about to start down anyway," I say, glancing at the flight computer and pressing a few buttons to ensure I give her an accurate estimate. "So, probably twenty-five minutes. Maybe twenty if we push it." On the navigation display, I see a blue circle to our left with the letters KFAT, the airport identifier for Fresno, California. "Fresno's probably ten or fifteen if that's better."

"Okay. I'll tell the doctor."

"Sounds good, Ashley. I'll call ahead to the station folks and have medical personnel meet the plane. I'll send dispatch a message, too. But we probably won't have time to call MedLink." Without a satellite phone, actually "calling" MedLink requires a cumbersome and time-consuming phone patch through a special ATC group, which is fine if time permits, but not when nearing the busy approach environment.

"Well, there's a very good chance I'll need you to call MedLink," she insists.

"Keep us posted. I'll see if I can squeeze it in."

"Will do," she replies before hanging up the phone.

I place the interphone back onto its cradle. My mind races as I consider options and alternatives. In situations like this, it goes without saying that getting the sick passenger the care he needs is my absolute top priority. So if minutes matter, a diversion to Fresno is absolutely the thing to do. Otherwise, I must also consider the needs of the other passengers, many of whom may have tight connections, or are racing to get to a hospital to share a few final moments with a loved one, or are heading to a wedding or an important business meeting. Once again, it's a fine line to walk, especially with medical situations that can change in an instant.

I turn to Lee. "Did you hear any of that?"

"No."

I fill Lee in and ask him to take over communication with air traffic control so I can coordinate with the flight attendants and our company.

"Sounds good. I've got the radios and the airplane," Lee says. "Did you say something about Fresno?"

"Just mentioned it could be an option that saves a few minutes if necessary. For now, it's S-F-O."

"Gotcha." Lee speeds the plane up as fast as it will go. Since the arrival to San Francisco is all but straight in, the faster speeds will save a few minutes at most, but it's worth the effort just in case. Lee radios air traffic control to inform them of our developing situation.

"United Sixteen-Seventeen, roger. Let us know what type of assistance you may need."

"Wilco," Lee replies, using pilot shorthand for "will comply."

I type a message to dispatch into the computer about our situation. I picture the dispatcher noticing the text message pop up on the screen of her high-tech workstation on the 27th floor. Then I see her calling over to the Ops Center leaders working on "the Bridge" in the center of the sprawling 52,000-square-foot facility. Those leaders highlight our flight on the massive computerized map along one wall that shows all airborne United flights. I can almost hear their chatter, both in person and on the phone, as they work to coordinate all the resources at United's disposal for our flight—the company liaisons with air traffic control, the medical advisors, the station personnel in

San Francisco, and more. Many passengers may worry that we are alone up there in the sky, but I know nothing is further from the truth.

DING!! The interphone chimes again.

"This is Korry," I say, my pen already hovering over the tiny piece of paper to take notes.

"This is Ashley. Passenger is male, mid-30s, possible diabetic seizure. Doc asks that you please get with MedLink ASAP."

"I copy all of that. Do you have his seat number or name?"

"No name. Seat is ten charlie," meaning 10C.

"Great. I'll forward this to dispatch and she'll reach out to MedLink, but we don't have time up here. Did the doc say if we should stop in Fresno?"

"Forgot to ask, but I'll do that now. *Please* call MedLink," she requests more emphatically before hanging up.

"Starting down," Lee says, as he begins our descent while I type another update to dispatch.

DING!! The interphone rings again. It's starting to get distracting… and annoying.

"This is Korry."

"Doc says continue to S-F-O. He thinks the medical facilities will be better there and are worth the extra few minutes." With Lee looking at me, I wag my index finger forward, mouthing, "S-F-O." Lee nods in acknowledgment of the plan. "The passenger is in and out of consciousness," Ashley continues. "Did you call MedLink?"

"No, I have not," I tell her, not understanding why she is so adamant about my contacting them since MedLink's service is for advisory purposes only. In the heat of battle, it's ultimately up to us to decide how to proceed. And then it dawns on me. Is it possible the doctor wants access to one of the onboard medical kits that requires special permission to unlock due to the types of medications it contains? Permission only MedLink—or the captain—can authorize?

"Ashley, do you need permission to open the E-E-M-K? Is that why you want me to contact MedLink?"

"YES!" She exclaims.

I feel stupid for not thinking of it sooner. "As the captain, I'm authorizing you to open the Enhanced Emergency Medical Kit if that's what the doctor is recommending."

"Outstanding! Thank you!" Ashley shouts, hanging up the phone once again.

Grad school flashbacks to a professor who constantly reminded us, "It is nearly impossible to communicate anything to anyone," flood my mind.

We will definitely debrief this on the ground, I think.

I turn to Lee. "Doc is opening the E-E-M-K. Let's declare a medical emergency."

"You got it." Lee keys the microphone. "Oakland Center, United Sixteen-Seventeen is declaring a medical emergency at this time."

"Roger that, United Sixteen-Seventeen. You are cleared direct to the San Francisco airport. Descend and maintain 10,000 feet for now. Speed your discretion."

And just like that, the Red Sea is parted.

Over the next few minutes, Lee and I complete checklists and set up for a visual approach. We coordinate with United and air traffic control to ensure paramedics are waiting at our gate. ATC changes our runway assignment to 28L, a non-standard runway for arrivals coming from our direction, but one that makes our exit onto the ramp much faster. United even changes our gate from one on the backside of San Francisco's terminal to one just off the runway, everything to save a few precious minutes here and there, and all because we have said the words "declaring an emergency," medical or otherwise.

DING!! I pick up the interphone...again.

"Ashley here. Doc gave the passenger some meds. He's regained consciousness for now. He's on oxygen and will probably be back in his seat for landing."

"That's great news. Thanks, Ashley. Our gate changed to F-82. Paramedics will be waiting for us there. I'll be sure to keep the seatbelt sign on and make an announcement asking the folks to stay seated so the paramedics can board quickly."

"Thanks, Korry. Hopefully I won't call again before we're on the ground."

I hope not, either! I think, but say, "It's fine if you do." After hanging up the handset, I turn to Lee and say it sounds like things are under control.

"Excellent."

"I'm back on the radios," I say.

"You've got the radios; I've got the airplane," Lee confirms. We are back to business as usual.

Like clockwork, we land, taxi clear of the runway, and park at the gate. Paramedics stand in the jetway as expected, and the passengers cooperate by staying seated until the professionals can assist our passenger. After the passenger is off the plane, I stand in the cockpit doorway, saying goodbye to the other deplaning passengers, who offer enthusiastic kudos to the flight attendants for a job well done. Ashley points out the doctor to me as he exits, and I make a point of offering a special thank you to him for stepping up in the moment.

Once everyone is off, I ask the flight attendants to quickly debrief the event with Lee and me before they head toward other flights. We huddle together in the jetway as the cleaners come aboard to refresh the plane before its next flight.

"First of all," I say, "I want to thank you all for your help. Judging from the constant string of positive passenger comments you just received, it sounds like you did a phenomenal job."

"We worked together really well," Ashley says on behalf of her team.

"It sure seems that way. So, well done," I say. "This was my first time handling a medical emergency as captain. And as I said in our preflight brief, I'm open to honest feedback, since that's the only way I'll learn how to be a better captain for you. And so with that in mind, I'd appreciate any insights you may have about how Lee and I could have done things differently on our side of the door to make your lives easier during the event."

The four flight attendants chatter back and forth. Then Ashley says, "The only issue was getting the medical kit authorization."

I nod. "You know, I didn't even put two-and-two together with that," I tell her, "but I should have. We were talking past one another."

"Completely," she says. "I should have thought to ask you directly about it. Missed it somehow in the heat of the moment."

"It happens," Lee says.

"Just keep it in mind for next time. You'll be seeing a lot of new captains in the near future, and I bet they will find it helpful, too. Good lesson for both of us."

"For sure," she says.

"Anything else?" I ask. But no one says a word. "Well, thanks again for everything. That turned out very well, all things considered. Can't tell you how much I appreciate your help."

Lee and I decide to debrief our portion of the event during cruise on our next flight back to Chicago. So we wave goodbye to the flight attendants and grab sandwiches at an airport deli before making our way to our next flight's departure gate.

Later, while cruising above jagged rows of snowcapped Rocky Mountain peaks, which cascade onward to the horizon and make me feel like I'm standing on the shoreline of a choppy, churning ocean, the two of us decide we're mostly pleased with how things went. The critiques we have are minor ones, mostly that words matter. And as a leader, I need to communicate effectively, using precise verbiage. I need to ensure I hear exactly what the other person is telling me, and

I need to listen carefully when I speak to ensure the listener actually hears what I say, too.

A few weeks later, after stenciling the airport codes for St. Maarten (SXM), Tampa (TPA), Sacramento (SMF), and Las Vegas (LAS) into my maroon pocket logbook, I try my hand again at another medical emergency when a ninety-year-old passenger collapses in a lavatory after passing out, literally breaking the door off its hinges while over Missouri on a flight from Cancun to Chicago.

Once again, the lead flight attendant calls for a doctor, and as it happens, one of the chaperones accompanying forty kids on a mission trip steps forward to assist. Right away, I authorize use of the E.E.M.K., and I pass flying duties to the first officer so I can coordinate with the flight attendants, who provide me the exact information I need at the exact time I need it. Since time permits, I set up a "phone patch" with MedLink personnel, who, together with the dispatcher, first officer, and me, evaluate whether a diversion is prudent. Ultimately, we decide expedited handling to Chicago is best. Because the passenger is fine lying down but keeps losing consciousness when she sits up, the doctor recommends she remain lying on the floor of the plane, even as we come in for landing. It's not an ideal situation, and it's not by the book, so I use my captain's emergency authority to permit the unusual setup. Once again, ATC parts the Red Sea and clears us direct to the airport. We touch down smoothly and are at the gate in no time. As planned, medical professionals are waiting for us, and the passengers cooperate as the EMTs board the plane and use a stretcher to carry our passenger off the jet. And just like the last time, exiting passengers rave about how well the crew has worked together.

The event reinforces to me that accomplishing great things requires a great team. There's no way I can fly the plane and communicate with air traffic control and coordinate with the dispatcher and assist the passengers at the same time. To do that, I need a great team—both on the plane and at headquarters—to ensure every resource United has at its disposal is utilized as effectively as possible.

As the captain, I figure my role isn't to play every instrument or even to dictate how each instrument is played; rather, my role is to conduct the orchestra, to harness the talents of the individual players, and to meld them together in a way that creates rich and beautiful harmonies. That's how great teams achieve great things. And, I believe, that's what we have done so well together on this day. Unfortunately, the unexpected events are not over, and the next one hits incredibly close to home.

The waiting room of Jen's obstetrician is rather drab. A single television in the corner plays some boring daytime show. Pregnant women, many with children and husbands in tow, fill up most seats. The magazine selection is lacking, especially for nervous dads-to-be like me who are looking for something to distract their overactive minds. I thumb through an issue of *People*, but I can't seem to focus on anything.

I just want to hear that heartbeat, I think. *Then I can relax.*

Mom sits beside me, glowing, as she flips through a magazine as well. She and Dad had come to Chicago for the weekend, primarily to meet our new Vizsla puppy, Jackson. And while Dad had had to return home for work on Monday, Mom decided to stay a few extra days after we invited her to join us for our baby's first checkup and ultrasound. Ours will not be the first grandchild in the family—my sister's daughter, Ari, takes that prize—but it's easy to tell Mom is thrilled to be getting another grandchild. And I know she's excited for Jen and me, too!

"You just can't imagine how much your life will change by having a child," she tells me.

"You mean all the stressful nights and gray hairs I've given you over the years?"

Mom rolls her eyes and shakes her head as she closes her magazine and turns to me. "You'll be a great dad, Korry Mike."

"I sure hope so," I say, not entirely sharing Mom's confidence. I know having a baby of my own will be a monumental adjustment—one I'm both excited…and a bit terrified about. After all, I've spent very little time around small children. I've never changed a diaper or tried to sooth a crying baby. Sure, I'll take a class with Jen, and I'll read a few books about the nuts and bolts of parenting. But will that really be enough to make me feel confident or ready? I mean, I'm 32, and one look at a fragile and delicate infant makes me feel woefully ill-equipped for my new role as a parent. "I don't know how you did it at twenty-four," I continue. "There's no way I would've been ready."

Mom smiles in a way that says she believes my fears are unfounded. "Korry, you're never ready. You just do it." And perhaps she's right. Perhaps I'll grow into my new role as a parent in much the same way I have grown into my role as a captain—by making a few mistakes here and there, but hopefully limiting them to the ones that are simply embarrassing, not life-threatening.

I turn back to my magazine, flipping another page. "I will say it's hard to imagine a better time for Jen and me to bring a child into the world. Our relationship has never been stronger. We've got stable jobs with solid incomes. It seems just about perfect."

"Well," Mom says, "God's timing is always perfect." She reaches over and places her hand on my knee. "And He never gives you anything you can't handle."

I smile and ask, "He just determines what that limit is and then backs it off a bit?"

Mom shakes her head again at my sarcasm. "No, He guides you through it." She closes her magazine and tilts her head slightly. "Trust me, Korry. You'll take one look at that little bundle of joy and the sleepless nights won't matter one bit."

I smile. "I hope you're right, Mom. And I'm very grateful to have had the two of you to model what great parenting looks like."

Mom smiles back. "I appreciate that, Korry, but your dad and I didn't know how it was supposed to be done, either. No one does. We just did our best, and that's what you and Jen will do, too. And you'll do great!" She pauses and starts grinning, saying, "You're both such honeys!"

Oh, Cindy Lou, I think. *Always the optimist.*

Just then a door opens across the room. "Korry?" a nurse calls out.

I raise my hand and start to stand up.

"Jennifer's exam is complete. They're ready to do the ultrasound now. You can follow me."

Mom smiles again, wrapping her arm around me and squeezing me tight. "This is so exciting!"

We follow the nurse back a short hallway, past a slew of exam rooms. Jen's room is at the end. She's sitting on the exam table, wearing a blue gown and smiling radiantly.

Dr. Summers is smiling, too. "It's so nice to meet you," she says to me with a wave. "And you must be Korry's mom."

Mom nods.

I walk over to Jen and hold her hand, lacing her fingers between mine. Mom stands beside me, her hand resting on my shoulder.

"The images will show up right here," Dr. Summers says, pointing to a small, portable black-and-white screen. "It won't be as clear as the ultrasound you'll get at the imaging center, but it's pretty good."

"And we'll be able to hear the heartbeat?" I ask.

"Most times, yes." She pauses. "I have to tell you, this is one of my favorite parts of the job. There's nothing like watching two new parents see their child for the first time."

I give Jen's hand a gentle squeeze.

"Are there any other questions before we begin?" Dr. Summers asks as she looks around the room.

"I think we're ready," Jen says.

"Well, then," Dr. Summers replies, "let's take a look at your baby."

Dr. Summers places the ultrasound machine's transducer on Jen's belly and begins sliding it around, her gaze and those of all of us fixated on the tiny computer screen. Images flicker across the screen, but I'm lost without the doctor's interpretation. I feel my breathing intensify, unsure of what to expect, and I squeeze Jen's hand a bit tighter.

"There's the gestational sac," Dr. Summers says, referencing a prominent black circle amidst the gray clutter along the screen's edges. I smile at Jen, offering another squeeze of her hand, as Dr. Summers continues to maneuver the handheld device atop Jen's belly. Dr. Summers pauses to examine an area of the image more closely. She leans in toward the computer screen and squints. "And how far along did you say you think you are?"

"Nine weeks," Jen says.

Dr. Summers sighs. "Hmmm."

Jen squeezes my hand more firmly. I look to her, noticing the mounting concern on her face, and I squeeze back. "Is everything okay?" Jen asks.

"Well," Dr. Summers says, pausing as though she's gathering her thoughts, "I'm not quite sure." Jen's squeeze tightens even more. "I'm afraid we may have a problem."

And my heart drops.

CHAPTER 13

Above the Fog

*"In order for the light to shine so brightly,
the darkness must be present."*
- Francis Bacon

Chicago, Illinois – April 2014

Jen and I lie in bed a few nights later after our visit to the imaging center, where the more detailed ultrasound gave us conclusive news about Jen's pregnancy. A dim orange glow from the streetlamps on Halsted Street bathes our faces as we stare at the cement ceiling of our apartment. A commuter train rumbles past on nearby tracks, its sound muted and almost wave-like thanks to the apartment's thick glass windows and concrete walls.

"What the heck's a blighted ovum anyway?" Jen asks, her head tucked up against my shoulder.

"I don't know, Wife," I say, caressing the skin on her arm. Later, I'll read that it's a pregnancy where the embryo stops developing for whatever reason.

"I told you something was wrong. I just knew it."

"But how could you know? You've never been pregnant before."

I feel her shaking her head. "I don't know. A sixth sense or something. It just didn't feel right." Jen sighs, bringing her hands to her face to rub her forehead. "And now we have to tell everyone. That's gonna be the worst part."

"They'll understand."

She pauses for several seconds, deep in thought. "Do you think it was my fault?"

"Your fault?" I ask, taken aback by her question. "Of course not."

"Maybe I did something or ate something."

"Come on, Wife. It's not your fault."

"I just don't get it, though. We are healthy people. We did everything we were supposed to do. And we got pregnant right away. Even the test in the doctor's office confirmed I'd been pregnant. So, what did we do wrong?"

"Wife, I don't think *we* did anything wrong. It just happened."

"Everything happens for a reason," Jen replies.

"So what's the reason?" I ask, continuing to caress her arm as I await her response.

"I don't know, Husband. I haven't figured that out."

"I mean, do you feel like God is punishing us or something?"

"No," she says. "I know that's not the case."

"Then what is it?"

"I don't know, Husband. I just don't understand."

"I don't understand either, Wife." I pause as another train rumbles past. "We may never understand. It just is." Jen sighs as I roll onto my side to look at her. "You know, when Mom and I were sitting in the waiting room, she said what now feels like the strangest thing to me."

"What's that?" Jen asks.

"She said God's timing is always perfect. She said He never gives us anything we can't handle and that He's always there to guide us through it. At the time, we were talking about how I thought this was the perfect time for us to bring a baby into our family and how I was excited and scared about doing so because of the stress and adjustment that comes with a new baby." I reach across Jen's stomach, letting the fingers of my left hand intertwine with those of her right.

"But now when I think about her comments, I wonder if they might mean something more."

"Like maybe the timing wasn't right?" Jen asks.

"Or maybe it wasn't *God's* timing," I say, squeezing her hand. "Maybe we're supposed to really listen to God right now, to let Him guide us through this."

Jen gently shakes her head, weighing this possibility. "I don't know, Husband. Maybe that's the case." She pauses for a moment. "And maybe one day I'll accept that answer. But right now, quite honestly, I'm just wondering why God would let this happen."

I nod slightly. "Me, too, Wife. Me, too." I lean in and kiss Jen's forehead. "Maybe this whole conversation is better suited for another day."

"Yeah," Jen says, her voice crackling. I can almost see the tears welling up in her eyes. "Maybe that's a good idea."

I snuggle tight against her again, wrapping my arms around her and kissing the back of her neck. "I love you, Wife."

"I love you, too, Husband."

I keep hugging her for a long time, staring into the darkness, praying for understanding and for help in finding peace.

A few days later, I pack up the Tank to begin another trip. I hate the thought of leaving Jen alone, but she insists we have to move forward. She also assures me that Jackson, our new puppy, will serve as an excellent companion for her while I'm gone.

I had expected to find comfort in the routines of the road, but instead, my trips only highlight how lonely and empty I feel. I share more cockpits with new single-serving colleagues, answering the same questions and debating the same predictable topics. And on my layovers, I go running—alone—and see other people experiencing life together: families building sandcastles on the beaches of Puerto Vallarta; couples swaying in unison with the Fountains of Bellagio along the glitzy Las Vegas Strip; Chinese Americans practicing tai chi together as the sun rises above San Francisco's Washington Square Park. And yet the one person I most want to experience life with is more than two thousand miles away in Chicago—alone.

At the end of one trip, my first officer and I race down Runway 28L in San Francisco toward a billowy fog bank that hovers over the runway's end after enveloping the nearby coastal mountains. We lift off long before reaching the cotton-swab-like clouds, climbing quickly into the Bay Area's brilliant blue skies. And as we do, the thought strikes me that maybe Jen and I need to rise above our own gloomy fog by changing perspectives. We have experienced plenty of death and dormancy during the long, dark, cold winter. Now, it's time to embrace the vibrancy and rebirth of spring.

After pulling the Tank into the apartment and giving Jen and Jackson a hug and a kiss, I suggest, "We need a vacation. And Europe is fantastic in the springtime. What do you say?"

A huge smile creeps across Jen's face as excitement instantaneously grows within her. "I say, when are we leaving?"

My answer is the end of the month, during a five-day break built into my schedule. It will be a quick European vacation, but plenty long enough for us to start to find ourselves again.

"The better question," I suggest, "is where are we going?"

But as with any vacation revolving around an airline's standby travel benefits, where we go depends on which flight has the most open seats. And so on the morning of the trip, we settle on our destination: the picturesque city of Amsterdam.

Hand-in-hand, we wander aimlessly for hours amongst Amsterdam's twisting roads and narrow canals. We comment on the crooked building facades and imagine what it would be like to live on one of the many houseboats we pass. We set no agenda; we just talk and enjoy whatever whim or fancy strikes us. When the line for a museum is too long, we move on, ducking into a quaint chocolate shop before strolling along the quiet paths of the city's massive Vondelpark, where, unlike Chicago, the leaves are already full and green. And since Jen is no longer pregnant, we end our day by stopping in several hole-in-the-wall pubs to sample the best Dutch beers we can find.

The next morning, we eat homemade breakfasts while sipping robust, aromatic coffees at an enchanting canal-side café. Using the café's Wi-Fi, we check passenger loads for return flights to Chicago a few days later, and decide that Frankfurt, Germany, seems to offer the best options for us. So we pack our bags and meander that way.

We hop a bullet train and zip through the Dutch and German countryside. Through our expansive windows we watch windmills spin amidst recently planted fields that are starting to show their first signs of new growth.

Rebirth, I think. *How refreshing.*

A few hours later, we arrive in Cologne, entering the city over the triple-arched Hohenzollern Bridge. Jen notices tens of thousands of multi-colored padlocks blanketing the fence along the bridge's pedestrian crossing.

"The lock bridge!" she exclaims, her face pressed to the train's window. "That's the one from the article I sent you a few weeks ago."

"Oh, yeah! How random is that!"

"We'll have to find our own lock so we can add it to the bridge."

That afternoon, we buy one in a downtown store and ask its jewelry clerk to engrave our initials and anniversary date on the lock's body. Early the next morning, we walk to the center of the bridge and look for an open spot on the fence. After snapping our lock into place, we close our eyes and make silent wishes while we hold the lock's flimsy key between our melded hands. I lift one of my eyelids several times to peek at Jen, and she catches me doing so as she finishes making her rather lengthy wish.

She slaps me on the shoulder as she shakes her head, chastising, "You're not supposed to look!"

I shrug my shoulders. "Couldn't help myself."

She slaps the key into my hand. "Well, now you get to throw it."

Smiling, I wind up, and with a giant heave, launch the key as far as I can. The sun glistens off it as it tumbles in the cool morning breeze toward the surface of the Rhine River. Without the key, our lock will now serve as a symbol of our unending love.

I wrap my arm around Jen, pulling her tight against me as we gaze upon the just-awakening city. "How funny that we ended up here!" Jen says.

"Guess it was meant to be."

"I guess so."

Hand-in-hand, we leave the bridge and return to the city center to trek up the winding stone stairways of one of the imposing bell towers in the massive gothic cathedral known as the Kölner Dom. As the humongous bells swing back and forth, dinging and donging at a thunderous volume, Jen and I peer out one of the tower's windows across the Rhine.

"Look!" Jen says, squinting—and grinning—as she points toward the bridge. "I think I see our lock!"

"Those eagle eyes are good!" I laugh. "With vision like that, maybe you should drive us to Mainz this afternoon."

"No way, José. That's all you!" Which, admittedly, is fine by me, since our Audi rental car makes twisting along the Autobahn and the two-lane country roads a blast.

We zoom up and down rolling hills that are blanketed by lush green grasses and brilliant yellow rapeseed blossoms. Several times we stop to take pictures, running our fingers through the fields' flowery tops and laughing as the warm breeze flaps Jen's pastel scarf across her face. We sample freshly baked pretzels while rambling through local artisan shops in a tiny red-roofed village, the name of which I never even notice. But the name doesn't matter; the village is simply a part of our journey—a journey that keeps creating itself. In fact, the only plan we make is to share dinner in Mainz, outside Frankfurt, with Jen's cousin and her husband, a U.S. Army lieutenant colonel stationed nearby.

From a crowded underground hall, we down steins of dark beer, cheering *"Prost!"* as we clink our heavy glasses together. We relish savory potato soup alongside huge plates of *jagerschnitzel*, listening as our friends recount stories highlighting the challenges and rewards of their multi-year German adventure. It's a perfect reminder that unexpected journeys often lead to unexpected growth and opportunity.

With dinner complete, we say goodbye to our friends and walk back to our hotel, longing for our European vacation to last forever. Thankfully, one final treat awaits us the next morning—a last-minute upgrade to the lie-flat seats and the impeccable service of United's first class for our long transatlantic flight home.

Halfway through the flight, after the gourmet meal service is complete and each of us is snuggled up with a plush navy blue duvet cover watching a movie in the dark cabin, Jen taps me on the shoulder. I pull my earbuds out and lean into her seat pod, asking, "Yeeeesssssssss?"

Jen shakes her head. "So I've been thinking," she says.

"That's never good," I say jokingly, "but go on."

"I'm wondering if God is trying to teach us something. With the miscarriage. And with this trip for that matter."

"Like what?"

"Like maybe we're not supposed to be in control."

I push the little electronic button to incline my seat a bit. "I'm not following you."

"I don't know if *I'm* even following myself," she says, pausing to gather her thoughts. "Take, for example, my small-group meeting at

Soul City Church a week or so before the miscarriage. That night our group was talking about how sometimes God makes things hard so you know He's in control. And ever since you and I left the doctor's office a month ago, I haven't stopped thinking about that talk. I keep thinking how maybe that's the case. Maybe God is making this tough for us so we know we aren't in control. Because we definitely tried to be in control. We planned out this whole getting-pregnant thing for at least two years. And it worked like clockwork, right on schedule. But it seemed too easy."

"What's wrong with it being easy?" I ask.

"Nothing, except—"

"I mean, shouldn't we be grateful everything went according to plan?"

"But maybe we aren't supposed to plan everything out in the first place. Maybe we sort of needed this to happen."

"But why?"

"So we could fully appreciate what an incredible gift a baby is. So we could understand that only He could create something so precious. And only on His schedule, not ours. Because otherwise, we might think that we did it on our own by planning it out and following a formula."

I find myself nodding along with her. "I guess I can see what you're saying. At least I can see that as a possibility."

"I don't know, Husband. I could also be way off. Maybe I'm reading too much into it. Maybe there is no explanation. But now I'm sitting here thinking about how awesome this trip has been, and it's been perfect—all of it."

"Even me?" I ask.

Jen rolls her eyes. "Even you. Which is surprising."

"Just checking."

"And the only thing we planned was dinner with Dana and Jon.

And we didn't even plan that until after we realized we'd be nearby in order to catch this flight from Frankfurt."

"That's true," I say. "It's been really nice to be somewhat spontaneous for once."

Jen nods. "I guess I'm wondering if the trip worked precisely *because* we kept it spontaneous."

I pause to consider that possibility. "But sometimes you gotta plan, Wife. We can't be spontaneous all the time."

"I know," she says. "I'm just wondering if we're not supposed to *overplan*. Maybe we're supposed to let God be in control and let Him guide us along like your mom said."

"I definitely see what you're saying, but I'm gonna have to think about that one."

"Yeah, dude. Me, too."

I reach over and squeeze Jen's hand, letting the low rumble of the engines and the rushing air's white noise fill the space between us for a moment. "I love you, Wife."

"I love you, too, Husband."

"We'll figure this out. I promise."

Jen smiles. Then both of us put our earbuds back in to finish our movies. But I pay little attention to what's on my screen. Instead, I stare straight ahead, mulling over Jen's comments for much of the remaining four hours until we touch down in O'Hare. She's right that the best moments of our trip were the spontaneous ones we never could have planned. And by losing ourselves in the many fortuitous moments the trip had gifted to us along the way, and by embracing each moment for what it was, not what it wasn't, the trip had been pleasantly distracting. It had been energizing and life-giving. In fact, as I think about it, the trip had been everything we needed it to be.

After returning to our apartment and repacking the Tank, I jet off to Los Angeles, Minneapolis, Philadelphia, and Austin. Then to

Tampa, Seattle, Orlando, and Portland. Each flight adds another line in my maroon pocket logbook, and each hour of flight time finesses my leadership skills.

Like the time in Chicago, when an air traffic control outage led to a massive, trickling delay after boarding was complete—the worst-case scenario for any delay, since passengers often feel like they're being held hostage, even though that's far from the case. Every ten minutes or so, I stood in the forward galley, making announcements I hoped would signal to the passengers complete transparency about the situation and my thought process for making decisions regarding it. I also hoped my announcements would help the passengers feel like we were all in this together. I knew I had achieved my goal when a flight attendant commended me for "staying ahead of the anxiety curve." I'd never thought of passenger announcements in that way, but I immediately committed to using the mantra as my guiding objective for every subsequent passenger announcement I would make, whether trying to manage expectations during a delay or to ease the minds of nervous travelers in flight. It was a huge *ah-ha!* moment for me.

Then there was the time when, after parking at the gate in Grand Rapids, I harshly admonished a much older first officer over his constant inflight prodding that had made me feel like he was trying to fly the plane for me. In the moment, it felt good to use my positional authority to seemingly put the first officer back in his place. But almost immediately, I regretted the overly aggressive way I had chosen to address the situation. I hadn't led with a desire to understand why he felt it was necessary to make such comments. Instead, I simply shut him down. And in the process, I built a giant wall between the two of us—a wall that could significantly affect our ability to work together on future flights. I knew I had to do something to rectify the situation, even though such a discussion would likely be awkward and uncomfortable. And so on our way to the airport the next day,

I unequivocally apologized for reacting the way I did. I told him I valued his experience and that I genuinely wanted his feedback. And then I suggested a few ways he might provide me such feedback in the future so that I would be more receptive to actually hearing what he had to say. I hoped our chat would show him that I respected him as a person and as a professional, that I wanted to tear down the wall between us, and that I valued his concerns and insights because I recognized they could help make me a better, safer pilot and a more effective leader. Judging from the changed tenor of our subsequent flights, I believe I was successful on all fronts.

But as spring turns into summer, it isn't just my leadership skills that are improving; it's also my confidence in putting those skills to use. Where I once would have been uncomfortable making any decision that is somewhat "outside the box," now such decisions fill me with much less consternation. Instead, I see them simply as decisions that need to be made, because they are the right calls to make, and as the captain, I'm the one who needs to make them.

Such is the case when I self-impose a delay on a flight from Washington, D.C., back to Chicago. With two back-to-back lines of thunderstorms tracking directly for O'Hare, air traffic control imposes a "ground stop" that prevents our flight from taking off. Several hours later, after the first line of storms clears O'Hare, our flight receives its "wheels up" takeoff time. The problem, however, is that both the first officer and I are concerned that departing at that time will put us in Chicago just as the second line of storms, which is only fifty miles behind the first one, slams into O'Hare. The result, we both believe, will be substantial turbulence, inflight holding, or possibly even a weather-related diversion. When the first officer suggests we delay our departure by an extra thirty or sixty minutes, I immediately warm to the idea. Doing so, we believe, will position us to arrive in Chicago after the second line of storms has comfortably passed by O'Hare, leading to a smoother flight and, quite likely, little difference in the

3 FEET TO THE LEFT

actual arrival time. We discuss the idea with our flight's dispatcher, and while she's receptive to the idea, it becomes clear that only the captain can delay a flight for such an atypical reason. I know doing so might mean having to explain myself after the fact; nonetheless, I make the unusual call. Following my newfound mantra of staying ahead of the anxiety curve, I take my company-issued iPad into the terminal and spend at least fifteen minutes discussing the weather and our reasoning for the delay with a substantial number of our passengers who are interested. A few hours later, my first officer and I look down onto the second line of storms as we glide over Lake Michigan's coastline, where only the wispy remnants of the storms' trailing edges are still slithering between the tops of downtown skyscrapers. Our arrival path to O'Hare, however, is clear as can be. We don't encounter even one ripple of turbulence all the way to landing. And while it's possible that such a turbulence-free arrival could have happened without my decision to delay our flight, I believe in my heart the delay was precisely the right call.

Week in and week out, Jen listens to me talk about these types of flights and how I feel like my personal growth rate is off the charts. I tell her I can't believe it will soon be a year that I've been in the left seat. I rave to her about how much I've learned from my first officers, both from the flying we've done and the first officers' unique outlooks on life and its meandering paths. But she's never heard me complain about someone as much as I do Justin. He's in a league all of his own.

Jackson's rust-colored feet scamper ahead of us in a quick trot, his lean and sporty frame built perfectly for outdoor adventures like this.

"You're doing so well, buddy," I tell him, interrupting my story about Justin's negative outlook for a moment as the three of us hike along the dirt trails and wooden steps leading to another one of Starved Rock State Park's sandstone canyons and pristine waterfalls.

"Guys, I'm a vizsla," Jen says, speaking for Jackson in a childlike voice. "Hiking ain't no thing."

"I guess not," I say, wiping the sweat from my brow with the sleeve of my blue Boeing tee-shirt. "We're gonna be exhausted after this, and he looks like he's gonna want to keep going."

"And going...and going...and going," Jen says, hinting at the highly energetic nature of the breed. Turning back to my story, she asks, "So what's an example of Justin's negativity?"

"Well, when one of our flights got delayed, he made it seem like *all* United flights are delayed. When a couple checked bags arrived planeside a few minutes late, he made it seem like the bags *always* arrive late. And if I tried to help move the process along, he'd look me in the eye and tell me our jobs are to fly the plane, not put out fires."

"Oh, man," she says. "That had to be draining."

"Tell me about it," I say, "By day four of the trip, the negativity was really starting to wear on me."

"I bet," Jen says. "And you think it was all because of his furloughs?"

"Well, that's what he claimed. But I don't know, Wife. There had to be something else going on. Even the charity group he managed on the side was a source of frustration. The volunteers were too hard to schedule. They didn't share his passion. On and on. I mean, if I had said it's a beautiful day, there's a good chance he would have told me, 'Yeah, but tomorrow's forecast is rain.' I'm not exaggerating."

"Like you said, Husband, there must be something else going on."

I move to the side of the steps to let a group of hikers going the opposite way pass by. "And I truly feel for him if that's the case," I say as we start to move again. "I just don't understand how you get to the point where it seems like your optimism is completely gone."

"Well, if you're stuck in a rut, how long can you keep spinning your wheels before you start to feel like you'll never get out?" Jen asks as we continue weaving up a seemingly endless staircase.

"Yeah, I don't know, Wife. I've just never flown with another furloughee who seemed so consumed by the furloughs or so resentful of United. Somehow the others made peace with the fact that their furloughs were simply a function of their low seniority numbers. I mean, it definitely wasn't personal."

"But clearly it felt that way to Justin."

"For sure," I reply. I wipe my brow again with my sleeve. "And in fairness to him, maybe I just caught him on a couple of bad days. Lord knows I have my moments from time to time, too."

"Noooo, never," Jen says sarcastically.

I roll my eyes. "But it still got me thinking, and since we weren't chatting that much during our flights, I had a lot of time for thinking."

"Oh, man," Jen jokes.

I roll my eyes again as we reach the top of the hill and pause to pull our water bottle out from my black backpack to take a few swigs. "I started thinking about what might have happened in my life if the pilots I met on the flight to Orlando as a five-year-old or the flight to London as a junior had been as negative about the industry and the career as Justin." I pass the bottle to Jen. "Would I have still pursued aviation? Would I have met Kurt, Paul, Dianna, and all my other aviation friends?" I look to Jen. "Would I have ever met you?"

She takes a swig of water and then hands the bottle back to me. "I don't know, Husband. I sure hope so. But that's crazy to consider."

"I think it could have changed everything," I say as I stuff the bottle back into my pack and lead us onward along the trail. "Don't get me wrong about Justin; there were glimmers of happiness in the way he talked about his organization. But they were so dim from the negativity that seemed to consume him because of his furloughs." We round a corner and enter a particularly large canyon the size of a baseball diamond's infield. At the far end, water cascades over the canyon's rocky top, landing on its sedimentary floor and splattering forward before regrouping into a small stream that flows toward us.

The three of us pause to take in the serene setting. "And I just hope we don't let our own challenges consume us in the same way."

Jen nods.

"Because there must be a reason our paths have led us to them," I say. "And if we let those challenges consume us, we might miss the beauty of the moment that's right in front of us."

Jen looks up to me with a forced smile, knowing I'm alluding to our miscarriage—a painful setback in our life plans, but not one the doctors think will prevent us from getting pregnant again. "I know, Husband. I know."

The three of us carefully maneuver along the sloped sandstone walls until we're standing behind the falling water. I extend my hand into its forceful stream before quickly yanking it back, saying, "It stings!"

Jen smiles. "And sometimes life does, too. Sometimes it stings so bad you can't see the beauty it's creating."

A small smile perks up across my face, and I reach over to hold Jen's hand, squeezing it firmly for several moments. Then, breaking the silence, I say, "Come on," as I look to Jackson, who is sitting back on his haunches after pulling his leash as far as it will go. "Jackson's terrified of the waterfall. Let's keep going."

Jen shakes her head. "You can't be serious for more than one minute, can you?"

"Nope," I say, grinning. "Not when we've got a hike to finish."

"Uggghhhh," Jen moans. "Sometimes, you really are the worst."

Chuckling, I say, "I know."

It's several weeks later when Kurt plops the pizza box and container of wings onto his kitchen table, where Kim has already set out napkins and paper plates for the three of us to use. She opens the box and runs a pizza cutter over the pre-cut lines on the pie.

"Are the kids asleep?" I ask her.

"Yep," she replies. "Told them you were getting in too late tonight for them to stay up. But they're excited to see you in the morning."

"I'm excited to see them, too," I say, reaching in and grabbing a big slice from the half topped with cheese and mushrooms. "You know, I'm thinking the last time I saw them was when Jen and I were here last June."

"That's probably about right," Kim says.

"Hard to believe that's been more than a year already."

Kurt shakes his head. "That *is* wild."

Kim chooses a slice from the half with pepperoni and then asks, "So how is Jen?"

"She's good," I say.

Kim's face grows more serious. "With . . . everything?"

I shrug one shoulder. "She's better. For the most part, at least. Both of us are."

"That's good to hear." She pauses. "We've been thinking about you guys."

I smile. "Thanks, Kim. That means a lot." I reach for the small container of red pepper flakes in the center of the table. "It's really just the little things that get us every now and then. Jen especially." I shake the red seasoning onto my slice. "Like when she sees a pregnant woman and thinks about how far along she would've been by now."

"Which is when you take her by the hand," Kurt interjects, "and tell her, 'We're going out.'"

I chuckle. "Or jetting off to Europe," I joke.

"Exactly," he says.

"Kurt, it's not the same," Kim says with a stern look.

"I know that," he says, opening the white foam container of chicken wings. "But it's not like they'd be going out for cocktails if Jen were eight months pregnant."

Kim rolls her eyes as she takes another bite of pizza.

"I get what you mean, though," I say to Kurt as I pull a few meaty wings from the container. "And you're right. It's like we got some extra time to be just us before a kiddo comes along." I lick my fingertips. "Which is probably good, because the doctors tell us we can try again. So until then, we'll just try to take it as it comes and be as intentional with our time as possible."

Noticing how saucy the wings are, Kim rises from the table to get more napkins. "Well, you know we're pulling for you guys."

"Thanks, Kim," I say. "It's been a crazy year, that's for sure. Filled with all sorts of highs and lows."

"Highs like how United hasn't pulled your fourth stripe yet?" Kurt jokes.

I laugh. "Somehow I guess I've slipped through the cracks."

Kurt chuckles. "Well, you better stay on your A-game," he says, sipping his drink.

"Always," I respond. I bite into my pizza slice, savoring the firmness of its crust and the juiciness of its cheese. "Believe it or not, this trip actually wraps up my first year in the left seat," I say. "Well, a year since my first flight after I-O-E."

"Where did you say you've been this time?" Kim asks, returning to the table with a stack of napkins.

"Day one was D-C-A, then Montego Bay on day two, and now Houston on day three." I dab the edges of my mouth with my napkin. "Tomorrow afternoon we shoot out to L-A-X and then back to Chicago to finish up. Not a bad trip."

"Who you flying with?" Kurt asks, biting into a wing.

"Guy named Todd." I pick one up and do the same. "He was one of the first F-Os I flew with."

"Good guy?"

"Oh, yeah," I reply. "Crazy life story, though. This is his seventh or eighth airline."

"Seriously?" Kurt asks.

"Yep. You should hear his stories, though. He's done some fascinating flying. Stuff you and I will probably never do."

"Like what?" Kurt asks, still chewing.

"Seaplanes, cargo, overseas flying, you name it."

He finishes his bite and then offers, "You know, a big part of me wishes I could have done that."

"And a big part of me enjoys knowing your paycheck comes on the first and sixteenth of every month, " Kim says, picking up her slice of pizza.

I chuckle.

"Oh, come on, Kim," Kurt says. "It would have been an adventure."

"Mmhmm," she says mid-chew. She covers her mouth. "Plenty of adventures to be had right here in Texas."

I laugh again. "Well, it would have been educational, that's for sure."

"Yes, it would've," Kurt agrees.

"Anyway," I redirect, "I'm not sure Todd likes me too much." I reach for the soda container.

"Why's that?" Kurt asks.

"I told you about the issue I had in Vancouver not long after I upgraded, right? The problem with the hotel van?"

"Sort of rings a bell."

I twist off the bottle's top. "Well, Todd was my F-O on that trip." The soda fizzes as I pour its contents into my glass. "Seems like an eternity ago. Knowing what I know now, I'm not sure what my hesitation was that day."

Kurt places a cleaned wing on the side of his plate and says, "I do. It's called being a new captain and learning the ropes."

"I think you're right," I say, setting the soda bottle back down. "I've definitely grown a lot as a leader since then."

"And do you think Todd agrees?" Kurt asks with a sly smile, somewhat busting my chops.

I pause to actually consider his question. "You know, I really can't tell. It sort of feels like he barely remembers me."

"Maybe that's because he doesn't," Kurt says, opening the pizza box to pull out a slice of his own.

"Maybe," I say. "But I would think a young guy like me would stick out, especially after botching that event so badly."

"Dude, I can barely remember who I flew with a few weeks ago, let alone a whole year ago." He closes the box after choosing pepperoni.

"I know."

"And how many F-Os have you flown with now?"

"Oh, man," I say, trying to quickly tabulate the number in my head. "I have no idea."

"Seventy? Eighty?"

"Something like that," I say. Later, I'll count the names in my logbook and discover the actual number is 91.

"You gotta figure he's in the same boat," Kurt says.

"True."

"And, I hate to burst your bubble, Korry, but I'm sure you aren't the only young guy he's flown with."

"No, I know. All valid points." I bite into another wing.

"So relax and don't worry about it."

"Relaxing. Definitely one of my specialties," I joke.

Kurt laughs as Kim interjects, "Speaking of F-Os you've flown with, Kurt tells me you flew with Paul."

I nod. "Just two legs, but yes. A few weeks ago."

"How cool is that?" she asks.

I smile. "Very. It's surreal to fly with your buddy. Doesn't feel much like work."

"I bet," Kim says, polishing off her slice of pizza.

I look to Kurt. "At some point, we've gotta find a way to fly together, too. Hopefully for more than just two legs."

"Yes, we do," Kurt says, sipping his drink. "That would be a blast."

"And if we don't do it soon," I say, "you're gonna upgrade and the moment will have passed."

Kurt smiles a half-smile. "Judging from the latest bids that have come out, I suspect we'll have plenty of time to make that happen before my number is up for captain."

Kurt takes another sip of his drink as an uncomfortable silence settles over the table. I look down at my glass, knowing I may have touched an understandably sore spot. I didn't mean to, of course. That's just how it goes with the seniority list. It's always there, looming above us like the omnipotent being that it is, always ready to remind us that it can, at any moment, grant favor to some while passing over others.

I look back to Kurt. "Well, hopefully not too long, because I'm eager for you to upgrade."

He looks to me, asking, "Why's that?"

I pause for a brief moment. "Because I think you'll make an excellent captain."

He smiles. "Thanks, Korry."

"And I can tell you this," I add, setting my cleaned wing on the side of my plate, "it's worth the wait."

Kurt nods. "I'm sure it is."

I reach for another slice of pizza and joke, "As is the captain party I'm sure you'll throw."

Kurt's face fills with an eager smile. "It's going to be epic!"

"And *that's* what I'm afraid of," Kim says, shaking her head as she slaps her hands down on the table.

We all laugh.

"All joking aside," I say, looking to Kurt, "there is one thing I will guarantee you without a doubt, my friend: You're in for one hell of a ride."

Kurt nods his head, grinning. "Just waiting on my number to come up."

"Soon enough, my friend."

The next day, one of the Tank's wheels squeaks as Todd and I march down a long jetway in Los Angeles. The squeaking stops when the wheel thumps against the metal kick plate stretched across the 737's main entryway as I pull the Tank aboard.

"Hi, I'm Korry," I say, offering my hand to the flight attendant standing in the forward galley. "Korry with a K."

"I'm Dawn," the flight attendant says, smiling with her hand outstretched. "Dawn with a D. It's nice to meet you, Korry with a K."

I smile. "Nice to meet you, too, Dawn with a D."

"Did you say Korry with a K?" another flight attendant asks from somewhere in first class.

"The one and only," I reply in jest. I hear her footsteps tapping against the 737's hollow floor as she walks up the aisle toward us.

I peek around the forward bulkhead and see Rebecca, instantly remembering her from a challenging flight we had shared the month before.

"Alright!" Rebecca exclaims.

"So I see you two know each other," Dawn says.

"We do," Rebecca exclaims. "Flew with Korry to LaGuardia last month. We'd probably still be there if he hadn't put his foot down."

"What happened in LaGuardia?" Todd asks.

"It's a long story," I say. "I'll fill you in during cruise."

Two hours later, as Todd and I race eastward above the Rockies, watching the clearly delineated shadow of the earth — the night line — rise higher into the sky as the sun creeps farther below the horizon behind us, I give Todd the full rundown of the cascading series of events that had transpired for Rebecca's and my LaGuardia-to-Chicago flight.

"The real takeaway for me," I tell Todd, "and really one of the main takeaways from my entire first year in the left seat, is that sometimes the role of the captain is simply to take a stand. To say, no, we're not going to do that; we're going to do this. And so long as your decision is reasonable and you're not totally off your rocker, my experience is the company will support you every time."

"That's good to hear," Todd says, his foot kicked up on the footrest.

"It really is. And yet I know I worried about that a lot when I was a new captain. An issue would come up, and I'd find myself torn on what to do, fearing that if I made the wrong choice I'd have to do the carpet dance in the Chief Pilot's office."

"Worse things could happen, I guess."

"And you're right," I continue, growing more passionate by the second. "But now I know that's not the case. Because the company realizes it can't write a policy or procedure to cover every possible scenario we may face on the line, so they give us broad priorities to consider. They give us policies and procedures to cover most of the routine issues that come up. And then they trust us to use our captain's authority in a responsible way to address the rest. Because, after all, if we're capable enough to be trusted with a hundred-million-dollar jet and the lives of so many passengers, then we're capable enough to be trusted in the moment, too."

"Yep," Todd says. "Sometimes the captain—and only the captain—can make a call that gets things moving."

"Exactly," I agree.

"Which is why it drives me crazy when a captain seems unwilling to do so." Todd shifts in his seat, turning toward me and leaning slightly forward. "Take for example this one captain I flew with a while ago in Vancouver."

Vancouver!! The mere mention of the word sends chills down my spine.

"It was like four-thirty in the morning," Todd continues, "and our van to the airport was very late."

Adrenaline rockets through my body. My heart thumps. My palms start to sweat. And a lump grows instantaneously in my throat.

"I suggested we call the company, but for whatever reason, the captain didn't want to do that, even though it was likely we would now be late to the airport."

This can't be a coincidence, I think. *Surely he remembers the captain was me!*

"Eventually a van arrived for another crew, so we hopped in. But get this: The driver refused to take us! He actually turned the van around and kicked us out onto the hotel's curb!" Todd grows extremely animated, as though he's wanted to get this off his chest ever since that day. And with my LaGuardia story as his opening, I've given him the perfect opportunity to unload on me with both barrels. I feel a mountain of stress welling up inside of me. "You know, I would have expected any captain worth his fourth stripe to have done something at that point, wouldn't you?" He pauses momentarily, staring right into my eyes. "I mean, make a phone call. Get a taxi. Do something. Anything at all. And that's why I kept suggesting as much." He shakes his head. "But not this guy. He wouldn't do a thing. He just stood there, paralyzed from head to toe by indecision."

I want to run, but there's nowhere to go. Todd and I are locked in this tiny room with two more hours until we land at O'Hare. *What do I do??? What do I say???* So I say nothing and just stare back at Todd, knowing full well he can see the surprise and awkwardness on my face.

Todd raises his hands up exasperatedly, continuing, "And if this captain was unwilling to take a stand on a miniscule issue like a hotel van, it sure made me wonder if he'd ever stand up and act like a captain for an issue that really mattered. Or, perhaps, maybe I'd have to do it for him." Todd pauses momentarily. "I mean, seriously, what kind of leader is that? What kind of *man* is that?"

Todd stares at me with a look somewhere between anger and amusement as he awaits my response to his questions. An awkward silence drifts over us, and then it lingers there, obscured only by the *whoosh* of the wind that rushes past the cockpit.

He has to know, I keep thinking. *There's no way he doesn't know. None whatsoever. Right?*

My heart feels like it's going to pop out of my chest. I'm at a loss for words, completely taken aback by either Todd legitimately forgetting the captain had been me, which seems unlikely, or the passive aggressiveness with which Todd has confronted me.

"You know, Todd," I say eventually, breaking the silence, only to let it return as I continue searching for what to say.

I almost think I see Todd's head nodding as if to say, "That's right, Korry. I said it. I went there. I've wanted to do this for almost a year now. And it feels good to get that off my chest."

"Todd, I'm…" I let another brief pause fill the air. "Todd, I'm certain that captain you're talking about was me."

Todd sits back into his chair. His brow tightens and his mouth drops open slightly, as though he's genuinely surprised, which is either the truth or an A+ acting job.

"And you know what?" I ask rhetorically, letting another long pause fill the air. "You're right about the whole damn thing."

Todd *is* right. In fact, he's spot on. And I couldn't have painted a clearer picture about how much I've grown over the past year. Because this isn't about the hotel van; it's about being a captain in more than name only. It's about stepping up and taking command. It's about leading from the front, even when that's uncomfortable. It's about taking care of the people on my team, about really listening to their stories, and about channeling our pasts—whatever those pasts may be—in a constructive way that helps move the team forward. It's about understanding myself, especially my triggers, like when I'm feeling disrespected, so I remember to breathe and see such moments as opportunities for growth. It's about capitalizing on my strengths as a communicator and team-builder, while leveraging my weaknesses as opportunities to empower others. It's about constantly evolving and knocking off the rough edges, understanding that those rough edges are the very things helping me to grow and become better, more knowledgeable, and more adept at handling issues that come my way. It's about pushing forward hard enough to get the job done while still managing the downside risk and not exceeding any limits—whether mine or the airplane's. It's about owning my decisions, even when they're wrong, and learning from my mistakes. It's about integrity and responsibility and humility. And it's about accepting the most brutal kind of honesty, even when that honesty is difficult and tough to hear. Because ultimately, that's what makes a great leader. That's what makes a great man. And that's what taking command is all about.

It's very late in the evening when Todd and I arrive at our gate in O'Hare. I'm still not sure what to make of Todd's repeated insistences that he didn't remember the Vancouver captain was me. But in the end, I guess it doesn't really matter either way. What matters is simply that I accept Todd's points, because they're valid. And his raising them in such a candid and vivid way is, in reality, a gift.

With the parking checklist complete, I jot the flight time down in my maroon pocket logbook and then reach across the center console, extending my hand toward Todd. "Thanks, Todd," I say. "For everything."

He smiles, giving my hand a firm shake. "Hope we get to fly together again soon, Korry."

"Me, too," I say. And I mean it.

Todd collects his things and then heads for home. After he leaves,

I pull the Tank out of its cubby and stand beside it near the flight deck door, saying goodbye as the final passengers exit the plane. I nod and smile as many of them offer "thanks" or small waves. Others are on their phones, undoubtedly letting loved ones know they've arrived safely in Chicago. Still more carry sleeping children in one arm while pulling a rollaboard bag with the other. I know many of them are United loyalists, but I also know many others simply found United offering the cheapest ticket. I suspect many of them love to fly, while others see flying as a necessary evil or perhaps even something to fear.

Standing in the flight deck doorway looking into the cabin, however, I can't see any of that. Instead, all I see is the incredible responsibility of the job staring back at me. I see what an awesome privilege it is to be entrusted with these passengers' lives. Me. A complete stranger they don't even know. And yet they trust that I'll safely guide them through winds and weather, across states and even oceans, to some distant destination where a client is or a loved one lives. It's the sacred bond Captain Crawford had described in the *Role of the Captain* class. And it's a not-so-subtle reminder of how incredibly important it is for me to be on my game, every moment of every flight I command.

How humbling is that? How awesome is that responsibility? It's a lot to put on the shoulders of a now-32-year-old captain…or a captain nearing his or her 65th birthday for that matter. But I say load my shoulders up, because I absolutely love bearing that burden. I'm excited by it. It energizes me. And I'm ready to step up and meet whatever challenge comes my way.

When the last passenger is off the jet, I flip several overhead panel switches to turn off the cockpit's lights and shut the jet down for the night. Then I walk with the flight attendants into the deserted terminal, wishing them well as they go on their way.

Then it's just the Tank and me. We head toward baggage claim and the underground tunnel leading to the L train. We walk slowly, looking at the long, colorful murals painted on the empty tunnel's walls. And after passing through the L's turnstile, I hoist the Tank onto my shoulder and traipse down the steps to the long boarding platform. Halfway down, I enter one of the paused rail cars, taking my usual single seat near the car's emergency exit.

The whole ride home, I stare straight ahead, thinking about Todd and the many other first officers with whom I've flown. I think about their journeys and how much they've taught me about life. I reflect on the many difficult flights I've commanded, the times I made mistakes and felt unbelievably small, and the times I felt like I'd been every bit the captain my passengers deserved. I think about my grandfather and the sage advice he offers in his book. I think about Jen and the challenges we've faced.

What a year it has been, I think as the train rumbles into the Grand Avenue station, knowing all too well how much I've grown as both a leader and a man.

When the doors open, I pull the Tank behind me and step off the train. We ride the escalator up to the turnstiles, and then climb the red tile stairs to the quiet streets of the West Loop. Three blocks later, I reach the front door of our apartment building. Since the doorman has already gone home for the night, I use my key fob to buzz myself in. I grab the mail from our box and sift through it as the Tank and I ride the elevator to the sixth floor. Then we walk down the long hallway to our apartment's door on the left side. I try to slide my key into the lock as quietly as I can, but it's a lost cause; Jackson hears me right away, and he pops up, barking, as I open the door. His nails click constantly against the wood floors as he scampers down the hallway to greet me.

"Hi, buddy!" I whisper as he wags his tail furiously, rubbing up against me. He runs circles around me as I slip off my shoes and hang my keys on the tiny hooks by the door. "Shhhh!" I exclaim in a whisper as he darts between my legs, his nails clicking away the whole time. "You'll wake your mom!" Examination complete, Jackson wiggles back down the hallway as fast as he came, eager to return to his cushy dog bed at Jen's side.

As is normally the case after I return home from a trip late at night, I'm too amped up to sleep. This is especially true tonight, since so much is racing through my mind given Todd's comments and the reflection that comes with my first year in the left seat now behind me. As I set the Tank next to the little office nook, pull my tie off, and drape it over the Tank's handle, I decide a celebratory scotch is in order.

I walk into the living room, turn on one small lamp on the end table beside our couch, and grab a monogrammed glass tumbler Kurt gave me as a groomsman gift at his wedding years earlier. Then I open the black cabinet along the wall and begin sifting through my small collection of whiskies.

I have a particular bottle in mind—a bottle that I bring out only for special occasions. It's the first bottle of whisky I ever purchased, a bottle of cask-strength Edradour that I acquired on a layover in Edinburgh, Scotland, in 2007. After maneuvering a few bottles out of the way, I see it tucked into the back corner of the cabinet.

I pull it out and hold the bottle in my hand, admiring its elegant design and the three fingers of brown whisky remaining within it. The distillery's name is etched on the glass along with a picturesque image of the distillery's grounds. The bottle's sides are tall and straight, but they narrow suddenly at the neck, where a thin crimson ribbon separates the bottle's body from its wide cork top.

The cork sticks as I start to twist the cap, which isn't a surprise; the last time I opened the bottle was the night Jen and I celebrated my captain award on Bid 14-02. Once it begins to move, however, it slides freely, making a soft popping sound as it escapes from the bottle's mouth. I tip it toward Kurt's tumbler, watching the liquid drizzle into the bottom of the glass. I add a few tiny drips of filtered water to the glass, and then place the bottle on the end table as I settle onto the couch.

I hold the tumbler up to the light, watching the water slowly diffuse itself through the whisky. I twist the glass from side to side, watching the spirit cling to the glass's edges before regrouping along the bottom. And then I lean back and take one small sip, closing my eyes and letting the whisky roll around in my mouth.

The spirit's bite is instantaneous, and it's followed immediately by a slight hint of smoke and a robust oaky finish. As I swallow, the whisky warms the back of my throat with a subtle burn that goes all the way down into my chest.

And then my eyes pop open.

No, I think. *Can it be this simple?*

I lean forward, intently examining the short stubby glass and its caramel-colored contents. I take another tiny sip, again letting the liquid swirl around in my mouth before swallowing it. And just like that, my mind returns to the cramped whisky shop along the Royal Mile in Edinburgh, where an old shopkeeper had taught me all about whisky. Only now, I'm wondering if the real lesson of his masterclass might actually have little to do with whisky at all. So I close my eyes, let the lights dim, and then watch as the whole memory unfolds in my mind's eye as though it's an old movie I haven't seen in years.

CHAPTER 14

The Shopkeeper

*"In every walk with nature,
one receives far more than he seeks."*
- John Muir

Edinburgh, Scotland – 2007

It's only fitting, I think as I step out of the hotel and find mist falling onto the granite sett streets of Edinburgh's Royal Mile. It's not enough mist to be obtrusive, just enough to be noticeable. And it's precisely what I'd expect for the storied Scottish city.

Besides, I think, *it adds a bit of mysticism to the city.*

Not that Edinburgh needs any help with that. From the soot-stained sandstone blocks of the regal buildings lining the streets, to the rocky crags that flank the city—most notably those of Holyrood Park to the east of downtown and Castle Rock, the perch for Edinburgh Castle at the end of the Royal Mile—the city is full of character.

As I make my way toward the castle, I join a group of tourists who are listening to a skillful kilt-wearing bagpiper play "Scotland the Brave." His cheeks puff out as he works to keep his pipes' bag full of air, and his fingers flutter along the chanter to play the anthem's soulful melody. It's then that I first notice the shop's reddish wooden door out of the corner of my eye. And after the piper is finished, I walk across the street to take a closer look.

Nearing the shop, I see the storefront's windows displaying

dozens of whisky bottles, some resting on special shelves built into small wooden casks.

This seems perfect, I think as I push open the door and step inside.

I'm hoping to pick up a souvenir bottle of scotch during my layover, and I don't want some bottle I can find in any American liquor store. I want something unique. Something memorable. Something quintessentially Scottish. But admittedly, I have no idea what that might be.

"Well, good day to ya lad," says the gentleman seated behind the worn wooden counter in his heavy Scottish brogue. "Can I help ya ta find anything?" His gray hair, which is slightly whiter than the three-day-old beard on his face, pokes out from underneath his plaid touring cap.

"Just browsing for now," I reply.

"Very well, lad. Ya know where ta find me if ye change yer mind," he says, returning to the newspaper that is sprawled across the counter.

My eyes drift around the room. It's no larger than the inside of a small moving truck. Wooden shelves blanket the walls from floor to ceiling. Above them are carved wooden signs that read Highland, Lowland, Islay, and Speyside, although I have no clue what differentiates these terms from one another.

Making matters worse, each rack is crammed with different variants of whisky originating from distilleries like Abelour, Ardbeg, and Auchentoshan; Balvenie and Bowmore; Cardhu and Cragganmore; Dalmore and Dalwhinnie. Then there are the Glens—Glen Elgin and Glen Mhor; Glenfarclas and Glenfiddich; Glengoyne and Glenlivet—which are followed by Hazelburn and Highland Park; Lagavulin and Laphroaig; Macallan and Mannochmore. It's a seemingly endless list of brands. And if that weren't confusing enough, within each particular brand, there are 10-, 12-, 15-, 18-, and 25-year whiskies. There are whisky maker blends and pure single malts. There are cask-strength whiskies, oak whiskies, port whiskies, and sherry whiskies. Looking at the racks, I feel more lost than when I peruse the wine selection at our local store back home. And clearly, the shopkeeper can tell.

He watches me from behind his paper as I roam from rack to rack, picking up a random bottle here, reading another's intriguing label there. But I can't make sense of any of them; the sheer volume of selections leads to analysis paralysis.

The shopkeeper's stool creaks when he stands up. He folds his newspaper and walks toward me, rubbing the stubble on his chin as he approaches. "Might I be correct in assuming yer a bit lost, lad?"

I smile. "It's that obvious?"

"Well, let's just say ya don't do a very good job of keepin' a secret!" To which he chuckles at his own joke. "After all, you've been staring at that one rack for a good twenty minutes now."

A slight exaggeration, I think, nodding my head nonetheless.

"And if I let ya keep goin' like that, I might have ta close up the shop before I can actually make a sale."

I laugh a bit. "It's just that I don't know much about scotch," I tell him. "And I'm hoping to bring a bottle back to the States."

"Oh, lad. If yer lookin' for scotch, I'm afraid you've come ta the wrong shop, because here we sell whisky, and nothing but!"

Scottish humor, I think. *Very witty.* Although I do see his point.

"Do ya mind if I tell ya a little bit about whisky? Because it's a most fascinating drink."

"That'd be great," I reply. I have all day to kill anyway.

"Excellent. Let's start with the basics. Do ya have any idear what 'whisky' means, lad?"

I shake my head; I haven't the foggiest idea.

"It means 'the water of life.' So as ya might expect, water's the first ingredient in any fine whisky. Look at this," he says, pointing to a map of Scotland that hangs on the wall. Tiny red dots are speckled all over it, each one corresponding to a different distillery's location. "Do ya notice how the distilleries are often clustered together?" And I do. "Well, that's no mere coincidence, lad." He traces a few waterways with his fingers. "Ya see, the whisky makers discovered that the water flowing in those parts is particularly well-suited for whisky making."

"Why's that?"

"Because it's so fresh, lad. So full of life, as though it's been collected from heaven, which, in a sense, it has. Ya see, when the rains fall upon the mountain hillsides," he says, using his hands to simulate the rain falling, "the tiny droplets slide down through the lush grasses and across the fertile loam, picking up tiny bits of precious minerals along the way. Eventually those drops collect inta small springs, which combine ta form streams, which feed ever-larger rivers. So by the time that water reaches the distilleries, it's simply perfect for making whisky." I nod along, entranced by the shopkeeper's excitement. "Of course, ya might imagine the minerals and character of each mountain stream is slightly different. And that leads ta different tastes, which is why the racks are labeled the way they are. Because a Highland whisky tastes different than a Lowland whisky or a Speyside whisky. And there's absolutely nothin' comparable ta an Islay whisky," he says. "Those whiskies are true explosions of flavors, lad. But I'll get ta that."

I smile, feeling like I'm watching a carefully rehearsed performance by the shopkeeper. He's so animated, at times leaning in and lowering his voice, while at other times he waves his hands around in big, flowing motions.

"Next comes the barley," he continues, leading me to a small barrel in the corner filled with barley grains. "Go ahead, lad. Grab a handful and hold them up ta yer nose." My fingers slide effortlessly into the barrel, scooping up a handful of grains as instructed. I raise them close to my nose, breathing in deeply as a few grains trickle out between my fingers. The shopkeeper leans forward and takes in a full breath, using his fingers to waft the smell of the grains toward his nose. "Can ya smell that, lad? The rich nuttiness?"

I breathe in deeply, suddenly smelling it, and I smile.

"It's delightful, isn't it?"

I nod again.

"It gets even better once the barley is malted."

The shopkeeper launches into an explanation about how the barley grains are spread out and wetted down to begin the germination process. But, he tells me, it's a tricky process, because if it's not done at just the right temperature and with just the right amount of moisture, the barley will germinate too much or too little. And if that happens, the barley won't produce the right amount of sugar. And without the right amount of sugar, he tells me, you simply cannot make a fine whisky.

"So how do you know when enough is enough?" I ask.

He smiles and leans in again. "Lots of practice, lad. Years of it."

Of course, I suspect there's a more scientific answer than that, but I appreciate the way he's turning whisky making into an art form.

The shopkeeper continues, describing how, at just the right time, the grains are toasted in a kiln to stop the germinating process. He tells me this is where the Islay whiskies really take their form, since those whisky makers dry their barley by burning large chunks of peat from the shore, which infuses those grains with the very taste of the sea.

I catch myself dabbing my tongue on the top of my mouth, imagining the richness and boldness of such flavor.

Next, he tells me how the malted barley is ground into a coarse flour and how water is then added to soak up the sugars. The introduction of yeast then starts the fermentation process, which is when the remaining liquid is placed in the large iconic copper stills. The shopkeeper chuckles. "I bet ya never knew so much went inta making a whisky, did ya, lad?"

I shake my head. "Not at all! It's so much more complicated than I had thought."

"Ahhh, lad," he says, winking at me as though I'm playing right into his hand, "the best things in life are complicated."

What comes out of the copper still, he tells me, is a clear spirit known as white whisky. It isn't pleasant to drink, but he says that's because it isn't finished yet. "Ya see, lad, we need ta enrich the spirit. We need ta add character to it. We need ta give it some spice and flavor and a bit of color. Because without that, the bottles behind us wouldn't come alive, lad." He waves his hand all around the room. "Without that, these whiskies would be bitter and dull, boring and incomplete."

"I'll bite," I say. "So how do they do that?"

"Why, I thought ya'd never ask!" he exclaims, chuckling again. "What's needed is a little magic." He smiles brightly as he tells me that in Scotland, whisky is aged in big oak barrels, but not new ones, because new ones don't have enough character. So they start with barrels that once housed bourbon. And to help those barrels begin their second life, they light the insides aflame to char and seal the wood boards together. "Only then are they ready ta store our whisky, lad. Only then are they ready ta help our spirits become complete by adding the most critical ingredient of all: time."

Three years, it turns out, at a minimum, but the longer the better. He tells me this is because as the spirit sits in that barrel, it transforms. It soaks up the character of its surroundings, like the oak and the char, and it evolves from a bitter white whisky into something beautiful and robust. "But that process takes time, lad. A *lot* of time. And the more time we add, the more the spirit evolves; the richer, more complex, and complete the spirit becomes."

I realize I'm smiling along with him, captivated by the nuances of a drink I never before appreciated.

He tells me how the whisky makers will often transfer the

partially aged spirits to sherry or port wine casks to continue the aging process and add even greater complexity and completeness to the spirits. "But even that process takes time, lad, because no spirit instantly acquires the character of its surroundings. No spirit can be shaped and completed overnight. Instead, a spirit does so slowly. Painfully slowly. So slowly that the process might take a decade or two ta complete. And that's why the longer that spirit ages, the more valuable it becomes. The more exceptional it is. The more unique and robust its flavor. And only then is it complete."

"I had no idea," I say to the shopkeeper.

"Most people don't, lad," he says, smiling as he takes a deep breath and runs his hand across his chin. "But now ya do. So when ya look around this shop, I don't want ya ta see bottles of 'scotch.' I want ya ta see the water of life. Rich. Complex. Valuable. And complete. Each one unique and different from the next. Each one carefully crafted over many years. Because that's what whisky is, lad. So look around and take yer time. I'll be here if ya'd like any suggestions."

I open my eyes and pick up the bottle the shopkeeper eventually suggested, tracing my thumb across its white etching and reading from the tag that still wraps around its neck: Edradour Distillery 1993. Distilled 16.06.93. Bottled 22.11.06. Cask No. 257. Decanter No. 48 of 646.

Can it really be this simple?

I start to wonder if, perhaps, it's not that my formula for success is incorrect, but that it's incomplete. Because success clearly requires a goal, a detailed plan, disciplined execution, and some fortunate timing here and there—just as has been the case in my own life thus far. But are those elements just the ingredients that get put into the still? And is the resulting spirit nothing more than a dull and bitter white whisky success? One that lacks character, complexity, and completeness?

Sure, those ingredients serve a vital purpose, but for a lasting and fulfilling success, is it possible that what's needed most of all is simply the peat and the loam? The oak and the char? The sherry and the port? The surroundings and experiences that, over time, gradually shape a spirit and make it unique, robust, complete, and fulfilled?

I consider the thought for several minutes as I recall the many conversations I shared with pilots over the previous year. I wonder what it must have felt like for Todd as he gracefully slipped his seaplane onto a glassy Florida lake, or as he climbed the final step to summit a Cambodian temple, or as he rode his BMW motorcycle across the bridges leading into Key West. I try to imagine the rush Vince must have felt when he catapulted his F-18 fighter jet off the deck of an aircraft carrier, the roar of the engines as deafening as the G-forces on his face were powerful. I attempt to envision the red and pink hues of the majestic sunset Lee described watching as he sipped wine with his girlfriend, their fingers intertwined, while their campfire crackled next to his fifth-wheel trailer in some wide-open expanse of Utah. I wonder if he ever looked up at the contrail of a jet crossing the sky above him and questioned his decision to take the voluntary furlough. *I suspect not,* I think.

And then I close my eyes and do my best to picture my grandfather as a young man on a train heading west from Pennsylvania. Alone. What did he think as he gazed out his window onto the Nebraskan plains rolling onward to the horizon? What went through his mind as he worked in Bremerton, Washington, repairing the vessels damaged at Pearl Harbor? And when he eventually arrived in Alaska, was he mystified by the mountains that were far larger than any he'd ever seen before? For as much as I can almost see him with his pack on his back, hiking for hours, limping slightly from the effects of his polio, I don't know what the breeze felt like when it blew across his face. I can't hear the babbling of the brook where he cast his fishing line. I can't taste the purity of the water he likely sipped from his cupped hands. So try as I might to feel and see those moments, they're blurry at best. Then again, they're not my moments to feel and to know. And maybe that's precisely as it should be.

I play with the idea in my head, thinking back on some of the powerful moments I know have shaped my own life. I see the brightness of the sunrise that greeted me as I stepped into the cockpit of the Boeing 747 high above the Atlantic Ocean, mesmerized by the flight deck and its panoramic view. I hear my high school teacher's voice echoing off his classroom's walls as he questioned my dream of becoming an airline pilot, kindling a fire inside me that drove my chase to the left seat. I feel the warmth of the ocean breeze as Jen and I walked along the water on the last night of the conference in Florida where we met, knowing in that moment she would change my life forever, in ways I could never expect. I sense the pride that filled me the day I was fitted for my first airline uniform; the staccato accents of Italian locals chatting as I stepped off the crew van in Rome following my first transatlantic flight as a major airline pilot; the energizing and terrifying sight of my name on the captain list of Bid 14-02; the texture of the paper notecard containing my new captain wings; and the uncanny way time seemed to stand still after my first takeoff as a captain. Each of them a vivid and powerful moment, forever etched into my memory, just like the roughness I can still feel of my grandfather's fingers on the day I sat beside him in his hospital room, or the sadness that still burns inside me from when I saw Jen's broken face after we realized she was having a miscarriage. All of them were moments that changed me. Moments that shaped my spirit. Moments that were slowly distilling my soul. And they were all solely and uniquely mine.

I take another sip of the whisky. As the liquid slips down my throat, I become more convinced that it's not just the major moments of my life that are shaping my spirit, but the simple and mundane moments, too. The sunrises and sunsets. The feeling Kurt described of the ground falling away on every takeoff. The cockpit conversations I shared with colleagues that have challenged me to think differently. The discomfort I felt from being pushed as a new leader. The laughter I shared with friends at the top of the Hancock Building. The sound of the crowd and the determination on Jen's face as she ran the last hundred yards of her marathon. The fluttering of the key I tossed off the lock bridge in Cologne. And perhaps even the moment when the taste of an aged whisky jogs a long-forgotten memory of a passionate whisky shopkeeper. Each moment slowly chiseling away at my spirit, helping to make it a little more unique, a little more robust, a little more complete, and a little more fulfilled. And then I wonder about the man I would have become without any one of these moments in my life.

Perhaps, I think, *it's not that a fulfilling success comes in spite of whatever circuitous life journey I may take; perhaps it's that the fulfilling part comes precisely* because *of that circuitous life journey.* Each moment combining with and amplifying the others, creating a success far greater and richer than I could ever imagine on my own.

I realize I could be reading too much into this, but I know for certain I don't want an empty spirit. I don't want some white whisky success, a mere sugar high that fades away and leaves me craving some fruitless chase after more. No, I want a complex life, a complete life, a fulfilled life. That's the life I want. That's the success I crave. And if I'm fortunate enough to climb to great heights, all the better. But if not, perhaps that's okay, too. Because what seems clear to me now is that no title will ever make a spirit whole. No title will ever fulfill a soul. But a rich and diverse journey might. One complete with tiny, insignificant moments as well as grand adventures and misadventures. One with side roads and scenic routes. A journey with joy *and* pain. A journey full of all sorts of moments—including moments just like this.

EPILOGUE

Onward

"Go as far as you can see; when you get there,
you'll be able to see farther."
- J. P. Morgan

Chicago, Illinois – January 2016

I kneel down next to the Tank, which is in its usual spot in the corner of my closet. As I unzip its top to refresh its contents, I feel excited about the new adventures that await us. It has, after all, been nearly two months since the two of us last ventured out on our own—and almost a year and a half since I completed my first year in the left seat.

Piece by piece, I fill the Tank's cavernous belly with a few spare uniform pieces and four days' worth of tightly rolled clothes for both warm and cold climates. I slide in my bagged-up running shoes near the bottom and wedge my brown leather Penn State toiletry bag into a space near the top. Then I squeeze the air out of my down winter coat, fold it, and place it over the bag's other items, careful to ensure its edges remain tucked inside as I zip the Tank closed.

After propping the Tank upright and extending its handle, I slide my laptop bag overtop and grin adoringly at my trusty sidekick. I wonder what the Tank thinks of our life on the road. Is it bored or humored by the many conversations it hears on the flight deck? Conversations like those I'd had with the 91 different first officers during the 267 flights of my first year in the left seat? All told, that year I had safely carried 36,237 passengers, which is more than one-and-a-half times the capacity of Chicago's United Center sports arena, more than 320,000 air miles—a distance equivalent to nearly 13 times around the globe. And the Tank had been with me for every takeoff, every landing, and every hotel in between.

Do you prefer Hiltons or Marriotts? I wonder. *Northern climates or the tropics?* But I suspect the Tank doesn't much care where it goes... so long as it goes with me.

But these are all questions for another day. The road beckons. And as I glance at my watch, I know it's time to go.

"Wife?" I call from the bedroom in a loud voice as I begin rapidly weaving my striped uniform tie into a tight Windsor knot around my neck. "Are you almost ready for the picture?"

"Almost," I hear her bellow from the living room.

I slide the knot perfectly into position and turn down my crisply pressed uniform shirt's collar. I clip my United ID onto the flap of my shirt's left breast pocket and slip my tiny maroon logbook into the pocket on the right. Then I pluck my blazer off its hanger and place it around my shoulders as I slide my arms in. My captain's hat is next. I flex its felt-covered brim and place it atop my head, noticing the captain I see in the mirror and thinking about how far I've come since first taking command.

Then, looking at the Tank, I think, *It's time, old friend.* I grasp the Tank's handle and pull it behind me, out of the bedroom and down the long hallway toward the door.

"Wife, I've gotta go," I implore, kneeling down to put on my polished black leather shoes. "So it's now or never."

"I know, I know."

Moments later I hear Jen's footsteps coming my way from around the hallway's corner, accompanied by the rapid scampering of Jackson's paws, which only slightly precede his ever-so-helpful kisses as I finish tying the thin laces on my shoes.

"It's just a couple days, buddy," I tell him, rubbing his velvety ears and giving him a kiss on the top of his head. "I promise I'll come home. Just like I always do."

As I stand up, I see Jen rounding the corner. "Someone is refusing to get up and say goodbye to her dad," she jokes, smiling at the tiny month-old infant in her arms.

I chuckle, although admittedly I feel more like crying at the thought of leaving my little baby girl for the first time. Reagan looks so precious nestled in her mom's loving arms, even though the pink newborn onesie with red polka dots dwarfs her tiny frame.

"This belongs to you," Jen says, handing Reagan to me.

Reagan furrows her brow and whimpers slightly during the handoff. "Hi, baby," I say, kissing her forehead and pulling her tight against my chest, careful not to let the pointy metal wings on my suit jacket snag her delicate skin. "Daddy's gonna miss you a whole lot, okay?" I look to Jen. "Like a whole, whooooole lot." And then Reagan falls right back to sleep, even as I turn her around to face Jen for the quick photo.

"She's clearly bored with this," Jen jokes.

"Better than a crying fit," I say.

"Truth! Okay, Husband, on three," Jen says, framing the two of us on her iPhone's screen.

I smile brightly, my whole new world in my arms.

"One…two…three." Jen snaps a few pics and then pauses to review her work.

"Well?" I ask.

"Awww, these are good!"

"Let me see!" I say.

Jen turns the phone around to show me the best one, instantly melting my heart.

I think back to the miscarriage, then to the day we found out we were pregnant again, and to the classes Jen and I took together at the hospital during the ensuing nine months of worry and wonder. We hoped and prayed this pregnancy would be okay. And it was. Until it almost wasn't.

I think of the dark, quiet delivery room where I stood next to Jen, squeezing her hand as Dr. Summers and a nurse guided her. I hear the tapping corresponding to Reagan's little heartbeat. Then I hear it slowing. And slowing. To the point of causing concern. I hear Dr. Summers saying, "Come on, baby. Come on." I see her changing into surgery scrubs between contractions. I recall thinking, *She's the professional, Korry. She's done this before. She's walking right up to that line, but she won't walk past it. Trust her.* And so I do.

And now I look down and see this perfect little baby girl in my arms. And I wonder if I ever would have met her if each of the preceding moments hadn't played out the way they did collectively for Jen and me. Each one shaping us. Preparing us. For now.

I give Reagan another kiss, saying, "Daddy loves you whole bunches!" My vision grows blurry as tears well up in my eyes. I hate the thought of leaving my family and returning to work, but I know it's what needs to happen. I rub my thumb across Reagan's soft, tiny cheek. "You be good for Momma, okay?"

Reagan's heavy eyelids open slightly, and I decide to take that as a sign she understands my request.

I smile again, and then look to Jen. "Okay, Wife. Time to go." Reagan lets out another small whimper as I pass her back to Jen. "I'll check in with you when I get to San Juan."

"Sounds good, dude."

I grab the Tank's handle. "It's just a couple days, Wife. You'll do great."

Jen nods and sighs. "Yeah, man. We've got this!" And I know without a doubt she's right, despite how hard it will be for her with me on the road and no one else nearby to help her out. Parenting is just one more part of our grand adventure together, and I can already tell it is shaping our spirits in ways I never could have imagined.

"Okay, Wife," I say, leaning in to give Jen a kiss before pulling the Tank over to the door. "I love you. See you in a few days."

"I love you, too, Husband! Fly safe!"

"Always."

I open the door, offer a little wave, and then pull the door closed behind me as the Tank and I step into the hallway.

It's just you and me now, I think as the Tank and I walk toward the elevator at the end of the hall. *And we've got work to do, adventures to seek, sunrises to admire, and new cities to explore. We've got people to meet, problems to solve, and lessons to learn.* I press the down button. *It's anyone's guess as to where we'll head over the next year or what we'll experience.* The elevator doors open and I walk in, pulling the Tank behind me. I press the button for floor 1. Then I pause, looking down at my friend. *It's time to go back where we both belong—on the road.*

And the elevator doors close.

There's no doubt the greatest journey I've ever taken in my life was the one to the captain's chair, three feet to the left. It pushed me in ways I never imagined, teaching me more than I ever could have expected in the process—about myself and about life. Perhaps the best part of all is that my journey isn't over. In fact, it's barely even begun. But now I know that each step, each up, each down, is shaping and distilling my spirit—one tiny moment at a time. And I wouldn't want it any other way.

I hope you find your own personal journey equally as rewarding. I doubt you'll end up where you expect, but that's the nature of journeys. Side roads and scenic routes steal your attention, compelling you to go just a little farther to see what's around the bend. But even if you get lost along the way, don't worry; journeys always have a way of leading you exactly where you need to go. My only advice is to start yours by moving three feet to the left, because that small change in perspective may make all the difference.

Of course, I hope your journey takes you into United's friendly skies. And if it does, be sure to peek into the flight deck and let me know how it's going.

Until then, safe travels wherever you go. It's been my true privilege to serve as your captain during our brief time together. Thanks for flying with me.

HIGHLIGHT REEL

Memorable Moments

Like the book?

If so, will you please leave a 5-star review on Amazon and Goodreads before sharing with your friends?

Be sure to tag your social media posts with **#3FeetToTheLeft.**

Thank you!

View from Korry and Jen's 37th-floor Chicago apartment

Korry's captain wings

Captain Jen in the Boeing 777 simulator

Leaving for work on Day One as a captain - August 6, 2013

One of Korry's last visits with Papaw

Cancun...just before Jen texts that she's calling the locksmith

Taking Command: A checklist for new captains of any industry

Congratulations! You're a new leader. Now what? How do you succeed when the torch is handed to you? Captain Korry Franke offers a simple checklist with techniques and tactics to ensure new captains of any industry can step up and succeed, even when the pressure is on.

Book Korry today by emailing him at korry@korryfranke.com.

Jen after the Disney Marathon in January 2014

Jen, Jackson, and Korry on the Kinzie Street Bridge

Keeping Your Wings Level:
How to strive and climb when adversity arrives

We all face challenges, whether it's a painful diagnosis, a project that goes off the rails, or an external event that shakes the realities of a business like a powerful earthquake. Captain Korry Franke offers a framework for how to prepare for challenges, manage through them safely, and turn those events into drivers for personal, professional, and corporate growth and success.

Book Korry today by emailing him at korry@korryfranke.com.

Korry and Jen in Amsterdam   Hiking Starved Rock State Park with
Jackson

Plotting Your Career Flight Plan:
How to define direction and soar to success

Young leaders face daunting career landscapes today. So how do you plot a course that builds on itself and accelerates achievement? And how do you respond if the path doesn't lead where it's expected to go? Captain Korry Franke offers a simple framework that helps students and young professionals find direction, plan a career that builds on itself, and navigate career "diversions" that accelerate advancement. **Book Korry today by emailing him at korry@korryfranke.com.**

Flying with Paul

You Can Help!

Donate today to the *Jason Dahl Scholarship Fund* and support aspiring pilots.

Credit Cards: http://dahlfund.org/donate/

Send checks or money orders to:

   The Jason Dahl Scholarship Fund

   9956 West Remington Place Unit A-10

   Suite 93

   Littleton, CO 80128

Leaving Reagan for the first time to go back on the road
in January 2016

You Can Help!

Donate today to the *United We Care Employee Relief Fund*
Credit Cards: https://www.crowdrise.com/unitedairlinesemployee
Send checks or money orders to:

United We Care Employee Relief Fund

c/o WHQHR

233 S. Wacker Drive, 25th Floor

Chicago, IL 60606

Finally flying together with Kurt in July 2016

ACKNOWLEDGMENTS

Helping Hands

"If you want to go fast, go alone.
If you want to go far, go together."
- African Proverb

Lehigh Valley, Pennsylvania – September 2018

Y ou should keep a journal."
It was the advice I received from more than a few captains after telling them I had secured a captain slot on Bid 14-02. They assured me that my first year in the left seat would inevitably be one of the most eventful and impactful years of my life. And, man, were they ever right!

Of course, I had no idea how right they would be when I first opened my laptop and started typing out my journal on June 16, 2013. Nor did I know that the stories it would soon contain would serve as my inspiration for writing this—my first—book. Sure, I have always enjoyed the idea of writing, but I had no concept back then of what truly goes into the *craft* of writing a book—the untold hours spent revising, editing, finessing, and obsessing over every word, phrase, sentence, and paragraph contained within it.

But I do now, thanks in no small part to the group of hearty souls who have assisted me throughout this process. Over four years, they dutifully trudged through three complete rewrites and at least three additional heavy refinements, offering feedback and advice along the way, slowly helping this project move from manuscript to memoir. I'm beyond humbled that their faith in me never waivered.

Truthfully, this book is theirs as much as it is mine, because without them, there's no way this book would have deserved to see the light of day. With the guidance, candor, and confidence they shared with me throughout this project, both this book and I have evolved and grown, especially regarding my skills as a writer and storyteller. I am and will be eternally grateful. I will also never read a book the same way again!

While this list is far from complete, I'd like to offer particular thanks to the people who have helped shape and craft this book the most.

Thank you to my team of readers and advisors: Father Ted Babcock; Anthony Beckles; Tim Bradley; Kim and Tim Custer; Robert and Francie Eyer; my parents, Steve and Cindy Franke; Jennifer Jamelli; my sister, Kristen Johnson; Dianna Klein; Ed and Christina Manfre; Pam Pollack; Joe Runyan; Kurt Schlesinger; Tom Schlesinger; Vishal Shah; Dr. Dennis Sheehan; David Sirott; Gail Smith; Robert Smith; Matthew Snyder; Paul Soporowski; and of course, my wife, Jen.

Special thanks to ad-man and high school friend Tim Bradley, who suggested the title change to *3 Feet to the Left* and helped shape this book in immeasurable ways. He saw what this book could become long before I did. He helped me tie it all together by zeroing in on what worked and what didn't. And he never stopped challenging me to write more vividly and engagingly so that readers like him could feel like they were sitting on the flight deck jumpseat with me. Tim also suffered through more versions of the manuscript than anyone else (except perhaps Jen and my family), and he read the various drafts almost exclusively while sitting on airplanes as he traveled to yet more business meetings in yet more random cities. I'm so thankful we reconnected in Chicago during one of his business trips as I was preparing to send out draft number 1. His guidance has been truly instrumental at every step along the way. I owe him big time. (Oh, and Tim? Sorry to hear about your seatmate with the cat breath. Brutal, man.)

Thank you to my editor, Stephanie M. Scott, for her excitement about the subject matter and for helping round out the manuscript so it can flow and sing. Thanks also to Kristen Johnson and Cindy Franke for their careful eyes while editing early drafts and proofreading the final one.

Thank you to Brett Snyder for not sending my out-of-the-blue email straight into the trash. As a longtime reader of his *Cranky Flier* blog, I'm humbled that he enjoyed the book and honored that he agreed to write its foreword. Hopefully, readers will agree that, just as Brett does on his blog, I've helped to demystify a part of the airline industry that is literally closed off from view most of the time.

Thank you to graphic artists and illustrators AKSARAMANTRA for the beautiful cover design and Khrystyne Robillard-Smith for the custom maps and charts she created to help tell this story graphically.

Thank you to interior designer and typesetter Roseanna White for readying the book for print.

Thank you to fellow United Airlines pilot Captain Karl Novak for the interior title page photography.

Thank you to the team at United Airlines who reviewed the manuscript and authorized the use of United's name with the project. I know their plates were full long before I asked them to read my 100,000+ word manuscript, but the suggestions they gave me were instrumental in shaping many of the stories within it. Additionally, the courage they've shown by letting me tell my story the way I wanted to tell it adds a level of realism and authenticity that simply wouldn't have been possible by using fictitious names for our two legacy companies. Yes, we've traveled a challenging road throughout our integration and beyond, but we are a *united* family now. And I'm excited to see to what heights our airline will fly now that our potential is being unleashed in a big way.

Thank you also to the many named and unnamed pilots and crew members with whom I flew during my first year as a captain and beyond. They will likely never know how much I've learned from them—about flying and about life—but I know with complete certainty that I would not be the man or the pilot I am today without each one of them. I look forward to seeing all of them again out on the line.

And now, a personal note to my daughter, Reagan: Thank you for being such a wonderful addition to our family. I'm thrilled you came along just in time to make the perfect cameo for this book! You're so vibrant and joyful, so strong-willed and determined. You bring both your mom and me more joy—and gray hairs—than you will likely ever understand. I have no doubt, however, that it is your magnetic personality that will power you forward in life, propelling you to success in whatever endeavors you ultimately choose to pursue. One day, I hope you'll take the time to read these pages. If you do, I suspect you'll learn a little more about your dad and the amazing grand adventure he shared with your mom in the Second City. Perhaps these pages will even encourage you to think a bit differently about how you define success in life. Either way, we can't wait to see where your path takes you. Maybe it will even lead you back to Chicago (you are, after all, a Chicagoan by birth!). If so, just don't be surprised if Mom and Dad become frequent visitors!

Finally, I offer my deepest personal thanks to the love of my life, Jennifer. Only you truly understand how much this project has consumed our relationship and me over the past several years. I just hope you know how incredibly thankful I am for the time and support you gave me as I pecked away endlessly on my laptop, usually in complete silence. I know you likely had your doubts about whether this project would ever end, but now it has, and I assure you, you will finally get your husband back! I love you and am so excited to continue journeying through life together with you!

Onward and upward,
Korry M. Franke
September 12, 2018

30707166R00227

Made in the USA
San Bernardino, CA
28 March 2019